Days to Remember

Days to Remember

Joshua Atkins Nickerson 2nd

*A Chatham Native Recalls Life on Cape Cod
Since the Turn of the Century*

*Illustrations and Cover Design
by Jeannette Fontaine*

PUBLISHED BY
THE CHATHAM HISTORICAL SOCIETY, INC.
CHATHAM, MASSACHUSETTS

Foreword

THE Chatham Historical Society has been a publisher for a number of years. Two major books, booklets, maps, and a coloring portfolio are included among the items.

In February 1985, the Committee on Publications was reactivated. A pamphlet, "Squanto—Friend of the Pilgrims," by Ernest John Knapton, former vice-president of the Society, was published as a contribution to the celebration of the Barnstable County Tercentenary.

Next came the fourth printing of "The Narrow Land" by Elizabeth Reynard—folk chronicles of old Cape Cod. Publication rights were bequeathed to the Society by Miss Reynard and Virginia Gildersleeve, and the Houghton Mifflin Company generously relinquished its copyright. Printed as a paperback, with an attractive cover design by Jeannette Fontaine, has helped to spotlight "The Narrow Land" in retail stores.

The Committee then turned its attention to a collection of 32 essays presented to the Society by Joshua Atkins Nickerson 2nd for publication. The essays covered Joshua's life in Chatham and on Cape Cod since 1901—fascinating descriptions of his early relatives, anecdotes and folktales, living conditions in Chatham and on Cape Cod in the early part of this century, plus Joshua's commentary on Cape Cod's growth and future.

Committee members assumed the responsibilities of preparing the essays for publication. Jay A. Ebel and Eric Hartell concentrated on editing; Jeannette Fontaine provided pen and ink drawings and the cover design; and Joseph A. Nickerson served as historian and supplied photographs from his extensive collection.

Working with Joshua to complete the final details of this book has enabled us to understand more fully this remarkable gentleman, whose life span of 87 years has been a part of the history of Chatham and Cape Cod. His ability to recall so many details of his long and active life, and the manner in which he has expressed his thoughts so clearly, are truly amazing. Not only his grandson Peter, to whom he has dedicated this book, but all who love Chatham and Cape Cod are indebted to him for his noteworthy literary achievement.

The Chatham Historical Society, organized in 1923, continues to be an active organization and to provide an important service to the Town of Chatham in preserving its history.

The Old Atwood House, built around 1752, was obtained by the Society in 1926 and has been open to the public ever since.

Several additions have been made to the Old Atwood House—the Joseph C. Lincoln Wing, the William Nickerson Wing—and the nationally known Stallknecht murals, presented to the Society in 1977, are on display in a special building next to the Old Atwood House.

All who read this book are cordially invited to visit the Old Atwood House and Museum, one of the few spots on Cape Cod where so much of interest to so many may be seen so easily.

Jay A. Ebel
Chairman, Committee on Publications

January 1988

Preface

For Peter

ALL history is divided into two parts: before I was born and since I was born. When my only grandson came into our lives in 1959, I wanted him to learn a little about Cape Cod, and Chatham as a particular example of Cape Cod, in the time before he was born. This seemed to me especially desirable, since he is an adopted child, and I might thus contribute to his sense of belonging, not only to the family, but to the local community. So from time to time over a period of many years I have written the "pieces" which comprise this book.

There has probably been no period in the history of mankind when changes in lifestyle have been greater nor more rapid than in my lifetime. This applies to everything about the way we live—transportation, communication, use of new tools, working shorter hours, more leisure, health care—life expectancy, personal comfort—even the food we eat. It is my hope that this book will help not only my grandson, but all grandsons and granddaughters who read it to have a better appreciation of their grandparents' time and of their own position in the flow of the never-ending thread that runs through and unites all our generations.

I am grateful, too, that there is a Chatham Historical Society ready, willing and able to undertake the publication of a book such as this.

JOSHUA ATKINS NICKERSON 2ND

East Harwich, Massachusetts
November 1987

Contents

How Chatham Came To Be Different

T HE first Europeans known to have died in Chatham were four Frenchmen who came with Samuel de Champlain in 1606, when he spent about three weeks in October in what is now Stage Harbor. The year before, he had spent some time in Nauset Harbor, where they killed one Indian who stole a pot. The next year, when he was in Stage Harbor, a number of Indians as well as the four Frenchmen must have been killed and wounded in the fighting.

At that time the French were intensively exploring the coast of New England, seeking a place for a settlement where the climate was more salubrious than in what is now the maritime provinces of Canada. If they had gotten along better with the Indians, several hundred of whom lived in Chatham at that time, we descendants of the original settlers would now doubtless speak French instead of English.

The English, however, were pretty mean to the Indians too, inveigling them onto their ships where they clapped them in irons and took them off to Spain to be sold as slaves. One such Indian was Squanto (Tisquantum); but he was a very special Indian. He had already been to England at least once and had learned to speak English. He did not come from Chatham, though he died here.

Somehow he made his way from Spain to England, where

he had visited before, and by the time the Pilgrims arrived he was back somewhere to the north or possibly, as we say, "down east". He came originally from Patuxet, which is now Plymouth. While he was away a plague wiped out every inhabitant of his village, about 1616. So he was the only survivor among the Indians who had tilled the soil and lived in Plymouth.

Early in the spring of 1621, having heard of the arrival of the Pilgrims, he went to their settlement and, speaking English, he became their interpreter, their mentor with the Wamponoags, and their teacher. It is doubtful indeed if the colony could have survived the winter of 1621–22 if he had not taught them how to plant, how to use alewives for fertilizer, how and where to fish, and the tactics of fowling.

In the fall of 1622 he came with Governor Bradford aboard the "Swan" into Pleasant Bay to trade with the Monomoyick Indians for corn and beans, which the colonists would sorely need to see them through the coming winter. He was able to reassure the Monomoyicks and persuaded them to barter peacefully with Bradford and his men. But before they left Squanto fell sick and died. He had asked to be buried in the white man's fashion and hoped to go to the white man's heaven. In all probability his body lies on the hill just west of Ryder's Cove, which has long been an Indian burial ground.

Relations between the colonists and the Indians of Cape Cod continued to be good and amicable. When William Nickerson came, the stage was set for a warm and friendly relationship with the Monomoyicks. Their Sachem Mattaquason and Nickerson became not only good neighbors but good friends.

What did William Nickerson see when he bought land in Monomoit (now Chatham) from the Indian Sachem Mattaquason in 1656, and later settled there in 1664?

He had sailed from England in 1637, when he was about 33 years old, with his wife Anne Busby (aged about 29) and their four children, ranging in age from two to nine, along with Anne's parents. They arrived safely in Salem after a voyage of more than two months. The following year he took the oath of freeman at Boston, where the Busbys lived. By 1640 he had moved to Yarmouth, where he had a farm near Follin's Pond (then called Little Bass Pond), which he held until he moved to Monomoit in 1664. About 1656 he purchased by verbal agreement land at Monomoit from Mattaquason, but because of a law passed in 1643, became involved in long and bitter litigation with the Plymouth Colony, which claimed that it also had to be bought from them.

From 1657 to 1661 he was in Boston so that his wife could care for her parents in their old age. Nicholas Busby died in August 1657 and his widow died in July 1660. Early in 1662 William with his family was back in Yarmouth, and in 1664 they moved to Monomoit, except for his oldest son Nicholas, then about 36, who remained on the farm in Yarmouth. Thus in 1664 William, aged about 60, his wife about 56, and eight of their children ranging in age from 17 to 34, with their families, were the original settlers in what is now Chatham.

During the next 10 years there was constant litigation and dispute about his title to the land, until finally in 1674, upon payment of 90 pounds to the Colony in addition to what he had already paid to the Indians, his title was confirmed in writing by both the Indians and the Colony. Thus he was about 70 years old when he came into undisputed ownership of about 4,000 acres of what is now the town of Chatham.

To each of his children he gave a farm of 40 acres of upland and 10 acres of meadow; so he started the community with nine families, all of them his own. Indian villages surrounded them to the west and north, and to the east of a line from the head of Oyster Pond to Frost Fish Creek, which he had not purchased. There were clearings and meadows, but most of the land was heavily forested.

Fish, shellfish and waterfowl were abundant. That crops were good is shown by the fact that the Indians at Monomoit had traded their surplus corn and beans to the colony at Plymouth in its early days. His house at the head of Ryder's Cove was by a bubbling spring. Nearby was Pasture Pond where his cattle could drink. Alewives by the tens of thousands in the spring provided plenty of fertilizer for his corn.

The forest supplied unlimited material for fuel, for building homes and boats, and for producing tar. The great cedar swamps not only provided logs for the fire and for fence rails, but peat for fuel and stoves and hoops for cooperage. Grapes and berries grew in profusion and salt could be made from sea water. Whales could occasionally be captured. Add to all this a mild and invigorating climate.

By 1664 he had come to know the Indians well, and they were friendly and helpful neighbors. The old Sachem Mattaquason lived only a stones's throw away. Pleasant Bay was big enough to harbor a fleet of ships, and yet he was far enough from the ocean to be well forewarned of any attack by pirates or French privateers.

In 1674 he made his first sale of land outside his family. In 1686, when he was about 82 years old, he deeded all his property to his daughter, Sarah Covel, a widow. The next year she and her parents deeded an undivided half interest in most of the property, excluding his own farm of which Sarah remained sole owner, to his son William. He had dedicated the hill at the head of Ryder's Cove beside his home as a burial place, and later his daughter Sarah gave it to the town. All but a small remnant of that burial place has since fallen into the hands of private owners.

What did William Nickerson see in Monomoit? A place where his clan could live in peace and security on farms which could support them well. And others could come: "Wee doe not desire to live alone, but are willing to receive soe many inhabitants as theire is land to accommodate them with." Here he would found not a dynasty but a clan.

He was a devout man, a thoughtful man, and a man of action, somewhat ahead of his time. This is demonstrated in numerous ways, but perhaps considering the legal status of English women in the 17th century, most spectacularly by turning over all his property, when he was over 80 years old, to his daughter Sarah.

The following is quoted from "A History of Chatham", written by William C. Smith. "He was in many respects a remarkable man—a man of large enterprises, of honorable intentions and strong religious convictions. He had the firm will and restless energy of the successful pioneer. In pursuing what he believed to be his rights, he was appalled by no difficulties and disheartened by no reverses. Drawn into the purchase of the Monomoit lands through a mistaken idea of the law, he looked behind the law to the equities of the case and strove long and earnestly to secure a favorable issue. The 'purchasers or old comers', however, whose rights were affected, were the governing class in the Colony and they would brook no compromise that seemed fair to him, hence the contest waxed warm. 'For I desier not to wrong any man of ther just right nor I would not be wronged myself', was his expressed principle."

In the first half of the nineteenth century salt was a major product, peaking in 1837 with 27,000 bushels. But by 1886 the last salt works closed down. In 1865 over 25,000 quintals of fish were salted and cured ("made") in Chatham, and 6,746 barrels of mackerel were inspected in 1864.

This little town, with a total population at that time of about 2,700, sent 292 men to fight in the Civil War.

But from that time on for the next 90 years, as the economic base of the town declined, so did its population. As sailing ships grew bigger, and when steamships replaced sail, many Chatham men served on them, but from larger ports. I can recall from my boyhood a nodding acquaintance with at least a half a dozen or more Chatham captains.

The census records show the growth and decline of Chatham's population. It increased from less than 700 in 1765 to a peak of more than 2,700 in 1860, 95 years later. It then fell steadily in each census until 50 years later, in 1910, it had dropped to 1,564, which was less than it had been 90 years before, in 1820. Even when the railroad came to Chatham in 1887, it did not check the decline in population, which fell from over 2,000 in 1885 to 1,564 in 1910.

And this is about the time when I became an active observer. My grandfather Nickerson was born in 1833 and died in 1915. I was born in 1901. So between the two of us we have lived to observe Chatham for 150 years, almost half the time since William Nickerson came here to live beside the old Sachem Mattaquason. Between us we have witnessed the pre-Civil War growth and prosperity of the town, its steady decline from the Civil War time until World War I, and its growth and prosperity from that time until now. This growth was interrupted by the great depression of the 1930's and by World War II, but has been consistent since then. And with this growth have come new problems.

Cape Cod as a whole—and Chatham in particular—has been a mecca for summer visitors ever since the railroad came in 1887. About 1890, for instance, the Hotel Chatham was built on what is now the fourth fairway of the Eastward Ho Golf Club by Eben Jordan of Boston and his friends. It was a very large and elegant summer hotel, complete with adjoining bowling alleys and croquet grounds. Its broad verandahs and its luxurious public rooms were most modern for their time. A special stop was made by the train at West Chatham, near the present Chatham airport, where passengers transferred to horse-drawn coaches to take them to the hotel. But it was far ahead of its time and failed.

In the village itself overlooking beach and harbor, there was the four-storied Hotel Mattaquason, built by Marcellus Eldredge, a Chatham boy who had made a fortune in the post Civil War period brewing beer and ale with his brother H. Fisher Eldredge in Portsmouth, New Hampshire. His summer mansion, complete with stables, carriage house, greenhouse and caretaker's gate-cottage, was on the broad acres of the knoll adjoining, known of old as James' Head, surrounded by a lovely high wooden fence with brick entrance posts.

He also gave the town the Eldredge Public Library and contributed largely to the building of the Methodist Episcopal Church across Main Street from the Library. But with all his wealth, he never lost touch with his local boyhood friends. Every summer he gave a great clambake to which they were all invited.

But simple lack of sophistication was beginning to change. Some of the more enterprising opportunities had developed from taking a few summer boarders, to more elaborate boarding houses by building on rooms accommodating 30 to 50 guests or more. Among them were the Hammond House and the Hawes Home in the "village" near the Chatham Twin Lights. There were the Dill Cottages and the Hawthorne Inn nearby, and the Old Harbor Inn and "Mrs Jones" in North Chatham, and the Cockle Cove Inn in West Chatham. These summer boarding houses were family affairs, run by the owners who for the most part had no professional experience as innkeepers. But their rates were reasonable, plumbing was minimal, the food was plain but excellent, and the same guests tended to come back year after year.

In the summer of 1912 Chatham celebrated its 200th Anniversary as a town. The program covered the better part of a week. It was "Old Home Week", with sons and daughters returning from afar. There was a great parade with two bands. It is interesting to note that the parade committee decided that automobiles should not be permitted in the parade. There were ball games, fireworks, special services in all the churches, lifeboat drills in which crews from the United States Life Saving Stations competed, (there were then four in Chatham), rowing races in dories, and sailing races.

A big banquet was served in a huge tent, seating over 600 people, which had been erected on "Rink Hill", overlooking the Mill Pond. *(See page 234, "Reflections" for more details on the 200th Anniversary.)* I was permitted to stay and listen to the long orations which followed the banquet and, more thrilling, to taste my first "frozen pudding dessert".

The celebration also marked a "slack tide" period, from which Chatham has grown since at an accelerating pace.

Many other things were happening to Chatham about 1912. Construction was begun on the Marconi Wireless Station in Chathamport. Originally it had six 400-foot steel towers stretching in a straight line from Chathamport to West Chatham. It was later found that such towers were not necessary and they have all been torn down. But at that time the engineers had great problems in lining them up just right to aim for Potsdam, Germany. This station was to replace the original Marconi Station in Wellfleet. It was completed in August of 1914 just as World War I started and the United States Government immediately commandeered it. *(See page 239, "Reflections" for more about the Marconi Station.)*

At the same time Charlie Hardy and a syndicate called the Chatham Associates were buying land in Chatham like mad. His group included several prominent men such as Willard Sears, the architect; Loring Underwood, landscaper and land-use planner; and Henry Fuller, attorney; also Herbert Windeler, a prime mover in the creation of the Eastward Ho Country Club. They purchased large tracts along the ocean front, on the Mill Pond and at Skunk's Neck, beyond the end of Cedar Street.

I heard some of the old-timers comment, "Charlie Hardy

must be crazy! Why I've heard he paid as high as $500 an acre for some of that sandy beach plum and bayberry bush land along the shore!"

He and his associates immediately built the Chatham Bars Inn and numerous cottages nearby. They built summer rental cottages overlooking the Mill Pond, a brick business block (Chatham's first) in the center of town on the site of the old post office and Kelley's ice cream parlor and Smallhoff's photography studio. Nearby they built a big garage (now a storage building) and quarters for visiting chauffeurs. This was just at the beginning of travel by motor car, and the trains still brought most of the summer visitors.

Hardy and his associates provided the sort of accomodations which appealed to the rich and successful. Many who came for a stay at his Chatham Bars Inn returned to take one of his cottages for the summer, and later bought land and built homes of their own. Chatham was lucky in all of this. For it occurred at the end of the Victorian style architecture and at the beginning of a period of simple and more functional architectural design. It was also lucky in that land values were *relatively* high compared with some other Cape Cod towns, so that there was little building of cheap camps and shacks. There was a tendency also to avoid selling tiny cottage lots, as happened in old "camp meeting" sites, such as Oak Bluffs, Harwichport and Eastham.

The game of golf was growing in popular favor at this time. So when the Chatham Bars Inn opened, it had from the start the added attraction of an excellent 9-hole golf course. I was caddying there on a warm August morning when a messenger called my golfer to the telephone at the Inn. Germany was on the warpath, France had declared war, England was standing by. There was utter world-wide confusion—and the New York Stock Exchange had closed! George Creel was appointed chief of propaganda—and the stories of German atrocities and horror that poured over us were unbelievable—

yet they were believed! Everybody started raising war gardens for food. The Home Guard was organized with civilians who trained each week with ancient rifles, even some muskets.

In 1916, the United States Navy acquired the land at the end of Nickerson's Neck, between Crows Pond and the channel southwest of Strong Island. By 1917 construction was well under way and the Naval Air Station was in operation. All through the war construction continued. *(See page 242, "Reflections" for more on the Naval Air Station).*

Glamour was added by the presence of hundreds of sailors, aviators, Marines, as well as civilian workers. The local people set up hospitality centers for them, a small one about opposite the present entrance to the Eastward Ho clubhouse and a larger one downtown on Cross Street. Both were in residences modified for the purpose. A few of the men came back or stayed on after the war and settled in Chatham. Chatham was booming. A few of the family names common in Chatham today first came then, among them them one named Farrenkopf.

Some of Charlie Hardy's friends who had been coming to the Chatham Bars Inn were dissatisfied with his 9-hole golf course. They dreamed of an 18-hole championship course with a spectacular view, such as they had played at Westward Ho! in Scotland—hence the name, Eastward Ho Country Club.

So about 1917 or 1918, Charlie and Herbert Windeler got together a number of men and bought all the land along the shore of Pleasant Bay, from Route 28 down to the Naval Air Station. They developed this into the Eastward Ho Golf Course of the Chatham Country Club. This included the site of the old Hotel Chatham, which opened about 1890 and failed after a few years. When it was torn down some of the materials were used to build several very ugly two-story cottages for a development called "Larchmont-by-the-Sea". This too was a failure.

They employed the best golf architects. They imported

a professional greenskeeper and golf pro from Scotland. They made it a really challenging course for the expert. The fairways were much narrower and the rough was much rougher than today. Summer residents and local people alike joined together to raise the funds to finance it.

Then came the crash and panic of 1921. Eastward Ho was in financial trouble, and Charlie Hardy bid for it and won it for a song at a mortgage foreclosure sale.

About 1927 Roy E. Tomlinson, president of National Biscuit Company and a director of several major national companies, and a long-time summer resident of Chatham, had been listening for several years to the former stockholders in the Club bemoaning their loss of Eastward Ho. Very quietly he bought the entire property for $75,000. He then politely suggested that his friends should either put up or shut up. They could have the property for a new club at just what he had paid for it, or he would hold it for real estate speculation. They decided to "put up", and a new club was organized, but under terms and conditions which Roy hoped would minimize the chances of losing it again.

Thus it came about that Eastward Ho again became a community venture, with a capitalization of $100,000—the extra $25,000 being intended to provide working capital. It did, but not enough. Various members loaned the Club substantial sums in return for unsecured notes, some of which were later paid off in land. But when the bonds (each member held a minimum of two shares of stock and one $1,000 bond) became in default, no more land could be sold. Thus Roy Tomlinson had provided against the hard times that followed by fixing it so the Club's land could neither be sold or mortgaged until the bond holders had been satisfied. This protected the property and held it safe from dissipation during the hard years of the '30's and '40's. It wasn't until about 1960 that the bonds were paid off with the proceeds of the sale of the land not used for golf purposes, and the Club was re-chartered as a non-business corporation. The Club now seems to be doing very well in every way. If it continues to do so, it will be the first financially successful undertaking on Nickerson's Neck since Ensign Nickerson's shipyard in the 1840's. The millions of dollars which went down the drain there may not have been lost in vain. It is so beautiful and such an asset to all who live or visit in this area!

The business crisis of 1921 turned out to be short-lived. By 1923–24 the country was booming again. The land boom in Florida was reflected on a much smaller scale by a speculative land boom on Cape Cod. In the mid-20's real estate operators "from away" were swarming all over the place. Tracts of land bought for $100 an acre a few months back were re-sold for $200 or even $300 an acre.

I was one of a group of five local people who owned a tract in Orleans overlooking the ocean. Not just once, but several times, we sold options to buy this land to speculators who thought they had customers lined up to pay them a big profit—but they didn't. We finally sold it, years later, to a local real estate man who did very well with it.

During the mid-20's the whole of Cape Cod was humming with an air of speculation. The Ferguson Hotel in Hyannis, which stood about where the main office of the Cape Cod Bank & Trust Company is today, was a favorite hangout for the "operators".

In Chatham fine new homes were being built at a slow but steady pace, many of them designed for year-round occupancy, though used mostly in the summer. But accompanying this frenzied speculation in land was a sound underlying development. High prices for land helped sustain high quality of structures *on* land. At Orleans, for example, Asa Mayo's farm at Pochet Neck was bought by the Orleans Associates, a group of speculators and land developers who went bankrupt in 1928. They employed a leading landscape architect to lay out their lots, and an excellent architect for the few houses they built. At that time they actually sold several lots at prices around three to four thousand dollars each—remember these were 100-cent dollars—so it would be equivalent to seven to ten thousand in 1965's deflated dollars. Later in the depression of the 1930's, these same lots were offered at six to seven hundred dollars each, but there were no buyers then.

But the summer residents of Chatham were faced with a problem. As their children reached their early teens there was no place for them to gather as a gang. Those around Stage Harbor scarcely knew the kids from North Chatham. And the summer season was so short! Something should be done to provide a place for these youngsters to get together.

So the idea was conceived of having a summer social club, with tennis courts and bathing as well as dancing and lunches, but no liquor! It was intended primarily for the teenagers, since it was felt that there was no convenient way for the young summer visitors to get to know each other. Parents were anxious to enhance the interest of their children in continuing to spend their summers in Chatham.

So in 1927 a group got together and bought a piece of land covered with silverleaf trees adjoining the site of the old lighthouse, which had been washed away a generation earlier. On the ocean side was a long inlet from Stage Harbor and beyond that a wide beach washed by surf. A clubhouse was built in the silverleaf grove in 1928. Its basement was at ground level on the side toward the water and was used for locker rooms and showers for men and for women.

At that time the point of North Beach was well north of the Chatham Lighthouse, and the "South Beach" paralleling the shoreline was reached by a 375-foot bridge from the Beach Club.

The beach itself was 200 to 300 yards wide, and it was here that hamburg lunches were grilled and served every pleasant day, and beach umbrellas and canvas wind shelters were stored in huge boxes for the use of members who were sun and surf bathing. At that time the entrance to Pleasant Bay was just north of the Beach Club.

Then as now there were three tennis courts. Every Thursday evening the Club was crowded for the buffet suppers and on Saturdays there was an orchestra for dancing. The young people gathered to play records and make dates during the day—all under the friendly and watchful eyes of the steward and his wife.

I served for several years as the original treasurer of the Club and was on the Building Committee along with Herbert Winslow and Charles Whiting, who built it.

In my boyhood there had been a clubhouse in East Harwich on Pleasant Bay, just north of where Wequasset Inn now stands. This was the base for sailboat racing for many years. But by 1918 it had fallen by the wayside. In that year a new Chatham Yacht Club was organized, with a class of "Bay Birds". There must have been about 50 of them, and the summer races, twice a week, were a source of great enjoyment to both participants and onlookers. Later a splinter group established the Stage Harbor Yacht Club for racing in Stage Harbor and Nantucket Sound. But the races and regattas on Pleasant Bay in the summer are colorful indeed, with nearly a hundred boats competing at times.

In 1930–31 the Chatham Band was reorganized under the direction of Thomas Nassi, a musician born in Albania, who brought the teaching of instrumental music to the schools of Chatham, Harwich and Orleans. The Band was (and still is) composed of amateur musicians from Chatham and nearby towns. They had no uniforms. So Mr. and Mrs. Herbert Winslow gave a huge garden party to introduce the new band to the summer colony. They had also given the band new uniform caps and jackets for the occasion. From that day to this the Chatham Band has continued active and successful. Nobody gets paid but they all have fun. Once upon a time they took great pride in the Christmas concert with Santa

Claus, out-of-doors for the children; and their Friday evening concerts with dancing on the green continue throughout each summer.

The shock of the stock market crash and the depression that followed did not really make their impact fully felt on Cape Cod until the summer of 1932. For the next few years almost no new homes were built. But the vacationeers continued to come, albeit with a tighter grasp on their purses than before. By 1937 we were beginning to climb out of the morass of depression. President Franklin Roosevelt declaimed on the radio that things were on the way up. "We planned it this way", he said, "and don't let anybody tell you different." Then the bottom fell out again.

But with the war in Europe the economy started up again, and Cape Cod too shared in it. After Pearl Harbor, Cape Cod had four long, hard years of struggling for economic survival. There were few summer visitors (gasoline was rationed). There was little social life (blackouts were in effect at night). There was almost no building (materials were rationed according to military priorities). No boats could have fuel, not even for a little 2 ½ H.P. outboard, except commercial boats.

I remember one summer day when my wife and I and another couple with three small children were sailing down to my camp on the beach in a big sailing sharpie I had at the time. We encountered both headwind and headtide and were making little progress toward the camp. It was past the time for the children's mid-day meal, so I pulled out my little 2 ½ H.P. outboard, which had been stored under the deck with a gallon of pre-war gas for just such an emergency. We had no sooner got it in operation than we were hailed from the beach by the Coast Guard and told to cease using our motor in violation of regulations.

At that time the Cape was swarming with Coast Guardsmen. They patrolled every waterfront beach in pairs and with dogs. In 1942 Germany, with her submarines, controlled our

North Atlantic Coast. Our ocean beaches were strewn with the debris from hundreds of sunken ships.

But in 1946 the war was over. By 1947 it was again possible to buy building materials without a military priority rating. Price controls were removed. Gasoline was no longer rationed, and Cape Cod, like the rest of the country, was off to a new era in its history. Its great growth period had just begun.

A Chatham Boy's
Neighborhood
1907–1917

—As Remembered In 1987

I ENTERED the Atwood Primary School in 1906 at the age of five and a half. My memories before that are vague, but none the less real.

There was old Mrs. Kendrick across the road, whom I used to visit as she lay on a couch under a paisley shawl. She always produced for me a large flat peppermint or wintergreen candy.

There was old Abner Nickerson, who asked to let me come to see him as he lay dying in his home, also across the road.

Afterwards there was his widow "Miz Abner". She and I would sit facing each other in rocking chairs, with her sewing table between us just to one side, on which perched a metal bird that held thread in its beak.

She would rock back and forth sighing, "Ho hum, hum-a-day", and I would rock back and forth sighing, "Ho hum, hum-a-day".

Then there was the house next door, where Uncle Joshua and Aunt May lived with "Aunt" Susan Gould as their permanent guest. From the kitchen windows there I could see the Chatham depot and railroad yard, and I delighted in playing with dominoes on the window sill in imitation of the movement of the railroad cars.

My neighborhood was my childhood world. It was an exciting time when they paved Old Harbor Road, passing our house, with water-bound crushed stone making it a macadam road. The steam roller compacting the stone looked huge, and the engineer who stoked it with coal and ran it seemed like a giant of the new revolution in transportation, which was barely beginning.

About this time too my father had a windmill installed which pumped water from a "driven well" to a metal-lined tank in the attic of our house, so that we no longer depended on the hand pump in the kitchen sink.

While a new world opened for me when I trudged off with my lunch pail to the Atwood School in September 1906, the center for me was still the neighborhood of the house where I was born.

Directly across the road was the bicycle shop of Arthur Edwards and next door to that was his home. He sold and repaired bicycles and he was a carpenter. But he was also a dreamer.

He sold the Victor talking machine. I remember being fascinated by the picture of a dog listening to "his master's voice", that being their slogan. Songs such as "In the Shade of the Old Apple Tree" and "My Irene Was the Village Queen" were heard on this machine above the scratching sound, as the cylindrical Edison record revolved against the needle.

Mr. Edwards also made and sold a great variety of toy windmills which were very popular as gifts and lawn ornaments. A few years later he was the inspiration for Joseph Lincoln's novel "Shavings", which was produced as a play on Broadway.

But his special love was his motorcycle. This was a relatively primitive affair, and his was particularly different because it was driven by a leather belt, which often slipped off with disastrous results.

Right behind his shop was a cranberry bog, separated from other swampland by an earthen dyke. There I used to catch turtles, some of which I sold to the Chinese laundryman in the village for a cent apiece, or maybe two cents.

Our next door neighbors to the north were "Captain Frank" Nickerson and his wife Olive, who lived in an old Cape Cod style house on the southeast corner of Old Harbor Road and Bar Cliff Avenue. I don't think "Captain Frank" Nickerson was ever really a captain. But we children were always taught to call him that.

They were poor by today's standards, but they owned their own home and "Captain Frank" managed to make a frugal living by clamming and fishing and raising his own vegetables.

I recall his delivering clams to mother, all neatly opened and ready to cook. He would then visit with her for a while, standing in the kitchen. Mother would politely inquire after his wife "Miss Olive".

He would usually say, "She's a little poorly of late".

Mother would express her sympathy, for which "Captain Frank" would thank her, adding, "But you know she's older than I be."

It was true—mother found out that Miss Olive was older. She had been born three months before her husband. But I guess it helped the old man to keep going, thinking how young he was!

He sometimes got confused when it came time to leave, and instead of going outside took the wrong door from the kitchen into the pantry. After a minute or two he would reappear, and without a word being said leave through the outside door. It was hard for us children to obey mother's admonition not to laugh.

I remember one occasion when "Captain Frank" had been clamming on a very hot day, he took his clothes off because of the heat. Naturally this resulted in his getting a very bad sunburn. So to relieve the burn he applied "oil" to his skin, but he made the mistake of using kerosene oil instead of a soothing emollient, with of course dire results. It damned near killed him.

Father used to say "Captain Frank" was the only man he ever heard of who saved his life by jumping overboard with an anchor lashed to him. It seems that "Captain Frank" was once offshore of the backside of the beach, just outside the breakers in his dory, when he lost an oar. There he was, helpless with a high sea running and a strong undertow setting back on the slope of the beach.

He soon realized that he was drifting right through the breakers to the beach. So he threw overboard everything but his anchor and a short length of rope, one end of which he fastened to the anchor and the other he lashed around his middle. Then he lay down in the bottom of the dory hoping the boat would ride safely through to the beach, which it did.

The moment the dory hit the beach, "Captain Frank" jumped overboard with his anchor firmly in hand and dug it into the sand as the undertow from the receding wave tore at him. The next sea sent him spinning upwards on the slope of the beach, where again he dug in with his anchor as the undertow tried to drag him back. After three such maneuvers he found himself safe and sound (but not dry) on the top of the dry beach. He had saved his life by jumping overboard with an anchor tied to him!

Diagonally across the road from "Captain Frank" lived "Miz Sophronie" Robbins. I didn't know her very well. But in her yard were mulberry trees which had been planted years before, when some people were advocating producing silk on Cape Cod made from the cocoons of silk worms, one of whose favorite foods was the mulberry. For me as a boy, it resulted in my enjoyment of eating the ripe fruit, even though it was soft, juicy and sickly sweet.

A few hundred yards west, on the north side of what is now Bar Cliff Avenue, lived the Bakers, a family with four boys. "Scrag", the oldest, I didn't know very well. But "Cal" (Alvin) and "Dodger" (Warren) were both about my age, and we saw a lot of each other. "The Kid" (Leslie) was a few years younger.

Across the street from their house was a big field, known as the "Cattle Field", and adjoining it another big field which had more recently been under cultivation. In the middle of it stood the "Old House", which had been unused for many years and which we boys took over as our own clubhouse. We had secret ways to get in and a secret way to get upstairs. It probably never occurred to us that we were trespassers and vandals—not even when we cut some of the lead flashing away from the chimney to melt down for keels on the toy boats we built.

Back of the Baker home were pine woods, which had grown up on land which was once pasture and on which someone had once tried to raise cranberries on upland. There was a small valley there too, in which we built a tepee out of rails and branches and pine needles. Beyond it we cut a labyrinth of "mystery paths" through the stands of young pines. Toadstools were abundant in season, and we used them as ammunition in "play-battles" with each other. Our only defensive armor were shields made of wood, cardboard, covers snitched from the tops of rubbish barrels, or once their mother's wash boiler. We made kites out of sticks of wood and newspapers, with tails made of bits of rags. We flew them in the cattle field.

In those days almost every boy set a string of jump traps for skunks and muskrats. When we caught one it was carefully skinned, and the skin was then stretched inside out to dry on a wooden form. Eventually it was shipped to St. Louis in exchange for a small amount of money. At school in the autumn and early winter, there were many days on which a boy would arrive smelling strongly of skunk.

I was still a boy when the Baker family moved to Orleans, and their home was bought by George and May Kendrick. George was a carpenter. They kept cows and I can remember going across the cattle field to their house to get extra milk when our supply ran low. I got it in a "lard pail" which had a wire bail. In those days lard was purchased in such pails, which were always saved to be used to carry liquids or to pick berries.

Raymond Eldredge was another of my boyhood friends. His father was George Eldredge, and they lived just north of the railroad tracks on what is now Hitching Post Road. Raymond had three older brothers—Wyman, Henry and Millard, and a younger sister Lois.

George ran a farm raising a wide variety of vegetables, and he kept a small herd of cows. Sometimes they would be pastured at "Tainter's Field," which overlooks Oyster Pond and lies between Queen Anne Road and Pond Street. One of Raymond's chores, in which I often participated, was to drive the cows home from there in the late afternoon, bringing them along Queen Anne Road and up thru the little valley between Depot Street and the cemetery.

His father also owned a peat bog, just south of the cattle field, where he cut peat into cakes and dried them for use as fuel in the cast-iron cooking range. It made a very hot fire. One or two summers Raymond and I planted a garden to the edge of this bog where we raised a few vegetables, which we peddled to our neighbors from my little express wagon.

When I was about 10 or 12 years old, I decided that I wanted to go into business for myself as a peddler. No doubt I was inspired by the example of the numerous peddlers who called at our house. In addition to the grocer, the milkman and the butcher, there were the shoe peddler, the tinware man, the bakery cart, the Grand Union Tea Company man, the junkman (buying, not selling, junk), the man selling flavoring extracts, and of course the pack peddler selling from a pack on his back.

So I would order from the catalog of Charles Broadway Rowse a few items which I could pack in a sort of suitcase, and then peddle them (at a small profit) among the neighbors. In this manner I got better acquainted with many neighbors. I'm sure that my parents did not wholly approve of this, but they did not restrain me from doing it for the rather brief period that I pursued the calling of a peddler.

Just south of Uncle Joshua's house on Old Harbor Road, in a small old-fashioned Cape Cod style cottage, lived the Crowell family, consisting of widow Crowell, her son Seth, her daughter Elsie, and Elsie's illegitimate son Sherman.

Poor Sherman was born crippled in both body and mind. He was a little older than I was, and I was much impressed by his hopping around on his one good leg, dragging his withered leg, and swinging his one good arm in wild gestures. He had red hair and when excited or angered poured forth a torrent of incomprehensible sounds.

Otherwise the family was quiet and industrious. Seth raised most of their food and kept a cow. Elsie did a lot of excellent needlework. Every fall they made "hulled corn", a process by which corn was soaked and cured in a solution which included wood ashes. The end product was used as a cereal food in the days before we had dry cereals from the grocery. My family always bought a small supply, even though we didn't like it very much.

Just beyond the Crowell's was a two-story building which had once been the Granville Seminary for young ladies. It was then occupied by Mrs. Shaw, formerly married to a Shaw from Boston, and a daughter of H. Fisher Eldredge, who with his brother Marcellus had been benefactors of the town of Chatham. Mrs. Shaw later married Keno Marble and ran a gift shop in the old seminary building. I used to sell her waterlilies (lotus) which I picked in nearby ponds. I remember that I sold them for a cent apiece or 10 cents a dozen. I still remember hearing the rustling of her satin skirts and the tinkling of the Japanese wind chimes as she came through the door.

Southerly at the corner of Old Harbor Road and Highland Avenue lived Nathaniel (Nat) and and Ethel Eldredge and their three children, Ethelma, Jonathan and Hudson. Ethelma was about my age and together we explored at a very early age the intricacies of making mudpies and playing hopscotch. Nat was the first manager of the Chatham Bars Inn, which opened in 1914. He carried the title of proprietor. With his genial skill in dealing with people, he got the Inn off to a good start in its early years.

On the opposite corner, now a part of the parking lot for the Catholic Church (there was no Catholic Church in Chatham until many years later), lived Frank Dill, who was a clerk at the Atwood store on Main Street. Just beyond his house stood the almshouse. This was a large two-story building which provided housing and board for those of the town's poor who had no family to look after them. It was run by a resident couple under the direction of Chatham's "Overseers of the Poor".

Across the street was Eugene Cahoon's blacksmith shop. I spent many hours there as a small boy watching him shoe horses while their owners waited and spun yarns. I was fascinated as the sparks flew from his forge or from the red hot iron as he pounded it on his anvil.

Across Depot Road on the corner lived Joseph W. Nickerson and his family of four children, Earl and Pearl (twins), Josephine and Luther. Weekdays he was a mason-contractor-builder. On Sunday mornings the Boston papers were delivered in bulk to his barn, where they were prepared for distribution. The price was five cents.

A little farther south on Old Harbor Road lived Captain Hezikiah Doane, who was "keeper" of a United States Life Saving Station. He had formerly been in command of the Chatham station which stood on the "South Beach" offshore from Morris Island. But I remember him as "keeper" of the Old Harbor Station on the "North Beach". To my boyish eyes he looked impressive in his blue uniform, as he walked between his home and the "Cow Yard" landing, where he kept a dory which he rowed across from the station on his leaves from duty there.

On Bar Cliff Avenue lived Richard and Rebecca Ryder and their children, across the street from "Captain Frank" Nickerson. He too was skipper of a United States Life Saving Station. Earlier when he was serving on Nantucket, he had met and married Rebecca. She is a bright and lively person— today (1987) she is 103 years old. My father always called her "Rebel" or "Reb".

A little to the north, on Old Harbor Road lived Captain Joseph C. Kelley and his family. He was also in the United States Life Saving Service. When I was a boy he was in command of the Monomoy Point Station, having been assigned there shortly after the disaster in memory of which stands the Mack Memorial, near Chatham Light. He was an exceptionally brave, daring, and skillful captain.

There are numerous tales of his crews' unusual exploits while he was at the Monomoy Point Station. Later he succeeded Hezikiah Doane in command of the Old Harbor Station. It was while he was there that he had a tower built onto the front of his house. From its upper room his wife used to talk with him every night that visibility permitted in Morse Code with flashing lights.

Between their house and the corner of Bar Cliff Avenue lived the Harry Berrys. He was a yacht captain, and in the summer Mrs. Berry took in a summer boarder or two. They had no children.

Across the street from Captain Joe Kelley lived Mr. O'-Neill, who was the conductor on one of the passenger trains which ran out of Chatham. I think he was a widower. In any case he had a housekeeper, who was a sincere believer in the occult. I remember her giving me at length the benefit of her ability to communicate with another world.

Just beyond Captain Kelley's house was a fine two-story mansion and barn once owned by a sea captain, but then serving as a summer home for the William Barclays. Mrs. Barclay was a Thayer, and her family summered in an elegant home at the head of Thayer's Hill, overlooking the "Cow Yard" and the Old Harbor. The Barclays lived in Pawtucket, Rhode Island, where he was much involved politically, serving for a time as postmaster. They had two children—a daughter Ruth, a lovely girl a bit older than I, who died in the influenza epidemic of 1918, and a son Bill, just a bit younger than I.

They had a beautiful Cadillac automobile, with acetylene head lamps, a folding canvas top, and even a new Klaxon horn, as well as the usual rubber bulb horn. But it had to be cranked by hand. I remember how thrilled I was when they took me as a passenger on a trip to Provincetown and back—all in one day. I remember too that out-of-season Mr. Barclay sometimes brought a few of his friends to their house for weekend "stag parties".

Across the street from the Barclays lived Mrs. Almena and her sister, in what had once been the home of Captain Hiram Harding. He was a deep-sea sailor, and the local legend was that he brought back with him on one of his voyages a young Hawaiian princess who went to school for a time at the Granville Seminary.

Just beyond lived Isaac Loveland, a man of small stature, but a virtuoso at building small boats, especially small sail-boats. My father had one that he built named the "Sculpin", which he kept in the "Cow Yard", moored just clear of what still remained of the dock which my great great grandfather,

Joshua Atkins, had built a century before. We used her for "scow-banging" trips, which consisted of going off for the day with fish lines and clam hoes, and coming back home with something to eat to show for it.

Back to Bar Cliff Avenue, just east of the Ryder's house was a small livery stable and next door to it the owner's home. When I was about 10 years old he added an automobile to his livery service. It was a Ford Model T touring car, with bright brass trim on the radiator. One Sunday he took my parents, my brother and me on a wonderful trip all the way to Marstons Mills and back.

It was only a year or so later that my father bought a car of his own. It was a Studebaker touring car, with side curtains which could be buttoned on in case of rain.

In a small but lovely old Cape Cod cottage across the street lived Mrs. Burgess and her son. They were "come-outers", that is fundamentalist religious people who had left the established church in protest of the frivolous introduction of such things as an organ in the "meeting house", and other signs of "frolic".

Beyond them lived Mrs. Rogers and her son Tommy. She occasionally took in overnight boarders. Among them was my father's Uncle Benjie Atkins, who used to come down on the train from Boston to stay for a few days between his trips. He was a pilot on the fast steamships which ran on tight time schedules between Boston and New York.

At the foot of Bar Cliff Avenue on Shore Road (then known as the Boulevard) was the home of Howard Eldredge and his wife and daughter. Just below it was his fish "shanty", where he kept his gear and stowed his salted fish in brine in huge casks. He also dried salt fish there on his "flakes".

In those days, what is now Tern Island joined onto the mainland abreast the Chatham Bars Inn. There was no channel through it. So when Howard went out fishing he went around the north end of what is now Tern Island, between it and Ram

Island Flat. There was plenty of water between it and the mainland, as well as in the "Cow Yard" itself, making Aunt Lydia's Cove a harbor even more protected than it is now.

Howard Eldredge was what would nowadays be called something of a "character". He claimed, for example, that he never needed a compass. When a friend gave him one he complained that it was useless, because if he ran ten miles off shore northeast and then turned around and ran ten miles southwest, it would never bring him back to his original starting point. He was also at times a bit noisy, as his normal talking voice was well nigh a bellow. But he was a wonderfully interesting man, from a small boy's point of view.

All in all, my boyhood in Chatham was a happy time to remember, especially when I consider how different it was from what it would have been—if I were a boy today.

The Old Folks

To describe Cape Cod as I have seen it, I must tell you first about how it appeared to me as a child, through the eyes of "the old folks". Although both of my grandmothers were living when I was born in 1901, the only grandparent I remember was my father's father, Warren Jenson Nickerson, "Grandpa Nicker", and my recollections of him are vivid.

Born in 1833, he died in 1915 when I was 14. He was a tall lanky man with a full white beard. He lived in East Harwich in an old Cape Cod cottage farmhouse in the southerly lee of a hill which sheltered the house, barn and outbuildings. In his youth he had taught school "boarding around", as the custom was then, as he made the circuit of the district schools. The public schools of that time were called district schools and included children of all ages, up to young men between voyages at sea "before the mast".

One of the essentials of a schoolteacher then was that he be able to lick any of the big boys who might egg him on to personal combat in the school yard. Most youngsters on Cape Cod didn't go beyond the district school in their formal education, although there were a few local academies equivalent to the modern high schools on the Cape, and many in New England.

My father left the district school at the age of 14 to "go to sea", and though he returned between voyages, he left for good at 18, when he received a telegram while at school of-

29

fering him a berth as mate on a coasting schooner sailing out
of Boston.

One winter the South Chatham school was pretty tough.
Several teachers were "thrown out" by the big boys, most of
them home for the winter from summer fishing trips to the
Grand Banks.

The School Committee came to see if "Grandpa Nicker",
who was known as a fine teacher and a good disciplinarian,
would take over. He did. This is the story as he told it to me.

"I was over six feet tall, thin as a rail. In fact they called
me 'Cedar Rail Jenson'. I took my place at the desk the first
morning in the new schoolhouse, called the roll, to which
thirty-five or forty girls and boys from the village answered—
all ages from five to 18 years.

"As an opening speech, I said, 'I have my rules and shall
expect you to obey them'. I read them aloud.

"When I finished, a scholar who was man-size, mum-
bled, 'I'd like to see you lick me, spindle shanks, if I don't
behave—and so would some of the rest of us.' "

That was enough for grandfather. He grabbed that fellow
by the collar and shook the daylights out of him, slammed
him down in his seat so hard that the fellow's head hit the
desk back of him and split a gash in his scalp from which the
blood spurted, and scared everyone half to death.

Calmly grandfather remarked, "I'll be ready anytime the
rest of you disobey."

But no one did and school went on quietly the rest of the
winter.

Grandfather said, "I didn't mean to split his head open,
but it was a good thing, I guess."

Later when those fellows grew to be men and captains
of mackerel schooners, they came to grandfather to be taught
how to "figure shares and lays" for themselves, the owners
and the crew.

"Grandpa Nicker" soon gave up school teaching, and

except for a few years when he served on the police force in Providence, he lived the life of a Cape Cod farmer and fisherman, and was involved in various civic duties ranging from the Harwich School Committee to one of the trustees of the Evergreen Cemetery.

Every summer my cousin Warner Eldredge, who was a year or two older than I, spent the summer vacation with him to help with the chores. I used to spend a week or two with them. This was high adventure for me, since my grandfather liked nothing better than a fresh and receptive young mind in which to plant his vast accumulations of local lore and general wisdom.

It was when I was 12 that he decided to give me his treasured leather-bound copy of the "Autobiography of Benjamin Franklin". I can still recall the impact of the chapter in which Franklin describes ceasing to be a vegetarian while on a short sea voyage, and especially the chapter on the choice of a mistress.

"Grandpa Nicker" imparted to me local understanding which I could have had only from him alone. I remember once when I was driving with him in his wagon from East Harwich to Orleans. We passed a large sandy area dotted with an occasional runty pine or bayberry bush which appeared to be completely fenced in. As we drove along beside the fence, the incongruity of fencing in these barren acres grew in my mind, til I asked him, "Why?"

After a moment's thought he said, "That is so no cattle can get in there and starve to death."

On a wall in my house hangs a pen and ink and watercolor picture of the schooner "Morning Star" of Chatham, Captain Joshua Atkins departing from the Port of Naples, Italy. He was my great, great grandfather and was but one of several Chatham men who sailed from here in their small ships owned in shares by Chatham people. They traded in the period between the Revolution and the Civil War to the Mediterranean and the West Indies, as well as along our own coast. Their fishing vessels went each season to the Grand Banks of Newfoundland.

In the mid-1800's ocean-going vessels were built in Chatham. My Great Uncle Albert Nickerson told me that as a boy, about 1850, he worked in Ensign Nickerson's shipyard, which was about where the seventh tee is now at the Eastward Ho Country Club. As many as 15 vessels were built in Chatham in 1855 alone.

When he was in his prime, Captain Atkins lost his ship. It was on one of his return trips home that he was captured by pirates. One version of the story was that it was a Barbary pirate; another was that it was an English pirate. My guess is that it may have been the former, and that in telling the story, after the hatred of the British was engendered by the War of 1812 and what led up to it, the pirate became an Englishman.

At any rate, he was returning home when he was captured and ordered to give up the money which he was known to have on board. This he refused to do, since he said, "The money is not mine, but belongs to poor men and some widows and orphans of Chatham, who would suffer from the loss of it."

But the pirate captain was not impressed and ordered him lashed to the mouth of a cannon. For hours he was left there while the pirate crew ransacked every nook and cranny of the vessel looking for the gold—but to no avail.

Finally the pirate captain had his gunner light a match to shoot off the cannon and blow Captain Atkins to "kingdom come". He asked him again if he would tell, to which Captain Atkins replied, "Sir, I shall *never* tell where that money is."

The pirate captain shook his head and then gave the order, "Unlash him. He is too brave a man to die *like that*."

So the pirates set him and two of his crew adrift in a

small boat. They kept the "Morning Star" and the rest of the crew, including an orphan boy whom the captain and his wife Mehitable loved dearly. They never heard of the boy again.

Eventually Captain Atkins made his way to his home by the harbor in Chatham, arriving on foot and at night. He tapped on the pane of the bedroom window. Presently he was greeted at the door by his wife.

He walked into the kitchen and tossed onto the table a package wrapped in a bandana handkershief and said, "Hittie, I've lost everything—the vessel, the money, even the boy. I've got nothing left, save what's in this bundle."

But Aunt Hit rose to the occasion. "Josh", she said, "You haven't lost everything. You've still got me. It will be easy enough to get another vessel. But I could never find another man like you."

It is hard for us to realize not only the conditions but the spirit of the people living in Chatham in the late eighteenth and early nineteenth centuries. Father used to tell stories about his old Great Uncle Jonathan, who lived just across the cedar swamp. He had fought in the War of 1812 and spent a long term in Dartmoor Prison in England. So had Aunt Hit's father, Nathaniel Eldredge. They neither liked nor trusted the English.

Father told how he and his brother Ernest Carleton Nickerson would go to call on Uncle Jonathan in his very old age. He knew their names, of course, but would always ask them.

Then he would say, scathingly, "Oscar Clinton—Ernest Carleton, couldn't your mother find no good Christian names from the Bible to give you boys?"

They would counter by asking him a question—about the musket he kept on pegs above the fireplace, and which he took down and carefully cleaned every Sunday.

They would say, respectfully I hope, "Uncle Jonathan,

that musket there. You take such good care of it. But it's no good for fowling. You never use is for hunting. What do you keep it for?"

His reply, invariably accompanied by a knowing smile, would always be, "I'll tell ye, boys, you always got to be ready and you always want to keep one eye on old England."

In the 1870's the boys thought that was funny.

I learned alot too from my grandfather's younger brother, Joshua Albert Nickerson, who was born in 1837 and died in 1923. By the time I was old enough to observe, he was a widower retired on a pension from the Providence police force. He spent his summers visiting around among his numerous Cape Cod relatives, including those of his late wife, who was a Snow from Orleans, for a week or two at each stop.

My father's older brother, Joshua Atkins Nickerson, lived next door to us in Chatham, so each year I usually got a double exposure to Uncle Albert. He lacked grandfather's devotion to books and reading. But he had a tremendous store of yarns and earthy philosophy.

I remember Uncle Albert telling me stories of when he was a boy of 10 or 12, he had a job of sorts working for a time in Ensign Nickerson's shipyard in Chathamport. There they built "bankers", schooners to sail to the Grand Banks of Newfoundland for codfishing. He told me he remembered seeing such "bankers" lying at anchor between Strong Island and Fox Hill, rolling their rails under in the heavy seas rushing in over the entrance to Chatham Harbor, which was then located just northeast of Scatteree. At that time, he told me, the Chatham Bar's entrance from the ocean into Pleasant Bay was opposite Strong Island and Scatteree.

Today the entrance has moved about five miles to the south, and in most of the area between Strong Island and the mainland, you can barely float a rowboat at low tide.

He told me about the numerous saltworks which used to line the shores of Pleasant Bay, and how men used to rush to slide the wooden covers over the evaporation "pans" when rain threatened.

Joshua Atkins Nickerson lived next door with Aunt May and an older sister of Aunt May's, Susan M. (Gould). Aunt Susan M's husband had disappeared years ago. There were rumors, which vaguely reached my childish ears, that he had been seen employed in the United States Life Saving Service near Cape Hatteras, living there with another wife.

Like most Cape Cod boys of his day, Uncle Joshua had gone to sea when he was about 10 or 12 years old. He served as one of two cabin boys for a time with a captain who required the boys to "learn to cipher" literally on the deck of his ship. Uncle Joshua and the other boy would holystone an area on the deck. The captain would then lay out their lessons in charcoal. When their work had been approved as correct by the captain, the boys would again holystone the deck in preparation for the next time. That is how they "learned to cipher."

Uncle Joshua said the captain's proudest boast was, "I never went to school a day in my life; but I can sign my name so *other* people can read it."

With such tutelage it wasn't long before Uncle Joshua became a mate, mastered "Bowditch", and got his captain's papers at 21. He skippered mostly on three and four-masted schooners in the thriving coastal cargo trade.

By the time I knew him he had given up going to sea and ran a grocery store near the depot in Chatham. For years he was also one of the three selectmen.

I remember, in my early teens, going with him in his new and very modern Studebaker touring car as he went campaigning through the county, seeking election to the post of county commissioner, an honor and duty in which he served conscientiously for many years.

He did a little insurance business on the side, and friends and neighbors used to come to him frequently for advice on both public and private affairs.

Uncle Joshua was one of the most self-disciplined men I ever knew. For example, if Aunt May had asked him to bring home from the store some small thing, such as a package of pepper—and if he forgot it—he would force himself to walk the one-half mile back to the store and get it. It made no difference that there was already sufficient pepper in the house for the next few days, nor that the mile round trip to get the forgotten item would have to be made in rain or snow. He should not have forgotten! This was his method of disciplining himself not to forget on some future occasion when it might be important.

During Uncle Joshua's several terms on the Board of Selectmen in Chatham, there would be occasions when an inquisitive citizen might try to find out from him just how the selectmen arrived at some decision, especially if it involved a controversial question. In those days, meetings of the board were conducted in privacy, unlike today when the "open meeting" laws require them to conduct their business in public with the press present, ready to pounce on any chance remark that might give the opportunity for an eye-catching headline, and providing a chance for an ambitious politician to make "grandstand plays" hoping for publicity for himself.

But in Uncle Joshua's time it was different. He would never disclose how the members of the board, including himself, voted on an issue. When asked, his invariable reply was, "The board voted (or decided) thus and so," with never an indication of whether the vote was unanimous or only a majority.

Mother told me that a day or two after I was born Uncle Joshua came to see her and the new baby. He asked gravely if my parents had chosen a name for me. Upon being told that they had not yet decided, he gently suggested that they might name me (the second son and third child) Joshua Atkins. He pointed out that this name was not only his, but that on his mother's side (Mary Atkins) there had been a Joshua Atkins for many generations.

He didn't mention that his own name was Joshua Atkins Nickerson, nor that he had no children of his own. Anyhow that is how I got to be Joshua Atkins Nickerson II.

Uncle Ernest, another of my father's numerous brothers, and his wife Aunt Hattie lived in Pawtucket, Rhode Island. He was a bookkeeper for a feed and flour merchant. He also had a substantial one-man-and-wife truck garden. He was an omnivorous reader. But most of all he liked to talk. Every spring he spent the first week in May fishing the fresh water ponds (now called lakes) in the area. Father usually accompanied him for a few days fishing, and by the time I was six I was allowed to go along. (*See "Fishing With Uncle Ernest", page 189.*)

Uncle Edwin was another brother. He was Chief of Detectives in the Providence Police Department. He was more a man of action than Ernest—tall, rangy, hawkeyed and perhaps dangerous. He was left-handed, I remember, because of the time in our living room when he pulled a gun from his hip pocket in one deft motion with his left hand. He did this while describing an exploit involving his chase after a criminal who had jumped through a window while being questioned at headquarters. Uncle Eddie had jumped right after him, and after chasing him up the street and exchanging a few shots, had recaptured him. It had all been in the papers, but the firsthand narration was even more exciting. Otherwise I might never have known that Uncle Eddie always carried a gun.

Uncle Carroll was quite different. He was inclined to be more of an introvert—occasionally moody, rarely angry, and the best man at handling a catboat I ever saw. He had to be good; except for a couple of cranberry bogs, his livelihood came from fishing in a catboat out on the ocean—alone, with no motor, just his one sail. He went out at dawn and often worked till dusk dressing and salting his fish. He was a handsome man with a beard, and when he wasn't too busy or too tired he was fascinating company. He was the only man I ever knew who could sail up the channel from the Chatham Bar to Pleasant Bay in a flat calm with a head tide—I've seen him do it.

Uncle Sears was the youngest brother. I heard that he had run away to sea, that he'd even been a cowboy in Argentina on the River Platte. By the time I first knew him he was married, had two daughters, and had a harness shop in Harwich Center. Uncle Sears was really gifted. He wrote verse—which scanned. He could do anything with his hands. He was a handsome fellow. He was popular and he knew how to make money. He became an undertaker, was in real estate and held important town offices in Harwich.

But right in his prime he had a bad heart attack which limited his physical activity. This was in the 1920's. So he shifted gears completely and devoted himself to things he *could* do, including becoming somewhat of an expert on local Indian history. Back in the harness shop days he had been divorced and had married again, a remarkable woman by whom he had three more beautiful daughters, and who helped him through the hard years of the great depression by teaching school while he tended store in his little shop in Florida.

The only one of my father's sisters I have known was Aunt Geneva. She had a large family. She was a great story-teller, she could sing, and I have always loved the sound of her speaking voice. It had a quality which I have heard only once or twice elsewhere, in the professional performances of a few successful actresses. Aunt Geneva wrote articles for the local papers and some verse. But her writing lacked the real thrill and charm of her spoken words.

(At this point, Aunt Geneva takes over. The following stories are in her words.)

One winter, "Grandpa Nicker" taught over in Punkhorn, a part of Brewster. He boarded around too. Said all went fine until February, when there came a spell of very cold weather—below zero most of the time. The Brewster flats were frozen solid, no digging clams or razor fish. Sometimes the bay was full of ice and no boat dared venture out for fish and the larders ran low.

Salt fish and potatoes, hull corn and plum porridge filled every menu of the homes where grandfather stayed. One night he went to the Walkers for a week. He had been there once before when roast pork chops and hogshead cheese were plentiful. But like their neighbors they were reduced to slim rations, with the fresh pork all gone and no clams or fresh fish. Mrs. Walker was bustling about when he went in, and supper smelled powerful good to grandfather.

"I don't know, Mr. Nickerson, whether you ever et a supper like this, but it's the nighest I can come to a biled dinner with what I have to do with."

Heaped on a big platter was what looked like—and smelled like—a real boiled dinner, but turned out to be lightly salted pork spare ribs with all the vegetables from down in the old cellar—even carrots which grandfather had always fed to the cow. There was stewed squash and tomato pickles to go with it, and everyone "fell to" with a relish and ate the platter clean. Dried apple pie was dessert, which all enjoyed. Grandfather brought the recipe of Punkhorn Stew home to grandmother, who made it now and then, much to her family's satisfaction, and grandfather's in particular.

Your father, Oscar Clinton Nickerson, had come home unexpectedly, leaving his ship at Providence, taking the train to Harwich, hiring a horse and buggy at Drum's Livery Stable, and driving home to East Harwich, picking up his sweetheart on the way.

It had been a particularly busy morning at the Nickerson homestead. Brother Ernest was home that winter to add to the family, which consisted of Lawrence and Carroll, Sears and me, father and mother, and the hired girl, Inez.

On the stove mother had the big black iron kettle full of Punkhorn Stew, and in the oven apple pies, each with a snip of rose geranium leaf for flavor, were baking. The dining table was stretched full length, covered with white oil cloth and all set for dinner.

Suddenly Inez said, "A horse and buggy has just drove in, Mis Mary (meaning mother)."

"For pity's sake, who is arriving just at dinner time?"

Then she saw. "Why, it's Oscar!"

And there was love and joy in her voice. "My sakes, he is helping a girl out of the buggy. Inez, who is it?"

"It's Eglantine Young, the girl he's been courting for some time. I guess he's brought her to dinner."

"I guess he has," says mother, "and I've got Punkhorn Stew."

"Well, you've got pies in the oven for dessert, Miss Mary. You'll make out real good, I'm sure."

"I'll have to!" said mother, as she rose to the occasion.

By the time Oscar and Eglantine got into the house, those who had been working outside came in for dinner. All were delighted to see Oscar, who had been gone for three months, and were eager to hear of his trip to Norfolk, Virginia, and Savannah, Georgia. Time went fast.

Father served from the great platter, full of stew with thick brown bread crumbs steamed on the top, to be eaten with homemade butter along with the stew.

Oscar ate plenty of the stew and the tomato pickles and stewed squash that went with it. Mother tried to make apologies for the plebian dish, but no one listened. The hot apple pie with whipped cream on top made a grand finishing touch. Soon the men went outside and mother took Oscar and Eglantine into the sitting room and sat down to talk with them, while Inez attended to the kitchen work.

Then Oscar put his arm around Eglantine, who blushed like a rose, and said, "This is the girl that I am going to marry in a few weeks, mother. I wanted to bring her home so she could meet you and father. I intended to tell this at the table, but I couldn't get the courage."

Mother congratulated them and kissed them both, apologizing for the Punkhorn Stew, but it evidently made a hit with Eglantine, for after they were married and came to visit a few days, she would ask mother to be sure and have Punkhorn Stew while she was there.

My grandfather, Warren Nickerson, was living at Aunt Emily Kenney's one winter when Louise (who married Joe D. Nickerson and lived on Mill Hill) and I were just going out with boys.

Two of them came to call for us one evening to go to a party, and grandfather saw them.

The next morning he asked, "Who was them young fellers you had here last night?"

We told him and explained who their fathers were. "Yes, yes," he said. "I used to know both their fathers—but remember this, gals, you want to look a leetle to the breed before you choose."

★ ★ ★

I never knew that Uncle Jonathan fought in the War of 1812—or spent time in Dartmoor Prison.

His wife was called Aunt Becky. She had a sharp tongue, but a warm heart. Was a Wixon from Dennisport, I think.

Uncle Jonathan was a methodical Eldredge. When he was town tax collector, he ate breakfast enough to last him *all day*. Because he said he was hired for a full day and didn't intend to cheat the town!

Both he and his wife were members of the old Methodist Church, still standing in East Harwich today.

When Uncle Jonathan's nephew, "Elnathan, the Mormon", once Aunt Becky's favorite, came back from Salt Lake City for a visit (by train—he had followed Brigham Young over the Rockies by ox team), Aunt Becky met him at the door and asked, "How many wives you got, Elnathan?"

"Only the one I took with me."

"Alright, then how many concubines have you got, tell me that."

"Not any, Aunt Becky."

"Well, you can come in and *set*, cause I'm glad to see you, but you can't stay all night, 'cause I won't have my good Methodist sheets used (sic) by a Mormon. Go over to Warren Jensen's to stay, they 'haint" particular."

So he did.

But though Aunt Becky thought she was a staunch Methodist and believer, she always put the Bible in the baby's cradle when she went to the well to wash, to keep the witches from carrying the baby up the chimney while she was gone.

This happened long before I was born, but I've heard father tell it many times. Aunt Becky called Sunday School a frolic in the House of God, and when the organ entered the picture, she said it was an abomination in the sight of the Lord. Stormy nights she put a lighted candle in the chamber window, hoping to guide some shipwrecked sailor to warmth and comfort. She had lost two boys at sea.

★ ★ ★

Aunt Hit's father, Nathaniel Eldridge of Red River (now South Chatham), married Betsey Allen, I think, and they had a little home not far from Deep Hole.

One day when Captain Nat, as he was known, was in his little boat fishing, an English "man-o-war" bore down upon him and took him aboard. He was told that if he would sign papers to fight for the English he could become one of the sailors. Otherwise they would take him to Dartmoor Prison— and maybe kill him.

Captain Nat had the spirit of his convictions and faced the officers with scorn.

"I would rather die in prison than fight with the British against the Colonists."

So they pressed him into service, took him back to England, threw him into Dartmoor Prison, where he remained two or three years.

Betsey, left alone in their little home with two small children, Mehitable and Zenas, refused to leave and go live with her parents.

"Something tells me that Nat will come back and I'm going to be here to welcome him."

She had a little garden and eked out a living.

One day when she and some of her neighbors sat knitting and sewing, the sun streaming in through the open kitchen door, Betsey said, "Hark! Here comes Nat, I know his step."

And sure enough, it was Nat. He had been set ashore from an English ship as an exchange for an Englishman or men, held in a Boston prison. What rejoicing there must have been at Nat's return!

Mehitable was my great grandmother, and Zenas was Charlie's (my husband) godfather. Captain Nat was a direct descendant of Jehosaphat Eldredge.

★ ★ ★

Ernest was an awful talker, but if you listened you learned a lot. For although he left school around 14, he had a searching mind and was a great reader.

One winter I remember he cut a deep gash in his foot with an axe, which my father sewed up with a flesh needle threaded with a hair from the horse's tail, which had been soaked in carbolic acid.

Ernest had to sit in the chair while his foot healed, so he studied Latin grammar to pass the time away, and read Shakespeare on the side. He would have made a wonderful professor if he had had the education, for he had what it takes and was well versed on the topics of the day. He could answer any question, from the Fall of Rome to the mechanism of a mosquito!

I loved him dearly. He read "The Fisherman's Ballads" to me, taught me to recite the "Wreck of the Hesperus" and "Paul Revere's Ride"; also "Marmion and Douglas".

I had a friend who traveled abroad. One day she brought snapshots she had taken. One was the picture of a palace, above which was printed, "Let the portcullis fall."

"I don't have the least idea what that means, do you, Mrs. E?"—and I explained just as Ernest had explained it to me. She listened in astonishment.

Then she said, "To think I traveled through Europe and came back to your old Cape Cod kitchen to learn what a portcullis is."

(*Back to Joshua* . . .)

It was largely through the eyes of my father's family that I first saw Cape Cod. Whenever two or more of them were together I listened, fascinated by their conversations and stories of "olden times". It was through them that I learned that there is a flow of individuals through the ages, starting we know not where and rushing headlong into the future. We see only those near us in time.

But if we are fortunate, those just before us can help us catch a glimpse of those just before them. In a time when the clock of man's destiny is accelerating madly, the lucky few who can feel this flow may be helped to understand.

How We Lived

Schools

I N September 1906, at the age of five and a half, I started my schooling at the Atwood School in Chatham. At that time there were six separate primary schools in the town, each within walking distance of its pupils—a radius of about two miles. Five of them—Old Harbor, Village, Atwood, Chathamport and West Chatham—each had one teacher who was responsible for grades one through four in one room. Her duties also included running the fire in the big stove in the corner of the room, supervising play during recess and, of course, maintaining discipline.

The sixth primary school was in South Chatham. This school was housed in a larger building than the other five and included also the fifth and sixth grades for that section of the town. I believe it had two teachers for the six grades.

We lived on Old Harbor Road, about halfway between the Atwood and the Old Harbor Schools. My parents sent me to the Atwood School, thinking that the teacher there was better than the teacher at Old Harbor. And Old Harbor Road was rutted and sandy. Usually I trudged the mile and a half carrying my dinner box and books. Sometimes I "hooked a ride" if Rufus Robbins happened to be carrying fish to the depot in his truck cart.

And there were the rare occasions when the weather was very bad that father sent Sam Clifford from the lumberyard with the "democrat" wagon to drive me to school. But rubber boots, oilskins and a sou'wester were the usual protection from foul weather. There were no automobiles then, so no one worried about traffic hazards. Parents' worries over children en route between home and school involved only such problems as getting soaked in a pond, puddle or swamp which might have proved too tempting to a child.

We learned fast in those schools with four grades in one room. It was so easy to learn when the higher grades were functioning in the presence of the lower ones. A bright student often skipped a grade and spent three years there instead of four. That happened to me—I skipped the third grade.

So before I was nine, I made the great jump to the grammar school. The grammar school and the high school were located in a two-and-a-half story building perched on a knoll right behind where home plate is now on Veterans Field. It was about halfway between the Railroad Depot and the Town Hall, which was on Main Street. The driveway came in from Main Street.

There was a sandy playground just east of the schoolhouse, but on the north and west side a fence ran close to the building. Beyond the fence were a field and a swamp which were our real playgrounds. It never occurred to us that we were trespassing when we played there, and no one ever called it to our attention.

The basement of this school building was half under and half above ground. So it was well lighted by windows set in its brick walls. In the center of the basement were two huge hot-air furnaces. Those of us who didn't go home for lunch ate our lunches in the remaining space, and we congregated there at recess and noontime when the weather did not permit outdoor activities. It was serviced by one janitor, George Eldredge, who not only started the fires and did the cleaning, but who had the added job of maintaining order among the adolescents crowded into his basement.

Beyond the north wall of the basement were connecting passageways, well ventilated by open slat walls, leading to the boys' and girls' toilets. I don't remember the girls' arrangements, but the boys had a slate-trough urinal and a row of five or six wooden backhouse holes with covers. Our drinking water was supplied by a hand pump outdoors in front of the building, to which a tin cup was usually attached by a chain.

The first floor above the basement was reached through two narrow wooden stairways. The boys went up the west one, and the girls the one to the east. When Charles Guild was principal of the school, we marched up these stairs to the cadence of his "left, right, one, two, hup-hup". There were also large double doors on each side of the building at this floor, reached by double flights of wooden stairs on the outside. But they were rarely used.

On the first floor were two large rooms running the whole breadth of the building and separated by a wide corridor and stairway leading to the floor above. The room on the north end of the building was occupied by the fifth and sixth grades, the fifth on the east side of the room and the sixth on the west.

When I arrived there in 1909, this room was presided over by Miss Madella Buck. She was a good teacher and countenanced no nonsense. The seventh and eighth grades were housed in the room on the south end of the same floor, and were presided over by Preston Chase, the first male teacher whom I encountered. He was a good teacher and rarely had to inflict corporal punishment, though he did not hesitate to do so when it was called for. This usually consisted of requiring a boy to stand before the class, with his palm extended, upon which the teacher administered a series of vigorous blows with a leather strap or the flat of a thin ruler.

The top floor of the building, reached by another flight of wooden stairs, housed the high school students. The main room where we all assembled for morning prayers and singing extended across the south end of the building, directly above the seventh and eighth grade room. The four grades (nine through 12) could be accomodated in this one room, since quite a few boys and girls dropped out after grammar school (grades five through eight) and went to work.

The principal, always a man, led the morning exercises and conducted his classes in the big room, at the same time maintaining discipline over those who had a study period there while he had his classes in session.

High school was for those who dreamed of going beyond it for further education, or whose parents wanted their children's chances of success in life to be aided by a coveted high school diploma.

On the north end of the building were two smaller classrooms, each run by women "assistants", who taught such subjects as English, algebra, French, Latin, or whatever they and the principal had decided best suited the distribution of the subjects which each of the three was qualified to teach.

We had good teachers. I remember particularly Miss Cochran, a blue-eyed blonde who taught French, and Miss Riley, a wiry outdoor type who taught Latin and mathematics. On Saturdays, when a small group of boys went fishing in the ponds beyond Great Hill, Miss Riley often accompanied us, and she was always welcome. She not only was a good fisherman, but she was a big help when it came time to cook our fish over a small open fire for lunch.

I have no doubt that today the Board of Health, the Department of Education, and various agencies of State and Federal government would unanimously condemn such a school building. But we were proud of it, and so were the voters of our town, as they compared it with the district schools which they had attended.

For we had good teachers, and unlike our parents, were given the opportunity to study specialized subjects under teachers who had been specially trained to teach these subjects. The principal, who was the only male high school teacher, had all the administrative and disciplinary responsibilities. He also taught some subjects, such as science, math and Latin. Our classes were small, and the young women who came from the colleges to teach us English, French, Latin, math, etc., were dedicated and excellent teachers, for the most part.

At every grade in the school system the day began with an assembly, at which there was a short reading from the Bible and recitation in unison of the Lord's Prayer, as we sat with hands folded on top of our desks. And then we sang songs usually of sentimental or patriotic nature. I thought that "America" (to the tune of "God Save the King") was our national anthem. "Columbia, the Gem of the Ocean" was a 10 to 1 favorite over "The Star Spangled Banner". Other favorites included "Flow Gently, Sweet Afton", "Aunt Dinah's Quilting Party", "A Spanish Cavalier", "Tenting Tonight" and "Just Before the Battle, Mother".

Our town school system was a part of a school union including Orleans, Harwich and Chatham, over which there was a superintendent of schools. This union supplied a music teacher (vocal) and an arts teacher. Their functions were combined in one woman who spent a day a week in each town. This was a decided recognition of the importance of the arts.

There were no school buses or school "barges", as such horse-drawn vehicles were called. The students attending the seventh and eighth grades and the high school who lived in the west end of town traveled on the trains, whose schedules were arranged to fit the school hours. Of course, these youngsters might have to walk up to two or three miles to get to the depot at South Chatham or West Chatham to take a train. But once on it they were transported to within a few hundred yards of the school.

The official athletic program of the high school was limited to baseball (and some basketball). But there were no paid coaches. For those not on a team there was plenty of informal "scrub up" baseball. Basketball was essentially a girl's game which they played clad in baggy bloomers and middy blouses.

Corporal punishment for infraction of rules was standard operating procedure. The culprit was made to stand in front of the class, while the teacher inflicted the appropriate number of blows on his outstretched palm with a thin ruler or a strap. To flinch or to cry under the lashes was considered a sign of weakness. But I must admit that occasionally a tear ran down the cheek of even the manliest boy.

I remember one occasion in the seventh or eighth grade when every boy, contrary to specific orders, ran off at noontime to a fire in the woods a mile or more away, which had been set by the noon train coming into town from Boston. Such mass disobedience called for mass punishment, so each of us had to walk to the front of the room and submit to the prescribed blows on our palms.

Nowadays a teacher would be accused of brutality for even upbraiding a pupil, let alone inflicting corporal punishment. But our system worked very well. It increased mutual respect between teachers and pupils, and I never knew of its ever being abused.

At Christmastime there were always "exercises" to which parents were invited. Mothers sometimes came, but rarely fathers. There were recitations of poems and other examples of literature, singing, and of course a Christmas tree with gifts for everyone—the name of every pupil having been previously chosen by lot.

It was customary, as part of their duties, for individual members of the elected School Committee to visit schools. The purpose was to enable them to get firsthand impressions of conditions and the efficacy of the schools in instructing the youth of the town.

I remember one school committeeman, a retired sea captain named Heman Francis Chase, who would pop in clad in his immaculate Sunday best, carrying a gold-headed cane. He wore a carefully trimmed beard. He would take over from the teacher for perhaps a half hour, after having spent the previous half hour inspecting us visually from the platform at the front of the room, and catechize us on such subjects as spelling, reading and arithmetic. Whatever one may think of this method, it did tend to tie the School Committee close to current situations in the school.

Of course the biggest event of the year was graduation. There were only seven in my graduating class in 1917. But a few years before there had been a class of 23, the largest number to graduate up to that time. There were many dropouts during high school years. But they were considered normal, and certainly not the object of intense political interest, as they are today.

My class of seven included one Catholic girl, but there was no problem at all about her attending the baccalaurate service at the Methodist Church, a service which alternated yearly between the Methodist and the Congregational Churches. There was no Catholic Church in Chatham then.

The graduation exercises were held in the evening in the Town Hall, which had been decorated with daisies and other wild flowers and greenery. There were also crepe-paper decorations, and of course a big banner with the class motto.

There was a salutarian, a historian and a valedictorian from the class. There were opening and closing prayers, a vocal selection or two, the principal speaker, and the awarding of diplomas. The speeches were all carefully rehearsed, complete with gestures. We took it very seriously, as did the crowd who filled the hall.

Transportation

B Y the time I was born, reliance on the packet boat and the stagecoach was well in the past. But as recently as 1887, the Chatham Railroad Company, of which the Town of Chatham was by far the largest stockholder, had been established from Harwich to Chatham.

The speed of changes in transportation is again illustrated by the fact that the Chatham branch was abandoned and its rails torn up, after only 50 years of use, in 1937. The rails were sent to Japan for scrap, only to be returned again with interest in World War II.

But around 1910 the Chatham Railroad was a busy branch. There were daily morning and afternoon trains out, and noon and evening trains in, to and from Boston, with connections for Fall River and Providence. In addition there were local trains running to Harwich or Yarmouth, and in summer an extra afternoon train from Boston.

On weekends these summer trains often were eight or ten cars long and carried one or two parlor cars. As the engine puffed to a snorting, steaming halt just east of the Chatham depot, the fireman from his seat on the left side of the cab could look down on the rotting remains of the old stage, left ignobly behind Eugene Cahoon's blacksmith shop and horse-shoeing establishment, which stood on the corner of Depot Road and Old Harbor Road.

As the train pulled in by the long wooden platform, there would be backed up to it and waiting—the express company's wagon; the mail wagon; in summer, "barges" from each of the summer hotels; and always the public "barges". These "barges" were covered by a solid roof, and the sides had removable canvas or leather curtains. The seats were two benches arranged fore and aft, facing in. The passengers entered through the rear by a set of short and narrow steps, on either side of which were racks for carrying trunks. Suitcases could be tucked on top as well as on the trunk racks, or beside the driver on his seat up front.

The owner and operator of the "barges" was Parker Nickerson, who was a constant source of interest to my eyes. He was very bald, a fact you might never have guessed were it not that he wore a gray wig on weekdays and a red wig on Sundays and holidays! He and his son, "Allie Parker", with a helper or two put in long days picking up for the seven A.M. train out, meeting all the Boston trains, and winding up the day after delivering passengers from the evening train, which got in—if on time—around seven P.M. But busy as they were, they carried only a small portion of the passengers.

Most of them walked to and from the trains, even though there was an occasional passenger who was met by a private carriage. There were "regulars" who rode the trains every day.

Conductors in those days were men of distinction. They wore the blue uniform cap with a brass plate on the front above the visor, with the name of the railroad and the word "Conductor" on it. But their formal Prince Albert coats, stiff starched shirts and collars and black ties were badges of dignity of their position. And they were known to receive high pay for those days, when in our town, at least, an income of $3,000 per year was looked upon as well-nigh unattainable affluence, rather than the edge of poverty, as it is today.

The conductor on the early morning train out and the evening train in was Mr. O'Neil. I remember him walking by our house daily in his blue uniform, with his white beard, carrying his dinner pail and puffing at a cigar, which he carefully put out and wrapped in damp paper when on duty.

Then there was tall and sprightly Clarendon Freeman, who went daily to his duties in the Courthouse at Barnstable, always walking the mile and a half between his home in North Chatham and the depot. There were many others—almost everybody walked to and from the train.

As a boy I was fascinated by the trains. With father having his lumber yard right on railroad land, I managed to see a lot of what went on there. The switching and sorting of cars was my special interest, and I was lucky enough to be allowed (contrary to regulations) occasionally to ride with the crew on the engine.

After switching the cars it was standard procedure to run the engine over to a sidetrack where there was a turntable, on which the train crew, divided into two groups, turned the engine by pushing against long wooden handles inserted at each end of the table. Thus the engine was turned to go out head-first on its next run.

Then the engine crew would replenish the coal in the tender from bins beside the track before backing it into the engine house, where water for the boilers would be added, the fires cleaned and the ashes dropped into a brick-lined pit below the engine. This last work was usually done by a hostler, who looked after the engines when they were between runs.

Something should be said about the railroad equipment used in those days. The locomotives, of course, were small, coal-fired steam engines, each with its tender attached carrying fuel and water. Mounted in front of the smoke stack was a big box-like lantern, lighted by a kerosene lamp which was backed by a large reflector to throw the light ahead onto the tracks.

Mounted on top, between the smoke stack and the engine cab were the bell, operated by a rope running back into the cab, and a sandbox from which sand could be released by a valve through pipes to the track just under the drive-wheels, to reduce spinning of the wheels when starting from a standstill. And right in front of the cab was the big steam whistle, which blew "Who-o-o Who-o-o, Who Who" before every crossing.

I remember one day in later years lying in a southwest rainstorm in the Eastham marshes hunting ducks with my good friend, Norman Hopkins. The train was going through from Orleans to Provincetown. At every crossing we could hear the whistle—two long followed by two short blasts. There were many such crossings. Finally Norman broke a long silence as we sat there in the rain waiting for ducks to come to our decoys.

He turned to me and said, "You know, it costs a lot of money to blow all the whistles in this country, doesn't it?"

It certainly did then, when there were about 35,000 steam locomotives in active service on the country's railroads.

The cars used on the passenger trains were of great variety. On the crack summer trains from Boston there were parlor cars and fine coaches lighted by gas instead of kerosene, and heated by steam led back from the engine through pipes and hoses. These cars were mostly made of wood, although a few steel cars were beginning to appear.

But on the local run from Chatham to Harwich or Yarmouth, the cars were quite different. Sometimes we had a full-fledged passenger car, but usually for the short haul the car was a combination baggage and passenger car, with a baggage room in one end separated by a partition from the passenger section. This was heated by a stove in one corner, for which the fuel was the same smelly, smoky, bituminous coal as was used in the locomotive. Of course the lighting was by kerosene lamps.

All the cars, except for a few towards the end of the era, had open vestibules, so that in passing from one car to another while underway, you stepped out onto an open platform at the ends of each car. Here you might be engulfed in a cloud of smoke, cinders and up-flung dirt, if conditions were right for it.

Of all the train crew my childhood favorite was Billy Wyer. As a railroader wearing a blue uniform, he was of course glamorous. But he won my heart completely. I can remember riding with him on the cowcatcher as the engineer moved the locomotive a few feet in the yard. But one day, when I was not there to see it, Billy Wyer slipped and fell between two moving freight cars which ran over and crushed both his legs. They gave him first aid, put him on a stretcher in a baggage car, and cleared the tracks to Boston to run him as a "special" to the nearest hospital. He died near Middleboro, they said, from loss of blood.

I have touched upon it already, but I cannot emphasize too greatly that in my boyhood the *normal* way to travel any distance up to five or six miles was to *walk*. We walked to school; we walked to church; we walked to meetings; we walked to work; we walked to entertainments; we walked to call on each other. I can remember the kids from Chathamport and North Chatham walking abreast down Old Harbor Road to school in the morning, and my scrambling to join them before they got past our house.

Sometimes on a lovely warm evening, when there had been a show of some sort at the Town Hall, all the people would come out at once, and the road would be full of people walking home. As they stretched out ahead and the men lighted their cigars, the aroma would come drifting back, and the bright tips of the lighted ends would dance like fireflies as the men up ahead removed them from their lips to discuss the evening.

For trips too short for travel by rail and too long or too formal for walking, we used horses and carriages. Almost no one kept a horse just for riding around. A few rich summer residents may have, and of course the doctor did. Most people would have frowned upon keeping a horse and carriage *just* for pleasure—even if they could have afforded it.

Our case was fairly typical in this respect. Father kept a light horse for light hauling and for occasional use with the carriage. He had two carriages.

One was the "democrat wagon"—of light construction, with good springs and two removable leather upholstered seats that set crosswise of the wagon. There was no roof over it. This was used for light work, errands, and such trips as going to the ponds in Brewster for the spring fishing.

Then there was the surrey—with the fringe on top. Painted black with fine gold scroll work by a carriage painter, it was elegant indeed to our eyes. This would be used when the family went to see grandfather, or for going to a funeral in a nearby village, or such.

I remember that mother used to tease her sea-captain husband about his lack of horse knowledge. He would drive holding the reins and moving them to right or left like the tiller of a boat, instead as mother would point out, of pulling straight back on the reins to guide the horse.

There was the story about the time when father had just given up seafaring for a landsman's life. He and mother drove to Harwich Center for some big affair at Exchange Hall. It was of considerable duration, so all the horses were unhitched from the wagons and put on the picket lines in John Drum's livery stable across the tracks from the hall. After the affair was over father went to get the horse and carriage and come back to pick up mother at the hall.

But he failed to return. Finally mother became worried and went to the stable looking for him. He was there, all right. He had been unable to recognize his own horse! So he was waiting till the others were all gone, thinking that the last must be his. Mother, of course, knew their own horse at once. Father never heard the end of it!

And there was one occasion when mother and I and Cousin

Edna were driving over to the yacht club in East Harwich on Pleasant Bay, when our horse stumbled on a loose stone and fell going down the hill just beyond Crowell Road. We couldn't get him up till some men came and helped.

But progress in the form of improved roads came fast. At first the new road building was confined to the installation of water-bound macadam. Here they just prepared the roadbed, then put in a layer of very coarse crushed stone, then medium, then layers of finer stone all the way down to dust. Each layer was rolled with a heavy steamroller and further packed by soaking with water from a sprinkler cart. The result was an excellent road, though dusty in dry weather.

With the advent of the automobile, a surfacing of oil and sand was added to the old macadam roads, and in some cases on secondary roads oil was spread directly onto dirt "hardening". This started taking place around 1910.

In 1912 father bought our first auto, a Studebaker touring car. For me this was the beginning of a new era. Now one *could drive* as far as Plymouth and back in a single day. Boston was only five hours (and several tire changes) away!

Entertainment

EFORE discussing what we did for entertainment in the early days of this century, we should remind ourselves of some of the forms of entertainment which we did *NOT* have. We had no television, no radio, no motion pictures, no electricity to provide lighting, no "reproduced" music such as by record players or sound-track, no "joy-riding" in non-existent automobiles.

But we did have entertainment. Much of it centered around the churches. In addition to the regular morning and evening services and Sunday School on Sundays, there were weekly prayer meetings on Thursday evenings; the Ladies Sewing Circle on Wednesday afternoons; and the children's parties in the vestry on Friday evenings, just to mention a few.

To me our regular Sunday attendance at church was prime entertainment. Even my insensitive ear was offended (but amused) by the off-key singing of the soloist in the choir. But the "hell-fire and brimstone" sermons, accompanied by long, loud and fervent prayers to the Old Testament "Lord God of Isaac and Jacob", provided vivid memories for a lifetime of reflection.

At least once a year the church was visited by an "evangelist", who stayed through a whole week of exhortation. He always converted a few, but even more rewarding were the confessions of sin by those already "born of God".

On the lighter side were the public performances of singing and "spieling pieces" by the children on "Children's Day" and at Christmastime. The latter was a joyous affair, with a big pagan Christmas tree in the vestry basement and presents for all.

For those who liked to eat out, there were no restaurants or dining places other than the dining room at the local inn. But the ladies of the various churches competed joyfully in attracting those of all faiths to their church suppers. Some were of the cold ham and baked beans variety. But the ones I remember best were the numerous chicken-pie suppers—m-m-m!

The annual Town Meeting might not be regarded by some as entertainment, but I am sure it was thought of by most of its participants as a combination of civic duty and self-government, a sort of religious rite of reaffirmation of manhood suffrage, with entertainment as a significant by-product. It was always held early in February, and started at eight o'clock in the morning on the day following the annual balloting for town officers, such as selectmen, overseers of the poor, constables, town clerk and treasurer, fence viewers, surveyor of bark and wood, pound keeper, road commissioners, etc.

Usually heat and excitement began building up a month or so before, and by Town Meeting day the issues and personal feelings among candidates for office had been well discussed and argued around numerous pot-bellied stoves at the depot, the post office, the stores, the fish shanties, in homes and elsewhere. For twenty years my father was moderator of the Town Meeting, and in my boyhood Uncle Joshua was a selectman for many years. So I was early conditioned to have a keen interest in town affairs.

The meeting was conducted according to a warrant which had been posted in each post office in town some weeks before. There was no mail delivery, so everyone who expected to receive mail or to send any had ample opportunity to study it in advance.

For a day or two before the meeting, father would study his well-thumbed "Robert's Rules of Order"; for he was sure to be challenged on parliamentary procedure during the course of the meeting. While it was generally true that the Moderator's rulings, right or wrong, had to be accepted, they had better be right! It would never do to have to resort to a vote of the meeting to sustain a parliamentary ruling. And there were sure to be plenty of "sea lawyers" present who would get a bang out of Captain Nickerson's discomfiture, if they could trip him up on a technicality.

I remember one occasion in the early years of Prohibition, when the question before the meeting had to do with a certain old road which led down to the shore. There seemed to be considerable confusion in the minds of the voters as to just which road was under discussion.

The moderator, of course, cannot participate in the debate; but in an attempt to be helpful, father stepped out of his role for a moment to explain its location, winding up by saying, "It is that road, you know, which leads down to the deep hole along the shore, where the rum-runners like to land." And of course everyone then knew exactly where it was!

But one of the constables (I believe it was the newly-created Chief of Police, the only full-time police officer in town), who had been standing in the rear of the hall, came striding down the aisle. "Mister Moderator," he said, "Mister Moderator, as a town official it is your duty, if you have knowledge of illegal activities of such a nature, to report them to the police for appropriate action."

He was right, of course. But he and most everybody else knew about it as a matter of common knowledge. He got a big laugh on the moderator from the crowd and established evidence of his own innocence of such knowledge. Everybody, including father, enjoyed the joke.

The articles in the warrant were taken up one by one and

disposed of in order; an article could be taken up out of order by vote of the meeting, but it was rarely done. The first few articles were of a routine nature.

There was one which has long since been dropped which always impressed me. It was the annual vote to "raise and appropriate" a sum of money for the care of shipwrecked sailors. In my childhood some of this was spent every year. The survivors' immediate needs for food, shelter and clothing were provided for, and they were shipped at the town's expense back to their home port or to their consul in Boston. The bodies of unidentified dead were given a decent Christian burial at the expense of the taxpayers of Chatham.

Then as now there was much argument over roads and schools. Town planning was howled down by a noisy minority group. The conservative oldsters wouldn't go along with building a new high school on the site of the old Town Hall, which had burned down, unless the old wooden high school building was moved over and incorporated in the new building.

A fire engine was acquired and a voluntary fire department created with surprisingly little opposition, following two successive fires in the center of the village in which the amateur bucket brigades were shown to be helpless.

It was a long time, however, before the old system was given up—whereby anybody who went to a fire and reported to a fire warden was entitled to an hour's pay. Similarly, after a snow storm, every man and boy who turned out with a shovel was entitled to be paid for clearing snow from the roads. They usually worked near their homes in gangs, clearing the biggest snow banks so a horse-drawn sleigh could get through. The more experienced men would carry a piece of pork rind in their pocket to grease their shovel so the snow would not stick to it.

At noon someone would always get up and move that, "The meeting be adjourned for one hour to reconvene at one o'clock this afternoon", in order that those who wished might partake of the repast which had been prepared by the Ladies of the Sewing Circle and was waiting to be served in the vestry of the Congregational (or Methodist) (or Universalist) Church. This dinner was always good, as the ladies of the churches, taking turns in serving it each year, vied pridefully to demonstrate that the culinary skills of their group surpassed those of the ladies of the other churches.

Promptly at one o'clock the meeting would reconvene, and even though there was unlimited debate, it was rare indeed that the annual meeting failed to wind up in plenty of time for people to walk home for supper at the usual hour of six o'clock.

Nowadays the Town Meetings are usually held at night and run for several successive nights. This results in meetings which are attended principally by those who are interested in articles which have not been taken up by previous meetings. The last meeting is heavily weighted with voters who have a special interest in the articles still to be voted on.

I think it was better when the meeting lasted all day and nearly everybody who came stayed through the whole meeting. It was more fun, and I think better self-government. In the old days there were no automobiles, radios, TV's or movies—whatever entertainment there was had to be right in your own town, so *everybody* went to Town Meeting and everybody enjoyed it—even those whose projects were defeated.

We did have some "imported entertainment from away", such as a Chatauqua series each winter—evenings of music, lectures and similar cultural programs.

But for me, at least, the big entertainment event of the year was the week that the Kickapoo Indian Medicine Show spent in Chatham. The Show arrived in a gaudily painted special train on which the performers lived, except for maybe a star or two who would go to the hotel while in town. The others lived on board the train on the siding in the freight yard. (But then so did the staff of the private car of the railroad president, when he came to spend a few days of summer at the Inn).

The Medicine Show presented a series of performances each evening for a week in the Town Hall. Before the flickering kerosene lights, with their tin reflectors which served as footlights, they performed everything from acrobatics to minstrel shows, to melodrama and prestidigitation.

The high point of the evening was always the entre act. Then the pitchman really hypnotized his audience as he extolled the virtues of "Sagawa—made by the medicine men of the Kickapoo Indians from a secret formula of herbs and roots, blended by a magic ingredient which produces a cure for all the ills of man or beast. Good for rheumatism, sore throat, aches and pains, spavin or worms, birth pains, death pains. Whatever ails you, Sagawa will cure. Step up, my friends, for Sagawa—only one dollar a bottle—and for the first three lucky friends to purchase this rare elixir, a special price of only 50 cents. Who will be the lucky three?"

Meanwhile his assistants, in costume, would be scattered about to aid the first three buyers to save 50 cents a bottle. It sounds pretty corny—and it was—but it was more forthright and less "cute" than the Madison Avenue drivel that offends our eyes and ears over TV today.

It was at one of these medicine shows that I saw my first motion picture. They set up a white sheet across the front of the stage, and with light produced from tanks of gas in the back of the hall, showed us our first "flickers"—and they did flicker! But they moved! I don't remember the plot, if there was one, but I do remember a couple of jerky flickering scenes in which the beautiful damsel escaped from the awful villain!

Soon after, about 1910 I'd guess, Charlie Lake got permission from the town to build a projection booth in the balcony of the Town Hall. Here, seated in settees, we viewed such classics as the "Perils of Pauline" (continued next week), interrupted at the end of each reel by a lantern slide which said, "Three minutes, please, while we change the film," followed in turn by a slide with the words of a popular song which we all sang to the accompaniment of the hard-working pianist, whose job it was to accompany the silent films with appropriate music of his own selection.

Most of the local dances were held in this same hall. There were signs on the walls around the hall which the authorities deemed necessary. Some of them read: "Spitting on the floor strictly forbidden". "Turkey Trot, Bunny Hug and throwing peanut shells on the floor not allowed".

There were two big stoves in diagonally opposite corners of the room. Evidently the spitting and the peanut shells were supposed to be directed at them.

And while round as well as square dances were approved and enjoyed—the Turkey Trot and the Bunny Hug were just too suggestive! One-step, two-step, fox trots, scottisches were tolerated, however. Girls, of course, were supposed to wear corsets at dances; but by the time I was in high school, it was rumored that some of the older girls "from away" sometimes left theirs in the ladies coat room!

In September of each year everybody went to the Barnstable County Agricultural Fair and Cattle Show on the fairgrounds in Barnstable. Crowded special trains ran from the Lower Cape to Barnstable, the trains from Chatham hooking onto the ones from Provincetown at Harwich. Literally everybody went, even those boys who routinely did not show up at school until the fall cranberry harvest had been completed. (In those days cranberries were picked by hand, and it took a lot of hands, including almost every boy and many women and girls).

At the Cattle Show farmers competed for prizes for their beasts. In the big, two-story agricultural hall were exhibited vegetables, fruits, preserves and handiwork, all competing for prizes.

But the real excitement of the Fair were the trotting races

on the track ending in front of the big grandstand, and above all the midway with its games, side shows, its hot dogs and pink lemonade, its merry-go-round, and barkers selling paring knives and glue to repair any "bric-a-brac or china", and the daily balloon ascension by a huge bag filled with hot air, followed by the daring parachute drop of the balloonist.

In later years there were the motorcycle riders who roared around the vertical inside curved walls of a cylinder only a few yards in diameter. And always there was the man who would give you a five-cent cigar if you could ring the bell at the top of a slide by swinging down just right with a huge mallet onto a plunger. You could also throw baseballs at a man who stuck his head through a hole in a canvas and dodged the balls. And of course "Hoop-La" was just as popular then as now. "Cover any prize with a tossed hoop and it's yours. Everybody plays Hoop-La".

There was a large tent over a permanent wooden platform where the W.C.T.U. (Womens' Christian Temperance Union) served steaming bowls of clam chowder and plates of apple pie. When it came time to take the train for home it was nearly dusk, and we were usually content with a bowl of crackers and milk before tumbling into bed at the end of a long, exciting, exhausting, and gastronomically dangerous day!

Each year Chatham had its own special kind of spectacular "spectator sport", when members of the Norfolk Hunt Club came for a week. They would arrive by a special train which included numerous baggage cars loaded with horses and hounds and gear. These would be unloaded across the freight house platform right next to father's lumber yard. The men in their pink coats mounted their horses as they were unloaded. The Master of Hounds in his black velvet cap and with his long whip was always hard put to control the dogs as they came out of the car after their long train ride.

Then off they would go, some to the Wayside Inn, but most to John Farmer's Monomyck Inn right beside Jo Eldredge's Livery Stable, both of which had been taken over for the week. The days that followed were exciting and romantic, to see them follow the hounds over hill and dale in what were then mostly open fields, yet to be taken over by scrub pine and new houses.

These were the high spots each year. But we also had high spots of entertainment which we created for ourselves. When I was about 10, there came to our town a man named Carroll Wight and his wife and son. He had been a professor of Latin and Greek, but for reasons of health had come to Chatham where he became a carpenter. Mrs. Wight, with his help, opened and operated a tea room called the Champlain Tea Room, which was very popular in those early days of motoring. Their son Frederick, later Curator of the Museum of Modern Art at Los Angeles, was in my class.

Dr. Wight, who was a man great in both energy and humor, wrote and produced a series of plays based on the local scene—one each year for several successive winters. What with writing, rehearsing and production of those plays in the then new (circa 1915) movie theatre, our lives were enriched. One of them, complete with songs and music, was written in blank verse, as I remember.

Our little world was not empty of entertainment. There were many facets besides those I have described, such as the Old Harbor Guild in North Chatham, where the neighborhood met for supper and songs and sometimes dancing. But none of us growing up in Chatham just before World War I ever heard music that did not originate where we were; nor saw pictures that weren't in books we could see at home, at school, at church or at the Eldredge Public Library. Our world was lacking in good music and art to a degree scarcely understandable to youngsters of today.

Along The Shore

IN my boyhood I don't recall ever having seen a "No Trespass" sign anywhere along our shores. There were innumerable footpaths leading to the shore and a few cartways across private land. But the most that any private landowner ever did, and then in only a few cases, was to have a sign posted by a deputy sheriff at infrequent intervals, so that such permissive use might not become a legal public right.

During the second decade of the century, there began to be a growing awareness of the need for legal protection of rights of access by the public to the shore. Some ancient "town landings" were re-defined and a few new ones established. This was done in Chatham when Uncle Joshua was on the Board of Selectmen. Whenever they could, the selectmen laid out these landings, in a fan-shaped design, at the foot of roads leading to the shore. Thus, in the event of erosion, there would always be at least the width of the road for a landing, and in case of accretion the shoreline of the landing would grow in length as the land extended to where water had been.

Although virtually all of the shoreline was accessible, certain spots were particularly suited for the uses of the time and so tended to attract traffic. Among those in Chatham were Ryders Cove, Scatteree, Cow Yard, Stage Harbor and Oyster Pond River.

There were still a few fishing catboats dependent entirely on sail. But the fishermen were mostly using extra-large-size

Grand Banks dories with a single cylinder Lathrop gasoline engine and outboard wooden stabilizers for fishing "outside". There were a few larger power boats for fishing. And there was an occasional small schooner. But there were no beam trawlers or even line trawlers. Everything was either hand-lining, seining, traps or weirs. There were always lots of skiffs and dories anchored along the shore with their oars tucked under the thwarts.

It was generally all right to "borrow" one of these if you didn't go out of sight or hailing distance, *provided* you returned it to the exact spot from which it had been taken. This meant putting the anchor back exactly where it had been with the same length of rope on which the boat could swing. This was important because a boatman, when leaving his skiff on the shore, usually did so in such a manner that it would be in just the right position in relation to tide and wind when he returned to use it the next time. It would no more enter anyone's head on Cape Cod to steal oars, a sail or other gear out of a boat, than it would have in Texas to steal a man's horse while he slept.

One favorite rig for getting around in the bay or harbor was a flat-bottomed sharpie with a centerboard, oars and a small "leg of mutton" triangular sail, which could be stepped through a hole in the forward thwart or deck and taken down and rolled up in the boat when not in use. You steered with an oar thrust over the leeward gunnel (gunwale), to which a small block of wood had been nailed to keep the oar from slipping when under pressure from the water. There were *no* outboard motors!

A small, light, canvas-decked version of the sharpie, designed for use by one man, was the favorite of "gunners" who hunted ducks and geese. I can just barely remember when there were "market gunners", who shipped their kill to the Boston market. And my own introduction to gunning in the marshes was shooting yellow-legs and beetle-head in the fall. The spring season, when birds were most plentiful, had already become a "closed season".

When the fishing boats came in from offshore with their daily catch, they would usually pitchfork their fish over the side into a dory. Then they would row the dory ashore into shallow water. Leading down from the fish shanties into the water were narrow planks secured and fastened down by stakes. On these the men would trundle down a wheelbarrow with an empty fish box and a "dressing table".

The dressing table would be set up in the shallow water and the men would dress the fish, throwing the heads and guts into the water and the dressed fish into the boxes. The "dressing" usually involved two operations—first, throating and gutting, and then splitting. There were various other methods used for the fresh fish market, such as "slivering" (filleting), and cutting out cheeks and tongues. But most of the cod were salted, before which the fish had to be split.

The size of the catch was always referred to as so many "kentles" (quintals), not boxes as today. The loaded box of dressed fish would be wheeled in the wheelbarrow up the rolling-plank to the fish house or "shanty". There the fish would be carefully packed in strong brine in huge hogsheads which lined the walls of the shanty. Sometimes the product would be shipped "wet salted", but usually the fish were dried in the sun or on flakes before shipping.

Some idea of the extent of this business can be gained from the fact that my father had a building devoted to the storage and sale of fishery salt at his lumber yard. This came in bulk in freight cars, from which it was unloaded by shoveling it into wheelbarrows and then dumped on the floor of the building which stood beside the railroad tracks. This building would hold nearly two carloads of salt.

It was sold by the 70-pound bushel, sometimes bagged in burlap (at a slight extra charge), but usually dumped into a horse-drawn "truck cart" to be taken to the fishermen's shanties.

It need hardly be said that these shanties were a constant source of attraction for us boys. But their owners usually kept them padlocked, and they were "off limits" to boys except on those bad weather days when the men used them as a place for mending gear, or making new.

There were a few places along the shore where people went swimming—even a few bath-houses for changing clothes. But lying in the sun on the beach in a wet bathing suit was not highly regarded. This should come as no surprise when it is remembered that both men's and women's bathing suits came down to the knees and covered not only the body but the upper arms as well. In addition, the well-dressed woman bather also wore stockings and shoes. And to cap it all, the suits were usually of cotton! B-r-r-r!

I have been talking of the "shore" as the shore of the mainland. But there is another shore. It is the ocean side of the outside beach. However, this was never referred to as the shore but as the "back side" of the beach. The word "shore", as applied to the outer beach, invariably referred to the inner side of the beach—never to the back side. This landward shore was (and still is) a favorite place for waterfowl, marsh birds and shellfish.

But the back side then was even more fascinating than now. Every winter saw its grisly harvest of wrecks, mostly sailing ships which failed to claw off the lee shore against the wind and struck on the outer bar, where they broke up, or if luckier, bumped over onto the beach itself. Every spring there was a new crop of wreckage from the winter's storms. Some of it was broken planks and spars, but often there would be a whole hull left almost intact and partly buried in sand.

Offshore was a constant stream of ships passing by. There was no Cape Cod Canal then, and all coastwise shipping had to go around the Cape. Sometimes you could count more than a hundred ships in sight at one time, as those which had been lying in Vineyard Sound waiting for a fair wind came roaring down past Monomoy and Pollock Rip to head north around the Cape. There were nearly always tows of barges in sight. There would be an ocean-going steam tugboat hawling a tow of barges strung out astern, mostly hulks which had seen better days, loaded with bulk cargoes such as coal, or grain or moulding sand.

There was no way to get to this outer beach except by boat, and no way to get round on it except on foot. It wasn't used much in those days, but I am told that a century before some cattle and horses had been kept there, when it was attached to and a part of Monomoy. But even then there couldn't have been much forage.

Monomoy was a special kind of place. Way down at the end was a small settlement around the "Powder Hole" which was a small harbor on the inner shore. Here, during the season, lived the families who made a livelihood of lobstering, running the "traps" as the weirs were called, and such strange occupations as anchor dragging and salvaging from wrecks. Along the inner shore extending far off to the edge of deep water were the fish weirs (in season).

At Inward Point, about halfway down on Monomoy, was another cluster of camps. But these were mostly used by gunners who hunted in the surrounding marshes. Just in from Inward Point toward Morris Island was an island occupied by the Monomoy Brant Club, a group of gentlemen hunters from the city. Morris Island itself was nearly a mile inshore from the ocean in my boyhood. Between it and the "back side" was a beach, on which stood the Chatham Beach Hotel and (landward from it) the Chatham Lifesaving Station.

Across the street in Chatham from the "Twin Lights", (now Chatham Light, and United States Coast Guard local headquarters) were a few bricks, all that remained of the second set of Chatham Lights. These had been washed away as the ocean eroded the mainland. But in my childhood the bank below the old lighthouse was safe again—for a time. At its foot was a long shallow arm of water from Stage Harbor, and beyond that the broad ocean beach, the South Beach. On this beach stood an old hut of the Massachusetts Humane Society and an ice cream and clam chowder "saloon" run in the summer by Tom Gill, who was a very skillful builder of small boats and skiffs the rest of the year.

There is one aspect of being along the shore which has a very special quality. It is as valid today as it was yesteryear. It stems from the ever-renewed sense of discovery which is involved in the littoral. It's name is "scow-banging".

I first heard this word from my father. He defined it this way, "In the early morning you start out with your skiff or little sailboat. Aboard you have a clam hoe, a quohog scratcher, fishing lines, a pair of binoculars, and maybe a gun and some decoys. You're gone all day. Late in the day you return home. You don't know where you've been, you don't know what you've done, but you've had a wonderful day. And in the boat you've brought home something to eat."

I still go scow-banging and I recommend it to anyone so inclined. But in my childhood, scow-banging was conditioned not on motors, but on sail and wind and tide.

Every year there was the special day with Uncle Joshua, when we'd start out in his sailing skiff on the flood tide and explore the flats and channels and marshes. Up past Scatteree we'd go to Strong Island and Little Sipson's, with maybe a brief stop at Stinking Hummock to pick up a few little necks in its pools not yet reached by the flooding tide. Then over to Hog Island, through the creek between it and Sampson's Island—or perhaps through Board Creek around the north end of Sampson's Island to Pochet.

Then across Little Bay to "the river", a crooked channel

leading up through the land to Meeting House Pond. If our calculations were right, we'd arrive there at the peak of the tide and have a fair tide on the ebb all the way home to the Cow Yard at Old Harbor in Chatham. But we had to figure it just right, because the tide at Meeting House Pond is three or four hours later than it is at the Cow Yard, and can vary considerably according to wind conditions. It was (and always is) lots of fun.

But even better than scow-banging days with Uncle Joshua were those with father. Somehow Uncle Joshua's preoccupation with tides were not quite as appealing as father's interest in where were we going to find clams?—and cook them—and had the gulls started to lay yet? With father we wouldn't start out with any sandwiches, just hardtack and water. We had to find something to eat. Of course he knew where the clams were and all that, but you got the feeling that we were really adventuring—no clams, no dinner!

Father might even start when the tide was still running *out*! But first we'd have to dig some clams. This having been achieved, we'd sail for Little Sipson's or Big Sipson's Island. There the gulls start to lay their eggs early in May. On a warm spring day we'd be sure to find some. In those days gulls were not protected. So we would pick up a dozen or two gull's eggs and punch a tiny hole in each end. Then we'd blow the contents out of the egg and take the empty shells home to show to mother and to add to our collection of empty birds' eggs.

By this time it would be getting along towards noon. So we would sail over to the rocky north side of Big Sipson's Island, and gather rock weed before the tide got too high. Then we'd build a fire of driftwood in the midst of a hollow cairn of rocks. When the fire had burned down to embers and the rocks were thoroughly hot, we'd put on a layer of rock weed, dump on the clams, then more rock weed, then more hot stones—then wait!

After a while we'd start testing the clams to see if they were done. By the time we had finished testing, the clams were all gone and our stomachs were full. Then home perhaps against the wind, surely against the tide. But we always made it, no matter what the obstacles and we always had fun. That was scow-banging—or at least one boy's version of it!

From Day to Day

DAILY living conditions in the early years of this century were certainly much improved over what they had been in the 19th century. But they were so unlike what we have come to take for granted today that it is hard for today's young people to visualize living conditions of 50 or 60 years ago. The two greatest factors which have contributed to this change are the automobile and the common use of electricity. Most of the changes in living habits could not have happened without these two developments, both of which were in their infancy when I was a little boy.

The lighting in our house was from kerosene oil lamps, most of which had a simple flat cotton wick which sucked the fuel up from the base of the lamp to the burner which was enclosed by a glass chimney. We soon acquired a Rayo lamp, which had a cylindrical wick and a metal nickeled base. This was much more efficient than the oil lamps, even when they were hung from the ceiling and trimmed with crystal pendants to reflect more light. The Rayo was placed on a table in the middle of the living room, and we would sit beside it parallel to the side of the table to read.

The old-style lamps were usually set in brackets above the kitchen sink and the cook stove, backed by an adjustable reflector to give better vision on the stove and in the sink. At bedtime we lighted a lamp in the kitchen and took it with us to the bedroom where we blew it out when ready for bed. Even Boston had just graduated from kerosene to gas to electric light bulbs with a single cotton filament. Signs in the rooms of the Adams House on Washington Street still read: "DO NOT BLOW OUT THE GAS".

Our water supply came from a hand-operated kitchen pump in the kitchen sink, which was heated by transferring it to the top of the kitchen range in a tea kettle or large container. Some ranges had a reservoir at the back end for warming water which was bailed out with a dipper. Most people bathed in a wooden tub placed in the middle of the kitchen floor, but we had a separate bathroom which was solely for that purpose. It was just off the kitchen and contained a zinc-lined tub which was filled by buckets of water warmed on the stove. It had a drain that let outside the house, because there were no cesspools or septic tanks. The dirty water from the sink ran off outside; in many homes it was merely thrown out the back door onto the ground.

When I was about six or seven years old the great change came in our plumbing arrangements. Father had a windmill of galvanized steel frame erected in the back yard to pump water mechanically from a "driven well". The water was pumped to a metal-lined wooden storage tank which he had built in our attic. But most such mills had a tank near the top of the mill itself. Pipes were installed leading the water by gravity to faucets in the kitchen sink and into the bathroom. A flush toilet and a wash hand-bowl were installed in the bathroom.

And miracles of miracles—we had hot water supplied from a 30-gallon cylindrical copper tank, which stood behind the kitchen range in which was installed a "hot water front" to heat the water. This worked fine in the winter, but we had to build a fire in the range to get hot water in the summer. In any event, if your bath followed someone who had been over-generous to themselves with the hot water, you had to wait a while for the water in the tank to reheat.

Even though the flush toilet had been installed in the bathroom, we continued to use the 3-holer privy for years. It was more convenient and was always available when the bathroom was being used for bathing.

I remember too the covered slop pail which was used each morning to collect the contents of the chamber pots which were placed under each bed. Of course, with the installation of the new plumbing, there had to be a big cesspool and from it a runoff taking the excess to an outlet down the hill, where the high bush blackberries grew in profusion.

Most houses were heated by the kitchen stove, in which we burned wood in the summer and coal in the winter, and by "gas burner" stoves in the various downstairs rooms. Upstairs was heated by registers in the ceiling of the downstairs rooms, which had shutters which could be opened or closed to control the flow of warm air from the room below. Needless to say, the temperature of the upstairs bedrooms was never very high on a cold winter's day, and many people slept in deep feather beds instead of on hard, cold mattresses in winter.

Our heating arrangements were slightly more sophisticated, for we had central heat supplied to the first floor from a hot air furnace in a room in the cellar. But we did have the ceiling registers.

As for refrigeration the only source was natural ice. This was delivered (in the warm season only) by an "iceman" driving a wagon with a canvas cover stretched on hoops over the body of the wagon. First he would hop from his seat, then come in and measure with his eye the amount of new ice which the icebox would take. Then he would go back to his wagon and haul a piece of appropriate size to the tailgate with his ice tongs. He would then trim it with a very sharp ice pick, weigh it on spring scales suspended on a retractable steel arm fastened to the back of the wagon, brush it off briskly with a whisk broom and carry it into the icebox. He would replace and stow all the food he might have had to remove temporarily, and then of course write down on a tally sheet beside the icebox the weight of the ice, so that the charge could be correctly computed at the end of the season. That tally card was the only paperwork involved in the transaction.

In the process of trimming the block of ice to the right size, chips and shards of ice would fall to the ground. These would be eagerly picked up by children and sucked until they had dissolved—after, of course, having been allowed to drip themselves clean.

Some people had iceboxes in their back entry-way. Ours was a small, varnished, wooden, metal-lined "White Mountain" model, located in a back room or "summer kitchen", with a lid on top opening to the ice storage area and a hinged door on the lower front, opening to shelves for food storage. The water caused by the melting ice ran down a tube to a metal pan set under the icebox, which had to be pulled out and emptied every day or two.

This use of ice as a household refrigerant was relatively new. Most houses still depended on a cool room such as a pantry like ours, located on the north side of the house, a buttery or a cool, small, round cellar. Only a few still continued to depend on the spring house, which was an almost perfect place to keep things cool—if you happened to have a spring!

The ice which supplied our domestic needs was entirely natural ice and of local origin—except following an occasional winter so mild that none could be harvested locally. Then it had to be shipped in "from away" in refrigerator cars. In the railroad yard there was a small icehouse big enough to hold a carload or two to care for this emergency.

On the south side of the Black Pond, just below our house, there were two good-sized icehouses. I remember similar ones on Emery's Pond, Newtie Flynn's Pond, South Pond (now Lovers Lake), all in Chatham, just to mention a few. It was always a thrill to be awakened at dawn of a winter's day by the sound of the ice plows at work. The harvest had begun! The desired thickness of ice was between eight and 12 inches, but it was taken thinner or thicker if need be. The first step in the harvest was to plow the surface of the ice with a horse-drawn plow, which cut sharply into the surface making evenly spaced parallel lines, first in one direction and then at right angles to the original set of lines. Then came men with long ice saws with wooden handles set crosswise at one end. They would cut the ice into long strips, two squares wide and of convenient length, to be guided by men with long-handled picks to the mouth of a channel out in the ice leading to the foot of a wooden chute outside the icehouse.

As they came into this channel the long strips were cut with a big ice chisel by a man standing on a plank laid astride the channel, into blocks of two squares each. These blocks were then turned lengthwise and guided to the foot of the wooden chute, where they were hooked onto by a claw fastened to a rope running over pulleys to a horse who whisked them to the top of the accumulated ice in the house.

The building itself was constructed with double walls filled between with sawdust. A door in one end was designed for unloading the ice with ice tongs, pulleys, and hand pikes at whatever level the ice piled inside had reached.

In those days our food was different as to method of supply, as well as to diet. There was always a barrel of flour under the counter in the kitchen to which access was had by lifting a section of the counter top. We made our own bread, of course. There was also always a barrel of sugar in the pantry, and lard came in a five-pound tin pail with a bale and cover. These pails were carefully saved for picking berries or carrying milk. Butter came in a five-pound wooden box.

Every fall there would be two or three barrels of apples put in the cellar. There was also a large barrel-like crock of fat salt pork and another one of lean. The salt pork was used freely for cooking everything from clam chowder to string beans, to "fish and potatoes", and of course baked beans, which were invariably the main dish for supper every Saturday evening. The beans were also used "warmed over" until the huge bean pot had been emptied in time for next Saturday night's meal!

Potatoes, beets, cabbages, carrots, turnips, squash and pumpkins were kept through the winter with varying degrees of success. Every family had its own vegetable garden as a matter of course, and a small flock of hens. Not everybody had pigs; but we always had two—"Napoleon" and "Caesar", who lived in a pen adjoining the horse stable at father's lumber yard. They met their fate every fall.

Some people had cows, but we didn't, preferring to buy our milk from Leonard Doane, who delivered daily in his milkwagon. There were several neighbors who kept a cow or two, so if we ran short I would be sent with an empty lard pail to get a couple of quarts. I can remember returning across the fields on many such occasions, swinging the pail of milk around and around over my head, without spilling a drop— at least not more than a few drops.

Fresh meat was provided from a canvas-covered butchercart which called once or twice a week. On the back end of the cart was a box containing the corned beef. The grocery cart came twice a week, once to take your order, and again to deliver it. There were no telephones then except a few for crucial use. A bakery cart came once a week; but we weren't very good customers unless mother could be wheedled into buying cream puffs. No self-respecting housewife could be expected to *buy* pies, bread or cookies—unless she was sick and couldn't make them herself. Then she would buy these obvious necessities.

Except for the apples in the cellar, a rare orange from the store, or an occasional banana, there were no fresh fruits or vegetables out of season. I can remember going with dad in the spring to gather young dock leaves and dandelions to satisfy our craving for fresh greens.

There was always plenty of fish. Shellfish we usually got

ourselves, or mother bought them from old "Captain Frank" Nickerson, a slightly demented and needy neighbor who eked out a living by clamming and such. For fresh fish, one of us children would be dispatched to the shore to buy from the boats coming in. And there was usually a fish peddler, highly unreliable as to what he'd have and when he'd come, but scrupulously trustworthy in other respects—such as freshness, quality, price and weight. His customers were always experts and connoisseurs when it came to fish.

There were many old men in those days who frugally supported themselves by clamming and odd jobs around the shores. They were not poor enough to be under the town's "Overseers of the Poor". They usually owned their own homes free and clear and kept them neat and shipshape. What with their gardens, their hens and pigs, and maybe a cow, and a woodlot of their own, or a friend's, they managed frugally but fairly comfortably on a couple of hundred dollars a year or less in cash income. And they were proudly "not dependent".

As I have said, everybody had his own vegetable garden. But there was some commercial traffic in vegetables, such as sweet corn, "hulled" corn (cured in ashes and served with milk and sugar like a modern cold cereal), potatoes, Eastham turnips and Orleans apples.

Every spring there were the peddlers of "smoked herring". We always had them roasted in the oven with the first of the season's cucumbers. They were delicious—but as father used to say, "Once or twice a season is enough."

A recent photo of the author, Joshua Atkins Nickerson 2nd, with Pleasant Bay in the background.

Warren Jenson and his wife Mary (Atkins) Nickerson, paternal grandparents of the author.

Lawrence and Mora Nickerson, brother and sister of the author.

At left, Oscar and Eglantine Nickerson (author's parents); at right, Joshua (Oscar's brother) and his wife Eliza May.

Edna Nickerson Matterson, cousin of the author, by her grandfather's woodpile.

Home of Uncle Joshua A. Nickerson, on Old Harbor Road.

Home of Oscar C. Nickerson, also on Old Harbor Road.

Family group at Oscar Nickersons—from left (standing) an unidentified friend, Edna Matterson, Mora, Bessie Young, holding the author; (kneeling) Eliza May, Lawrence, Uncle Joshua and Oscar.

Oscar and Uncle Joshua Nickerson standing in front of Joshua's retail store.

Old Harbor Road before it was paved—the old Granville Seminary building is in the foreground.

The author's Uncle Sears Nickerson.

The Atwood School (at right) on the corner of Stage Harbor Road and Cedar Street.

Typical of the many delivery wagons during the early part of the century.

On Frugality

AN old friend of mine once told me that, in going through his recently deceased mother's personal effects, he came across a large shoebox, carefully tied and labeled.

The label read, "Pieces of string too short to save", and he said, "When I opened the box, what do you think I found? You guessed it! It was full of pieces of string too short to save!"

Such frugality, though extreme in this instance, was not uncharacteristic of my parents and earlier generations here on Cape Cod.

My mother reserved a bottom drawer in the chest under the counter in the kitchen for paper bags, wrapping paper and string. In those days paper bags were used only occasionally. Wrapping paper or old newspapers were more commonly used for wrapping. In addition to the carefully folded paper bags in that drawer, mother always kept two balls of string there, one heavy and one fine, which had been retrieved from parcels tied in wrapping paper.

Our groceries were brought into the house in a basket by the delivery man (or boy), so the heavy brown paper bags now used in every supermarket were rare indeed. Our sugar and flour came in barrels which, when emptied, served many useful purposes.

Today almost everything comes prepackaged in various sizes. Then most things—for example, flour, sugar, crackers, molasses and kerosene—came in bulk in barrels and were weighed or measured out in the store into the customers' own containers. The kerosene presented a small problem when delivered along with the groceries, because the kerosene can usually had a small spout at the top which could spill when jolting along the road. This was usually prevented by jamming a small potato over the end of the spout.

Bottles were rare too. There was a ready market for the empty pints and quarts which we kids could find. At the hardware and paint store, we could always sell them for at least a cent a piece. You see, turpentine and linseed oil came in 55-gallon casks which, when laid on the side in a rack and tilted slightly forward, dispensed their contents through a spigot into a tin measure from which it was poured through a spout into the empty bottles. There were no small cans of such products. The bottles were in constant demand, since the only paint used was white lead and oil, mixed and "boxed" just before application.

Consider the matter of darning. A mother's workbasket was always full of stockings to be darned and rips to be knitted up or patched. This work was always done carefully, to make the repairs as inconspicuous as possible; not like today, when conspicuous contrasting patches and ragged or torn blue jeans are symbols of our "youth culture".

Perhaps the most obvious examples of frugality involved the most personal needs. Rolled toilet paper was unknown. Such as there was came in flat sheets cut to appropriate size. I remember that my mother used to save the tissue wrappings from the occasional oranges we had, to be used as toilet tissue. But even this was not common. About every privy was supplied with an old Sears Roebuck catalog—certainly an improvement on old newspapers and dried corncobs.

There was no "facial" tissue. Even in 1918, I remember being impressed that my college roommate used toilet paper to blow his nose when he had a bad cold. There was no

Kleenex. Nor were there any disposable sanitary napkins such as Kotex. The cloth napkins were washed and boiled and used again and again.

Any glass jars or tumblers which came our way were carefully saved and set aside to hold jellies and preserves, which would be sealed with paraffin poured over the top of the contents.

Mother used to make most of her own soap. There were no detergents. She saved all the grease that accumulated in the household, and when she had enough, she added wood ashes and lye and whatever else her process called for. The product was poured into a large flat pan. Then while it was still a little soft, she cut it into squares with a knife. The finished product was hard but not unpleasant to use. Perhaps this was because she always put in a little oil of sassafras which dad had been commissioned to buy on one of his business trips to Boston. It certainly made it smell good!

Bits of soap left when the cake had become worn down were saved and put into a "soap shaker". This was a wire mesh container with a metal handle which hung in the sink. It was swished about in the dishpan containing warm water for dishwashing to create suds. It was effective of course, but then there were no soapflakes or detergent powders, such as are piled high nowadays on supermarket shelves.

We did have a soft yellow soap which came in large bars from which we sliced thin pieces to be used in the laundry, much as you slice cheese today from a brick of processed cheese. Mother's favorite was Fels Naptha, which in addition to being a good soap, had a pleasant antiseptic odor.

Certain days of the week were designated for specific household chores. Monday was always washday. I remember when we graduated from using a tub and scrubboard to a patented washing machine, because the power for operating the new machine was often boy-power. It consisted of a wooden tub which sat on a frame fastened in such a way that the tub could be rocked back and forth horizontally by means of a small wooden handle attached to its upper rim. This forced the water back and forth through the clothes until they were clean. A perforated cover was placed on top of the wash to keep the water from slopping over the side of the tub.

After this was accomplished, the sudsy water was drained from the tub and replaced with clean warm water in which the laundry was throughly rinsed. The next step was to put the material through a patented wringer, which consisted of two rubber-covered rollers between which the clothes were forced by turning a hand-operated crank on the side of the wringer—(a big improvement over wringing by hand.) The damp clothes fell into a wicker or rattan basket, in which they were lugged outdoors and hung with wooden clothespins to dry on the clothesline.

Tuesday, quite naturally, was ironing day, when Monday's wash was carefully ironed and put away. Wednesday was mending day. Thursday was cleaning day, when any cleanup jobs not routinely covered daily were taken care of. When I was a boy, the acquisition of a hand-operated barrel-shaped vacuum cleaner was much appreciated by my mother—but not by me—as I was too often called upon to pump the wooden handle, which activated it back and forth.

I have forgotten what specific tasks were set for Friday, except that every Friday evening we prepared the dough for the bread to be baked on Saturday, which was baking day. We had a patented dough-mixer. This consisted of a large metal pail, across the top of which was clamped a metal brace through which was inserted an S-shaped metal rod activated by a handle on top, which was usually boy-operated by turning it horizontally. When the dough was stiff enough, mother would take over, knead the dough into loaves, and put them into bread pans which she put in a warm place where the dough would rise in readiness for baking the next day.

Saturday was baking day, which included baking cakes

and pies, as well as bread, and invariably a large pot of baked beans with salt pork and a little molasses, to which frequent additions of water were made to prevent their getting too crusty. "The Hearty"—entree to you—for Saturday night's meal was always baked beans and brown bread.

Saturday evening was always bath day; at least it was for us children. On other days, we had to be clean, washing the back of the neck and behind our ears, for example. But on Saturday evening, we were required to get into the tub and wash and scrub ourselves all over. The water was always warm at the beginning of the process, at least. In addition to the cold water from the pump in the kitchen sink, mother added steaming hot water from kettles heated on the stove.

I was still a boy, however, when this method of supplying hot water was superseded by the installation of a "hotwater front" in the stove through pipes in which hot water was circulated to a thirty-gallon copper tank set on end behind the stove, and thence through a pipe to faucets in the kitchen sink and a new bathtub in the bathroom, which was really, as its name suggests, only a small room in which to bathe.

While camping on Monomoy Point with Bradford Bloomer, my Sunday School teacher, I learned a little trick which I have occasionally found useful ever since, when no refrigeration is available. Our milk was evaporated milk which came in cans. The trick is to punch two tiny holes opposite each other at the edge of the top of the can. This enables you to pour milk out of one hole while air enters the can through the opposite one, displacing the milk that is poured out. Then to preserve the milk left in the can, you simply tilt it so that a little milk covers each hole. This little bit of milk will co-agulate to cover the holes, thus sealing and preserving the remaining contents of the can as effectively as before the can was punctured.

In my boyhood nothing was thrown away until it was worn out, and even then bits of old cloth were kept in a big rag bag, which was a source of materials for making braided or hooked rugs and patchwork quilts.

Attics were the repository of household goods no longer in current use. I remember in ours, where I often spent a rainy day, there was an old spinning wheel and the cards for carding wool into the strands for making thread. Old "Harper's Weekly" magazines were piled there too; and it was from some of them dated in the 1860's that I got my first vivid impressions of such matters as life in the Libby Prison during the Civil War.

All of these old items have now long since disappeared, but the one I regret losing most was my father's medicine chest, which he had taken to sea with him in his days as a sea captain. It was a wooden box about a foot and a half long and a bit more than half that in width, with a hinged top. Outside it was beautifully varnished, and inside were numerous compartments separated by little vertical wooden partitions, containing various glass bottles and jars with appropriate labels. One, I recall, bore the label "Cholera Cure"; another, "Laudanum"; etc. There were surgical needles and sutures and scalpels and a small bonesaw. I don't remember my father ever talking about using this medicine chest.

It wasn't only in attics that old things were stored. They were saved and kept in barns and woodsheds. For example I still have an old stub-hoe with a handle made of some kind of natural swampwood, and an old plaice-fish spear which belonged to my Uncle Joshua, who died in 1932. These were old then. I even have the piece of a tree trunk which he used as a chopping block. I use it when I split a little kindling for the fireplace. Somehow there is a peculiar satisfaction in using these things which bear the patina from generations which they have outlived.

In those days leftover food was never thrown away. Much of it was saved to be warmed over or added to a pot kept stewing on the back of the stove. What was not used in that way was fed to the animals, the hens, the pigs, the dogs and cats. "Waste not, want not" was more than an adage. It was a way of life.

And many other old sayings were given practical applications in daily living.

Father used to quote a saying of his mother's, "Weight and measure is every man's due, but price is another thing."

This is rarely applied in today's packaging techniques, but it was a statement of principle which few people in her day failed to honor.

Another of her sayings was, "Blessed be nothing", meaning that worldly goods, or the possession of too many of them, often turned out not to be a blessing.

A day's work in my youth had a different meaning than it has today. The standard workday was from seven A.M. to six P.M., with an hour off at noon for "dinner". The work week was six days, thus making the normal work week 60 hours. The hours were varied in some occupations to be from daylight to dark, but most jobs in the wintertime began and ended by lantern light.

As for pay, it was rarely by the hour, mostly by the day or week, sometimes by the month. Unskilled labor was paid about a dollar a day or perhaps a bit more. When Henry Ford announced his eight-hour day, with five dollars a day minimum pay back before World War I, men flocked to Detroit to seek this unheard of affluence. It marked the end of an era of frugality and the beginning of a new life style for most Americans.

Schooner, Abel W. Parker

Anecdotes And Words

Bedtime Stories

WHEN I was a small boy, my brother Ivan (two years my junior) and I shared a bedroom. In fact for some years, we shared the same double bed. Inevitably this led to bedtime quarrels and fighting in bed. On such occasions our father, having heard the commotion from below, would come storming up the stairs.

He paid no attention whatever to the protestations from each of us that the other had started the fight, saying, "It takes two to make a fight, and you both get the same punishment."

That usually consisted of a firm but not too heavy spanking and the admonition that, if he heard any more quarreling, he would come up again and give us both a much sounder spanking.

But often his bedtime administrations were of a very different sort. He would tell us bedtime stories. Many of them began with "Once upon a time".

So we begged for his "Once upon a time" stories, especially those about when he went to sea. There were others which we loved to have him repeat, such as intoning in his deep and resonant voice, "I have roamed through woods— where alligators hung from every bush—and the grizzly bear—was chewing—the gut of his master."

If he was in a hurry, his way of avoiding a story was to say,

"I'll tell you a story
About Jack Menory,
And now my story's begun.
I'll tell you another
About Jack and his brother,
And now my story's done."

But when he had the time, we were fascinated by his stories of "going to sea." Included in this category was the one about the time he was docked in Norfolk, Virginia, taking on a cargo of corn. This was about 1890. He described the bitterness of his southern acquaintances toward "damn Yankees." But we liked it especially when he demonstrated his version of the blood curdling Rebel yell, which he heard for the first time while attending some sort of a public affair in Norfolk.

Evidently it took considerable time to get his cargo aboard. At any rate, while he was there, he went with the local agent on a short hunting trip up the canal and into the Dismal Swamp. His description of how they found their way to a lake within the swamp, and their extreme difficulty in finding their way out again—where they had come in—was just the stuff to fire the imagination of two small boys when they reenacted it in the nearby huckleberry swamp.

By far the most thrilling were his stories of his own experiences during the great March blizzard of 1888. His ship was off the coast of Long Island when the storm struck, in company with about one hundred other sailing ships. It was several days later that they found themselves wallowing almost helplessly on the edge of the Gulf Stream, but at least in warmer weather. Meantime several other ships had foundered.

As for their ship, every bulkhead stove and the deckhouse, booms and gaffs were smashed; their boats and anchor with one hundred fathoms of chain were lost. The only dry space was right up in the bow below the deck and here the injured men huddled. Every man in the crew went to the hospital on Staten Island when they finally made port.

Father, a young mate, had been smashed against a mast, suffering cracked ribs. He was the only man aboard without frozen toes, even though he showed us where he had bits of frozen bone removed from the tips of two of his fingers. The reason his toes were spared was because they rationed out a bottle of rum for each man at one point, having had no fire or warm food for two days. The others used their rum in the obvious way. But dad said he poured half of his bottle down inside of each boot, thus saving his toes from freezing.

At one point in the storm, the captain was washed overboard by a huge sea but managed to grab the end of a trailing rope. After banging a couple of times against the ship's side, he was washed back onto the deck where they grabbed him and got him below, half dead but still alive and able to recover.

After father was smashed against the spanker mast, he too had to stay below. Just after dark he dragged himself on deck to see what a new commotion was all about. Two brothers had been lashed to the wheel to try to hold her on some sort of a course, scudding before the storm with a heavy hauser trailing over the stern. A huge sea hit them from astern, spinning the wheel out of their hands. One of the men was thrown over the wheel and suffered a broken shoulder. The other was thrown under the wheel and the spokes tore through the side of his head. He died later in a hospital.

When they finally made it to the Staten Island Hospital, they entered through a snowdrift so high it seemed like a tunnel. That was the blizzard of '88, when several people died from exposure while lost in the storm on the streets of midtown Manhattan.

Another of Father's stories, a sequel to this, was about the trial or inquest held later, in the Admiralty Court, in which the underwriter's lawyer tried to prove that the officers and crew had been negligent in their duties. They had not been able, for example, to keep the ship's log for two or three days.

At that time father was a strapping 200-pound athletic fellow of 21. The lawyer was a pint-sized little redhead, but very aggressive. He asked questions demanding "yes" or "no" answers. Dad was an uncooperative witness and resented questions of the "Have you stopped beating your wife yet?" variety.

Obviously there were no simple answers to some of the lawyer's questions, but he kept insisting and would shake his fist or finger right under dad's nose.

At this point, dad turned to the judge and said, "Your honor, this man is threatening me. I appeal to the court for protection."

The judge replied, "I can see that this line of approach is not being productive. Would you like to tell the court, in your own words, what happened?"

Of course this is exactly what dad wanted to do, and from that point on, in giving his testimony, it was smooth sailing.

There were many such stories, but I always liked the one about the Plimsoll Mark. It seems that father's ship, of which he was now captain, was in Portland, Maine, undergoing some sort of maintenance, and waiting for cargo at the time when new regulations governing such vessels were issued. One of these had to do with requiring a Plimsoll Mark on each ship. When the time came to sail, he applied to the port authorities for clearance and an inspector came on board to check out the ship. However he saw no Plimsoll Mark, as required by the new regulations. Dad told him it was there, just as the regulations required. If the inspector could not see it, that certainly was no fault of the ship's officers.

The discussion went on for some time, until finally dad said, "The new rule says that the Plimsoll Mark shall be clearly painted at a point beyond which it is unsafe to load. Isn't that correct?"

The inspector agreed that this was precisely what the regulation said.

"Well then," said dad, "if you will look on top of the taff-rail, you will find, in accordance with the rules, a Plimsoll Mark painted there. If anyone thinks it is safe to load beyond that, he's crazy!"

Needless to say, the regulation was soon changed by striking out "beyond which it is unsafe to load" and inserting "up to which it is safe to load".

I understand that since then the rules have gone even further in requiring ships to have two Plimsoll Marks, one for summer and a lower one for winter, and the choice depends upon the season and proposed sailing routes.

We loved to hear about life on shipboard. For example dad explained the expression, "Eat hearty and give the ship a good name."

It seems that it was common practice for the owners to pay the captain an allowance for the men's mess. Some captains tried to profit from this by giving scanty or inferior victuals. But good captains knew better. They would provide for the mess the best and most food the allowance would admit. Their ships were known to the men, and the word soon got around the waterfront as to which ships fed well and which fed poorly.

Hence, "Eat hearty and give the ship a good name."

Dad told us too a bit about discipline on shipboard. It had to be reasonably strict, but not abusive. The life of the ship and her crew depended on it. Remember there was no radio, and once at sea the ship was a world unto herself, and the captain was all-powerful. When he had signed on a new crew, he always called them before the quarterdeck and told them what his rules were. Then he required each man to produce his knife and drive the point firmly into the deck. He would then snap off the point of each knife and hand it back—no longer capable of stabbing.

In all the years of my youth, I never heard my parents quarrel or be anything but courteous to each other, though I'm sure they had their disagreements.

Sometimes, when mother seemed to scold a bit, father would say, "Eglantine, are you speaking to me—or to one of the men for'ard?"

That would usually take care of the immediate situation. If he really wanted to put on the pressure, he would call her "Eggie" instead of Eglantine. That was a name she hated.

There was one occasion when mother and father were having a serious disagreement. It had to do with a joint enterprise in which he and another man, whom mother did not trust, were involved.

"Oscar," she said indignantly at the height of their argument, "that man is making a fool of you!"

"I know it," dad replied, "I know it, and so long as I know it, it's all right. Now if he was making a fool of me and I *didn't* know it, then there really would be something to worry about."

Mother was a petite little woman, very active, very energetic, and with lovely brown eyes. They were, in fact, an extraordinarily handsome couple. Mother's father, Mulford Young, was frail in health, but strong on purposefulness. He built up a very small retail business in East Harwich to a successful enterprise, with a chain of delivery and order wagons fanning out from there in all directions, as far as a man could drive a wagon and return in the same day.

And that included the long, long days of summer. When

mother was fifteen or sixteen years old, she was permitted to go on the train to Boston, where she would buy bolts of cloth for the store, always selecting patterns from which she herself would like to have a dress made.

They were married on January 23, 1889, when dad was 22, and she was 18. The matter of her age was always a source of teasing from dad, who claimed she was a year younger, which she always denied. They had been married only a short time when dad took her with him on a voyage.

The mates and crew really put themselves out to have everything spruce and shipshape for the bride. Dad also loved to tease mother by telling of an incident which happened on this trip, perhaps just because she always blushed when he told the story, and she blushed beautifully.

Among the many things done in preparation for the captain's bride was a considerable amount of painting, which included varnishing the toilet seat in the captain's quarters. Shortly after coming on board, Mother had occasion to use the toilet, only to discover that the varnish had not dried completely, and she was stuck to the seat. After futile attempts to free herself, she managed to get father's attention and to bring him to her rescue.

But even he could not solve the problem and he finally called the mate, who came with tools to enable the two of them to take the seat apart with mother still on it. She was finally rescued, and knowing how modest and meticulous she always was about her person, I have often wondered which was the greater hurt she suffered: the physical or the psychological. At any rate, it was a helluva way for a bride to start off traveling with her seagoing husband.

It was their little misadventures that I learned about, rather than the long happy times together, such as the time she lost her wedding ring. They were at anchor in a harbor. I think they had been over the side, swimming. At any rate her hands were wet. As they stood chatting happily on the deck, she slapped her hand in laughter flat on the ship's rail. Off flew her ring, bouncing over the side into the water. No amount of diving and swimming down recovered it, though many tried. But I never saw her without a wedding ring.

Anecdotes And Remembrances

MY favorite Cape Cod story is about a commercial fisherman, who years ago sailed his catboat out of Pleasant Bay and into the ocean, hand-lining for cod and haddock every day, weather permitting.

Each evening as he came ashore with his catch, his old friend and neighbor would be there to greet him with the same question, "How did you make out today?"

Invariably the fisherman's answer was the same, "I didn't do as well as I expected—(long pause)—but I didn't expect I would."

To me this sums up the entire philosophy of the fisherman, be he professional, amateur, sports or neophyte, in a few succinct words.

UNCLE CARROLL

My father's brother, Uncle Carroll, was such a fisherman. He disdained having a motor in his boat. After all, that was in the days of the clumsy one-lunger engines which were unreliable. He depended on sail alone for his 24-foot catboat, which was broad of beam and whose boom extended some 10 feet or so out over the stern. She did have a cabin with red glass portholes to port, and green glass portholes to starboard, so he could hang a lantern in the cabin after dark and show his port and starboard lights. Along the gunnels of the boat and the rail around the cockpit were deep grooves worn there by the friction of the heavy codline which he used while fishing.

Like all the hand-liners of those days, he brought his catch in his catboat to his mooring, just in front of his fish shanty on the shore. There he pitchforked the fish into his dory, which had been left at the mooring, and then he rowed ashore. From the door of his shanty was a plank walk, securely held down by stakes imbedded in the ground all the way down to the low-water mark. Having rowed ashore, he would walk up to the shanty and get a wooden wheelbarrow, onto which he would load a wooden "dressing table", which he would then roll down and set up at the edge of and in the water.

Then would begin the arduous job of dressing the fish, throating and splitting them and tossing the result into the wheelbarrow. He always referred to the size of his catch as being so many quintals—never as pounds. When he had a barrow-load, he would roll it up to the shanty and carefully spread the flat fillets into hogsheads there, sprinkling each layer with fishery salt, with just enough water to make a very strong brine. Later in the season these fish would be shipped to market, either wet-salted as they came from the brine in the hogsheads, or dry-salted after having been dried in the sun on flakes built for the purpose.

Nowadays dressing fish on the shore or in the harbor is generally forbidden. But then it was the common practice, much to the joy of crabs, minnow and eels. Today the fish are usually dressed aboard the boats, all of which carry at least two men, as they come in from the fishing grounds, followed by clouds of gulls feasting on the guts as they are tossed overboard on the way. In this vicinity too, nearly all the fish are now shipped to market fresh, iced down in wooden boxes. I know of no fishermen who salt down their catch today.

In fact fishery salt, which used to be brought into Chatham in bulk by the carload, is scarcely available.

Characteristic of Uncle Carroll is an incident which occurred when I was in my teens, back before 1920. He was dressing fish on the shore when some summer visitors strolled by and stopped to admire his catch. A few minutes later I came along and found him still hard at work, but muttering and scolding under his breath. I knew he wasn't particularly fond of summer folks, especially those he called "health-eaters" or "sun worshippers", but I was hardly prepared for his comment when I asked what was bothering him.

"Did you see those folks, just now?"

"Yes, I did."

"Well here I am dressing haddock and one of them had the gall to say to me, 'Those are fine looking codfish.' Damned fools didn't even know the difference between a haddock and a cod!"

He was not about to be patronized by anybody, no matter how well-meaning they might be.

Uncle Carroll was a handsome and proud man, very skillful in his field. Long before we had weather forecasts, other than the almanac (there were no radios), he would look at his barometer, scan the heavens, squint at the clouds and wind direction, gauge the humidity, and whatever else he needed, and forecast the weather, usually for a day or two ahead, with amazing accuracy. In fact if he were alive today, I would sooner have his judgment about the weather just ahead here at the elbow of Cape Cod, than that of today's forecasters with all their elaborate instruments and reports to help them.

He was also most expert in the way he sailed his catboat. He would come up to his mooring in a spanking breeze, bringing the boat almost—but not quite—dead in the water, then walk deliberately forward from the wheel to the bow, step over the side into his dory, fasten the boat to the mooring, all with the most casual air of unhurried efficiency of movement. He was the only man I ever knew, who having come in over Chatham Bars, could sail his boat upstream against the tide in what appeared to be a calm, and get home promptly to the head of Pleasant Bay. He knew how to take advantage of every back eddy and swirl of the tide and every least puff of air.

Every winter he would go to his woodlot and cut and cord a year's supply of firewood, mostly pine, but some of it hardwood. He would cut several cords, because wood was the principal fuel used in his home, both for heating and for cooking. There was no oil, and coal was expensive. He would have the wood which he had already split for cordwood carted down to his house, where he sawed it with a bucksaw into stove lengths. Then he would stack it outdoors into the biggest, most carefully arranged and geometrically perfect woodpile I have ever seen. It always was just a little more than enough, to last until he could bring in a fresh supply for the next year.

UNCLE JOSHUA

Uncle Joshua was an active and busy citizen. After giving up going to sea as captain of sailing ships, he had a small grocery store near the railroad depot in Chatham. He was for years a selectman and county commissioner. His advice was often sought on personal matters, and he drew wills and deeds for his neighbors.

He had the first typewriter I ever saw. I think it was an Underwood, and the type came down onto the paper on long arms banked on either side of the machine. If you went too fast, this could result in snarling an arm from the right bank with one on the left.

Among other innovations, he was the first in our neighborhood to have a modern bathroom with a flush toilet right inside the house. To be sure, a few people had a small room with a zinc-lined tub for bathing, but the idea of using a flush toilet inside the house instead of an outside privy was new, at least in our vicinity.

His wife, Aunt May, was not nearly as forward-looking and up-and-coming as he. This is evidenced by a story about Uncle Joshua's brother Edwin, who came to visit them for a few days just after the new bathroom had been completed.

As he was leaving, Aunt May called him aside and asked, "Edwin, have you seen our new bathroom?"

He replied, "Yes, May, I have. I peeked in the door once as I walked by it."

Aunt May's attitude is quite understandable, when you consider that she had confided to my mother at that time that she herself never used the flush toilet.

"The seat is so cold," she said.

"But," mother protested, "the wooden seat is no colder than the one in the privy."

"Oh," replied Aunt May, "I wouldn't think of using the wooden part. I might get it dirty."

LOUIS BRANDEIS

The cantakerous independence of spirit of our local fishermen has been the subject of many a comment and story. One example occurred many years ago and involved the late Louis D. Brandeis, who at that time was a justice of the United States Supreme Court. Mr. Brandeis' home was near the Oyster Pond River in Chatham, and he liked to row his little skiff up to the head of the Oyster Pond on mild June evenings and then walk up to the post office to collect his mail.

In those days the post office was directly opposite what is now the entrance to the lovely little Kate Gould Park on Main Street. Directly across the street from it, on land now a part of the park, stood a small drugstore operated by Dallas Smith.

On this particular evening, the mail train was late in arriving at the depot, and consequently the mail was late in reaching the post office and being sorted into the various mailboxes. (There was no house-to-house delivery.) A few of the local fishermen were gathered in the drugstore while waiting for the mail.

Naturally their talk was mostly of their fishing. Mr. Brandeis too, while waiting, had joined the group in the drugstore. After listening for a while he vouchsafed a comment, and then later another or two on the subject.

At this point one of the local fishermen turned to Mr. Brandeis and very quietly said, "Mr. Justice Brandeis, we know you are a justice of the Supreme Court of these United States; we recognize that you are a great jurist and lawyer; we respect and admire your high intellect—but with all due respect, we don't think you know much about fishin'."

ERASTUS BEARSE

The local smithy and horseshoeing shop was, in the days before automobiles, a social center of sorts. While waiting for their horse to be shod, or an eel spear or clam hoe to be finished, the men would sit around and gossip. Naturally the talk often ran to local politics and local politicians.

On one particular day they were discussing Erastus Bearse, editor of the local weekly paper, jeweler, watch repairer and one-time representative in the Massachusetts legislature. There were, of course, differences of opinion between the men as to his virtues, as well as his faults.

The argument had been going on for some time when the blacksmith laid down his tools and said, "I'll tell you about Erastus."

Thereupon he walked across the floor to an empty wooden barrel that stood bottom up against the wall.

Leaning over, he rapped smartly on the bottom of the barrel and said, "Erastus, are you in there?"

He then imitated Erastus' voice and said, "Yes, I'm in here."

He then knocked again, "Ratty, are you sure you're in there?"

"Of course, I'm sure I'm in here!"

For a third time he knocked. "No mistake? You really sure you're there?"

Again in an exasperated tone, "Of course I'm sure I'm in here!"

Then ever so slowly the blacksmith turned the barrel up so all could see that it was empty. "My God!" said the smith in an amazed tone "he ain't there!"

As he walked back to his tools, he said, "That's Rastus."

UNCLE ALBERT

When I was a boy there was no radio, no television, not even movie shows. One great source of entertainment for me, at least, was to sit enthralled and listen to the yarns and discussions engaged in by my elders. This was particularly intriguing when the men on the Nickerson side of the family got together. They were all great talkers and given to telling stories which were *based* on their experiences.

One such was Uncle Albert, my grandfather's younger brother. He was a great pipe smoker and loved his old Meerschaum so much that, when it finally burned through a spot in the bowl, he had an inset piece inserted.

When he visited next door at Uncle Joshua's, Aunt May wouldn't let him smoke in the house. So he would settle his huge frame into a big wicker rocking chair just inside the open barn doors facing the street, with a cuspidor on one side and often me on the other. He even carved for me a little wooden pipe, so I could feel more a participant; but of course I did not need a cuspidor, even though I did spit occasionally, just not to be left out.

Spitting in the cuspidor was an important part of smoking for Uncle Albert. Later when my sister's husband-to-be came courting, he asked if he might smoke. As he got out his cigarettes, he was amazed when mother brought him a cuspidor. Mother's only experience with smokers at that time having been with Uncle Albert, she just assumed that using a cuspidor was an integral part of smoking.

Uncle Albert was given to philosophizing at times, not as a theorist, but as a very pragmatic realist. Like most of his generation he measured success in life, to a considerable degree, by the extent of the individual's financial success.

I recall his offering my older brother and sister this advice about marriage.

"Getting married is, in a way, like getting a dog. Now you can pick up some mongrel cur and keep it around for a while. Then pretty soon you'll get to love that pooch, even though it's no good for anything. On the other hand you can pick out a real thoroughbred dog, a good bird dog or a shepherd, for example. Soon you'll get to love that dog, just as you would the worthless mongrel. But now instead you've got a good dog, worth something, something to be proud of.

"Now it's the same way in choosing a marriage partner. If you associate with a bum, you may get to love that no good bum and end up married to him (or her). But if you associate with the thoroughbreds, especially people who've got some money, you'll end up marrying one of them. It's just as easy as associating with trash, and a hell of a lot better for you in the end."

At times, in talking to my older sister, he was even more specific and defined the choice of boys as between those destined always to be poor and those who were or might become rich.

I remember Uncle Albert telling me a little about what it was like around Pleasant Bay when he was a boy. At the age of 10 or thereabouts, he said, he had a job of sorts working in Ensign Nickerson's shipyard, about where the approach to the sixth green at the Eastward Ho golf course is now. There they built "bankers", schooners designed to go codfishing on the Grand Banks of Newfoundland.

JESSE'S FOLLY

Just to the east of the town landing, at the end of what is now Strong Island Road, was a location which was commonly designated in my childhood days as "Jesse's Folly". It seems that Jesse Nickerson had a farm there, near the end of Nickerson's Neck. But he was scarcely a top-notch farmer, deriving most of his income from the fisheries. He *was* imaginative and innovative, as well as being something of an amateur efficiency expert.

So he conceived the idea of building his barn on piling over the water, instead of on the land. Thus he could dispose of the manure from his animals, simply by pushing it through a trapdoor in the floor and letting it drift away on the tide. In a time when chemical fertilizers were unknown, his neighbors aptly named the place "Jesse's Folly".

This locale seems to have been the site of other "follies" since Jesse's time. In the 1890's Eben Jordan, a Boston merchant, and some of his friends built the Hotel Chatham on the high bluff overlooking Pleasant Bay, about where the fourth fairway and green are now on the golf course. It was an elegant hostelry, way ahead of its time in appointments and facilities. Even though the management had the train stop at West Chatham and provided carriages to take people from there to the hotel—even though they provided bowling alleys, sports, fishing and bathing—the enterprise was a dismal financial failure. Automobiles and roads for them to use had not yet arrived.

In the period from 1917 through 1919, the United States Navy bought all the land at the end of the Neck (now Eastward Point) and developed it into what was for that time a major Naval Air Station. I remember the hangars for airplanes, one in use in 1918, and the other, much larger, not completed until late in 1919 long after World War I was over. There was also an enormous blimp hangar, which stood for many years after, until it too was torn down.

For years the end of the neck was filled with the sad remains of the foundations of the many buildings which stood there. We dubbed it "Concrete Acres", but then the government sold the property, and an enterprising local general contractor named Fred Crowell took the place over, cleaned it up, and far from "folly", achieved substantial financial success in developing it as Eastward Point.

I remember the hot summer day in August 1918, when a German submarine shelled and sank several ships right off Nauset Beach in Orleans, even landing one shell, it was said, on the land at East Orleans. There was a fog bank hanging just off shore of the beach. One of the "flying boats" with Liberty motors was on a test flight from the Naval Air Station, out over the fog bank, when they heard the firing and came in to investigate.

The story is that either they were not armed or the bombs they carried failed to explode. At any rate the only missile directed at that submarine was a monkey wrench thrown at it by a member of an airplane's crew.

The word spread locally that the bombs stored at the Naval Air Station would not detonate—or maybe they just didn't have any. However that may be, that night, in the small hours of the morning, we heard trucks rumbling past our house on Old Harbor Road, which were said to be loaded with bombs that will explode, shipped from a mainland ammunition depot.

NICKNAMES

Up until well into this century, it was customary hereabouts for people whose names were similar to or the same as others, to be given distinguishing nicknames or designations by their neighbors and acquaintances.

For example, in Chatham there were two Walter Eldredges who lived near each other. One was always referred to as "Good Walter", and the other as "Wicked Walter". This had nothing to do with the character of either of them, but since one was conscientiously present at all church services, while the other was irregular in his attendance at church, it was natural to call the former "Good Walter", and of course it seemed equally natural to call the other "Wicked Walter".

Over in Orleans, there were two Joseph Rogers. One was known as "Joe Rich", and the other as "Joe Splendid". The former was not especially wealthy. Both men were prosperous by the standards of their times. But Rich was "Joe Rich's" middle name, and "Joe Splendid" was given to wearing clothes which were very natty and modish, perhaps a little more splendid than those worn by most of his neighbors. "Joe Rich's" wife was named Mary, but there was another Mary Rogers who lived nearby. Therefore she was called "Mary Joe" to keep her identity clear.

In Chatham there were numerous George Eldredges. Some of the names given to distinguish them come to mind. "Chart George" was obviously so named because he was known internationally for the accuracy of his charts and tide tables of the coastal waters. In fact they are still being used today. "Hungry George" got his name from the fact that he had a large family, which at times was said to have to go on short rations because he wasn't able to supply enough food to feed them well. "George Cornelius" was so called because his father's name was Cornelius.

"CHART GEORGE"

There were many anecdotes about "Chart George" Eldredge, mostly having to do with his skill as a cartographer and his intimate knowledge of the coast. On one occasion, along with several veteran captains and pilots, he was called as an expert witness in a case before the Admiralty Court.

One of the questions asked was the actual width of a certain main channel at a place between Nantucket and Monomoy, where a collision had occurred between two ships. The pilots had been called first and gave their estimates.

"Chart George" was the last expert witness. He gave his estimate of the width of the channel, and it was widely different from those of the other experts who were using that channel frequently. This gave rise to one of the lawyer's attempting to discredit "Chart George's" testimony.

At this point the previous expert witnesses held a whispered conference and sought the Court's permission to make a further statement.

It was, "We testified as to the width of the channel the best we could at the time, but if George Eldredge says that is its width, we all agree that that is what it is."

There was another occasion in court when the examining lawyer had been persistently insisting that the last previous witness give only testimony of what he knew from his own knowledge. He kept bearing down on the witness whenever his testimony drifted, ever so slightly, into what might possibly be considered as hearsay.

Next it came "Chart George's" turn on the witness stand.

There were the usual preliminaries of "What is your name?" "Where do you live?" etc.

But to the question, "How old are you?" he replied, "I don't know."

The lawyer was annoyed of course, and insisted that anyone who was about to testify as an expert should certainly know his own age, but "Chart George" stolidly insisted he did not know how old he was.

Finally the judge too became a little put out and said to him, "Surely, you must know how old you are."

"Well, your honor, since this lawyer has been insisting that testimony be limited to one's own personal knowledge, I do not know from my own personal knowledge, but if my mother was right when she told me I was five years old—I've been keeping track of my age since she told me that—if she was right about it, I am 63. But I can't truly say from my own personal knowledge that I am."

"TUTT RIND"

There was one Chatham man, George Gould, whom I recall as having the reputation of being an outstandingly successful small-time con man and panhandler. He was a flashy dresser, usually wearing a yachting cap at a jaunty angle, and had the most gold teeth I had ever seen in one mouth. He carried himself very erectly and had a sprightly air about him.

How he got the name of "Tutt Rind", I never knew. But he was known by that name, not only locally, but all up and down the coast where he succeeded in getting employment on yachts or along the waterfront. There were many stories about him, usually exemplifying his unmitigated gall and the brassy charm which got him by.

One, I recall, is about "Tutt Rind's" hanging around some docks in Florida, where several yachts were moored or tied up in slips. The story was that he would station himself, all togged out in yachting clothes, near a fine yacht where there was no one on board, and he had discovered that there wasn't likely to be on that particular day. As a few tourists came along he would get into conversation with them, drawing the talk toward this yacht. When they showed interest, he would invite them to go on board and inspect her under his guidance, but of course charging two dollars a person for that privilege.

"WASHY" TAYLOR

There were some whose names were just too long or too inappropriate to be used commonly. One such was Washington Taylor, whom I never heard called by any other name than "Washy". He had a small delivery service and used to carry parcels in his wagon from the express office at the depot to their consignees.

Since Chatham was a "dry" town in those days, this often included special shipments of cases of liquor. Chatham was not only a "dry" town, but the influence of the W.C.T.U. was so great, that on one occasion I remember there was a bonfire in the middle of Main Street to which the storekeepers contributed their entire supplies of cigarettes.

At that time cigarettes were smoked only by a few dudes or men of questionable masculinity, so it wasn't as great a bonfire as it would be today. There was still plenty of plug tobacco and cigars for the smokers and chewers. In fact chewing tobacco was in common use, and every store that sold it had a cast iron slicer with a steel blade, which was clamped down by a handle to cut pocket-sized plugs from the long plugs of tobacco.

Smoking cigars was a mark of distinction and a sign of affluence. Marcus Howard had a store in one half of what is now the Mayflower Shop. On a counter at the rear of the store he sold the newspapers that came in daily on the evening train from Boston.

One of "Washy" Taylor's favorite tricks was to wait until there were several men standing around to get their papers, then stride up to Marcus and say in a loud voice, "Give me some of them ten cent cigars, Mark, them ten cent cigars", but he added in a whisper intended only for Marcus' ears, "Those three for ten, Mark, three for ten."

And that was when a ten cent cigar was really a fine smoke!

"FISH" STORIES

In those days there were men of probity and deep religious conviction. One such, whose name I can't recall, was a buyer and shipper of fish. He also was a very regular churchgoer who would never transact any business on the Sabbath. However it was at church on Sunday that he would be likely to meet some of the fishermen from whom he bought.

Occasionally one of them would ask him what he was paying for fish. He would always answer that he could not say on the Sabbath, since this was the Lord's Day and we must remember to keep it holy.

"But, if this were *Monday*", he would continue, "the price would be such and such."

And on Monday, that would indeed be his price for fish.

There was another very religious man who was also well known for being stingy. He prided himself moreover on his complete honesty. He had one pocket in his trousers to which he gave the name "this world", and in which he kept a few small coins. He was comparatively wealthy for his community, but when approached for a contribution for some worthy cause, he would reach into that pocket, pull out those few coins and hand them to the solicitor saying, "There, that's every cent I have in this world."

Such equivocation in the name of pious honesty was fairly common in those days. I remember one time in my own experience when it had a little different slant. I was in my twenties and working hard to help build up my father's lumber business.

We had a good customer in South Orleans named Rogers, who was given to an occasional whimsical slant. He was developing a tract of high land overlooking Pleasant Bay, which he advertised as having a "million acre view", which it may have had if you could see over the ocean beyond the horizon.

One day he came in to pay his bill as he always did, promptly, taking his two percent earned cash discount. This time he tackled me for a bigger discount. Even though I assured him that no one, even our biggest and promptest paying contractor customers, received a bigger discount, he kept insisting that we did give bigger discounts to some. It got to the point where it became evident to him that I was getting really disturbed at his allegations.

Then he said to me, "Young feller, let me ask you, does everybody pay their bills? Ain't they some who never pay?"

"Of course," I reluctantly admitted, "there are a few who never pay. I must admit we have to charge a few off to bad debts."

"Well," he said, "you give *them* one hundred percent off. It seems to me that you ought to do as well by me, who pays right off, as you do for those who don't never pay at all."

Whereupon he left, cackling with laughter at my discomfiture over his little joke.

Another crusty character was Fobe Foster, a successful contractor-builder from Brewster. He was something of a mathematical wizard and also given to philosophizing at times. This may have been due, in part, to the fact that he was terribly afflicted with asthma and often went for weeks at a time without lying flat in bed.

But he didn't let that interfere with his hard work nor his civic duties, including several terms as a selectman.

Characteristic of him was his saying on several occasions, when we were in some serious discussion, "I never tell the truth when a lie will do as well."

"But Fobe," I would say, "when does a lie do as well?"

"Dunno," he'd say, "never had the occasion to find out."

One morning he came in to our store and said to me, "Josh, will you go bail for me?"

Somewhat taken aback, I said, "Yes, I guess so. But why?"

"Well, I had an argument with my wife this morning, and I got real mad at her. I guess I lost my temper, because I hit her, and a lot harder than I intended to. So I knocked her down. I may have to go to jail before night. You will go bail for me, won't you?"

Later, after his divorce, his former wife brought an action in court for an increase in her alimony which he could very well afford. Fobe told me how he prepared for his appearance in court. He wore an old gray suit which was just a little too small for him. There were a few darned mends in it, and the sleeves left his wrists well exposed, but it was carefully cleaned and pressed. He told the court that he was doing the best he could, and he hoped he would not be required to cut back on his already frugal way of living by having to pay more alimony.

I don't remember whether the judge let him continue with the payments as they were or raised the amount a little. But I'm sure Fobe enjoyed the considerateness of the court.

On another occasion he told me about the neighbor who came to get him "to go on a note for two hundred dollars with him at the bank."

The neighbor said that the man at the bank had told him they would be glad to accommodate him, if he would have

Fobe sign the note with him.

"I told him, no, but I'd do better than that," said Fobe, "I told him *I'd* lend him the money myself, and at a very low rate of interest, if he'd get the *bank* to go on his note with him."

Folk Tales And Anecdotes

As told while opening scallops in the fall of the year, or later in the season around the stove in the store while waiting for the evening papers to arrive—

These tales and anecdotes have stuck in my memory from my childhood and youth in the first quarter of the 20th century. In those days there were no soap operas —in fact no radios or television. Spinning yarns and recounting local anecdotes were a popular form of adult entertainment. And I enjoyed listening.

LANGUAGE DIFFICULTIES

In East Harwich there were, two brothers of Indian descent, Stephen and Billy Peters, who never quite adjusted to the guileful ways of the white man. One winter's day they went down to Round Cove to spear eels through the ice.

On the shore they met a neighbor bent on the same mission, who had brought along a sled with a box lashed on it in which to put the eels he caught. Noticing that the Peters brothers had not come so equipped, he suggested that they all go out on the ice together, put the eels in his box and divide them when they came back to shore.

In telling about it later to a friend, Billy said he couldn't understand how, when the neighbor divided the eels between them, he seemed to have more than either Billy or Stephen.

"He divided them fair and square," said Billy, "but somehow he seemed to have more than his share."

"Tell me," asked the friend, "just how did he do it?"

"Well, it was fair and square alright. He divided them one at a time. As he did so, he said, 'Now there's one for you two, then one for me too'. But he still seemed to come out with more than either of us."

This anecdote not only illustrates the perils of oral English, but has been used for comparison to some of the more preposterous proposals with which the United States has become involved in conducting its foreign affairs.

DISCIPLINE

Uncle Peter had a dog who was as stubborn as Uncle Peter himself. One evening when a neighbor was present, the dog was comfortably settled behind the kitchen stove when Uncle Peter decided he wanted him out. Upon repeated commands the dog remained right where he was.

Finally Uncle Peter gave up. "All right then. You stay there," he said, "and don't you move. I'll have you obey me anyway."

That is how it came about that a disobedient child was said to "mind like Peter's dog."

UNCLE PERCY

Uncle Percy was set in his ways. On one occasion he and his wife Emeline were discussing the wedding plans of a young relative.

"I don't think I shall go to the wedding", he said.
"But Percy", said his wife, "you ain't invited."
"Don't think I shall go."
"But Percy, you ain't even invited."
"Don't think I shall go, Emeline, don't think I shall go".

Once Uncle Percy and his neighbor Mr. Higgins rowed down to the east end of Pleasant Bay to mow salt hay. Late in the afternoon, after a long day swinging their scythes and swigging their "switchel" (a thirst-quenching drink made with rum, molasses and water), they started to row home just as a pea-soup fog settled around them. The two, both rowing, with Mr. Higgins at the stern pair of oars, pulled across the bay for home. At long last the dory "shushed" gently onto the beach, or so it seemed.

"You keep your sitting, Mr. Higgins", said Uncle Percy. "I'll pull her ashore."

Whereupon he stepped over the side, into a solid mass of floating eel grass, and disappeared into ten feet of water.

DO ALL STRIPED BASS MIGRATE?

My Uncle Carroll was a commercial fisherman who sailed his catboat out of Pleasant Bay, mostly hand-lining for cod and haddock. Since he depended entirely on sail, he was an expert observer of nature. His weather forecasts were more reliable than the scientific ones we get today. They had to be; for his life depended on the accuracy of his forecasts. He was also an astute observer of the ways of fish.

He used to say, "First you figure out where you would be if you were a fish, and that's where you'd go. If they are not there, you go where you wouldn't expect them to be, and often that's where they are."

My grandfather (his father) also went fishing out of Pleas-

125

ant Bay. But he was by no means as knowledgeable in that field as his son Carroll. Once they got to discussing the migratory habits of striped bass, which appear each year in Pleasant Bay when the alewives arrive, about the end of April or early in May, and disappear in the late fall. Grandfather insisted that none remained here out of season. But Carroll disagreed. They got into quite an argument about it.

Later, on a winter's day, Carroll was down at the shore working at his fish shanty. It was dead low tide when he noticed a commotion in the eel grass. Grabbing a pitchfork he waded out and managed to spear a nice fish, with stripes on its sides. Later he carefully took it home and then took it over to his father's house to show him.

"What kind of fish do you suppose this is?" he asked.

Grandfather took a quick look. "You know perfectly well what it is, Carroll. It's a striped bass."

"But father, it can't be; because I got it today, and you know for certain that no striped bass can be in Pleasant Bay at this season of the year."

GRANDFATHER'S CEILING

When grandfather was in his late seventies he had to live very frugally. There wasn't much money. His sons had noticed that the plaster ceiling of his front sitting room had been peeling badly for a considerable length of time. So they got together and decided they would like to make him a present of a new ceiling. My father and his brother Ernest were delegated to call on him and offer the present they had decided upon.

They did it as gracefully as they could.

Whereupon grandfather, after a long pause, said, "Well, boys, I thank you very much for being so thoughtful and generous. But I cannot accept. You see *anybody* can have a *new* ceiling."

SAM NICKERSON

This story is probably not quite true. But it is the way it was told to me by my father's Uncle Joshua Albert, who worked in Ensign Nickerson's shipyard at Nickerson's Neck in Chathamport as a boy, about 1850 or a bit later. Sam Nickerson's home was also on Nickerson's Neck, but he had gone to sea as skipper of a "banker", fishing on the Grand Banks of Newfoundland.

But Sam was not as good a fisherman as some of the others, and consequently when he finally filled his vessel with fish and got back to sell his fare in Boston, there was no good market for his catch. So he went on to Providence, New Haven, even New York, only to find a glutted market. By this time he was worried about the condition of his cargo but he kept on up the Hudson River to Albany, where he found a good market even though the fish were beginning to smell of age.

The next season he was again a little late in filling his vessel with fish. But this time, not bothering with the intervening ports, he sailed directly to Albany where he sold his catch for top prices. The Erie Canal had not long been open then, and it beckoned enticingly to the Great West, and Sam Nickerson kept on going till he finally arrived in Chicago.

There in a few years he built a fortune and became the first president of the First National Bank of Chicago. The marbled mansion which he built for a home is now a museum. And his wealth has sustained the generations of his descendants.

But as Uncle Albert said, "It all started with a load of stinking fish."

ANECDOTES AND WORDS

UNCLE JONATHAN

When my father was a boy (in the 1870's), Uncle Jonathan lived in an old Cape Cod house across the cedar swamp. A few hundred yards beyond his house, on a knoll overlooking Pleasant Bay, stood his windmill, where he ground corn and other grains for the local farmers.

My father and his brother Ernest were fascinated by the mill. They would grab on to one of its great arms as it came down near the ground, and ride it as it made its great circular turn, and then drop off as it swung down to earth again. While this was exciting, more thrilling perhaps than a roller coaster, it was also dangerous. If Uncle Jonathan caught them at it, he punished them and sent them away.

But the boys found a way of getting even. For the miller Jonathan often used to sit, nearly dozing, with his hands under the spout out of which the meal poured, testing it for coarseness or fineness. The boys would sneak into the mill and unnoticed climb behind him to the top of the mill, just above the place where the great millstones were turning.

There they would drop a nail or two into the whole grain above the stones. Then they would wait, convulsed with merriment, until they heard Uncle Jonathan yell with pain as the red-hot nail, having passed between the millstones, fell into his waiting hands.

CAPTAIN COOK

I remember a Captain Cook of Provincetown, a whaling captain, describing an amputation he performed when caught in the ice one winter north of Point Barrow in the Arctic off Alaska. One of his men got his leg crushed in the ice and gangrene had set in, leaving only a choice between amputation and certain death.

128

Captain Cook spent most of the day studying his "doctor" book on how to amputate. Then, having no other anesthetic except laudanum, they got the man thoroughly drunk on rum. They lashed him securely to a table in the cabin, and while four men held him down, Captain Cook amputated his leg at the knee. When this had been accomplished, they cauterized the stump with red-hot pokers which had been shoved into the coals of the fire.

It was pretty gruesome, Captain Cook said, but many months later when his ship finally got into San Francisco and they sent the man to the hospital for a checkup, the surgeons there declared they couldn't have done a better job themselves.

COPPER JOE

As late as the early 1900's, salvage of ships and cargoes was a fairly lucrative business for those few engaged in it. Among them was one Joe Bloomer of Chatham, who was more than ordinarily proficient at such mundane operations as anchor dragging, for instance. This consisted of dragging on the ocean bottom for anchors which had been abandoned there by vessels in danger, or even wrecked when their anchors did not hold.

But Joe Bloomer was more enterprising than just re-covering anchors and their chains. If a vessel came ashore he was skilled at getting the choicest things aboard it into his possession before the underwriter's agent came to protect them. It was said that on at least one such occasion he stripped the copper sheathing off the bottom of a ship. At any rate that was the reason, I heard, that he was called "Copper Joe".

PRAYER MEETING

Every Thursday in the vestry of the church there used to be held a "prayer meeting". This consisted of members of the congregation giving testimonials of their own religious experiences, as well as exhortation and prayer. The meeting was usually conducted by a deacon of the church or another layman. It was one of his duties at the close of the meeting to announce the time of the next one.

One deacon always announced in this manner, "The next prayer meeting will be held at seven o'clock here next Thursday evening—the Lord willing. But Friday evening whether or no!"

"BLUEY"

Back when I was a boy, there lived in the village in Chatham a lobster fisherman known to all as "Bluey". Why, I don't know. He lived alone, and in his old age developed "dropsy", as it was called then, to the point where it became increasingly difficult for him to take care of himself and keep his house in order.

In those days there were no visiting nurses or any organized service to help care for such people. The family or neighbors were expected to take care of such situations. But "Bluey" had no family. The neighbors did comment on what they found when they dropped in, but he refused to let them clean up the place.

Mrs. Heman Harding, the wife of a local lawyer, heard about the situation. She and my mother were good friends, and they decided that it called for drastic action—and by them! So they descended on poor "Bluey", with mops and pails and cleaning supplies, and of course some soups and good warm food.

They were appalled at the filthy mess which his quarters had become, especially the condition of his bed. His pillows were badly stained with what appeared to be tobacco juice. All this they cleaned up and replaced with fresh linen. But they still were puzzled by the tobacco stains. When they asked him, he explained.

"Well, you see, I've always made it my practice to eat my breakfast before I go to bed at night. It saves time in the morning, when I'm in a hurry to get going."

"But that doesn't explain the tobacco stains."

"Oh yes it does! You see after I have et my breakfast I always put in a chaw of plug tobacco."

TWO BLACK CROWS

Sometimes at the dinner table we children would gossip about a recent local event, and naturally we often were inclined to exaggerate, or at least to pass on an exaggerated version of it.

Then our father was wont to admonish us by saying, "Two black crows."

We knew that this was his signal for us to stick to the facts; for we were familiar with the family story.

East Harwich was a small village stretched not more than a couple of miles along the old dirt road. It seems that at one end of the village a man became deathly ill, with symptoms which were most unusual. His wife, in describing it to her nearest neighbor, said that he had vomited up something "as black as a crow."

The story was repeated from neighbor to neighbor until it reached the other end of the village, where the last to hear the story was told, "You may not believe this. But it is a fact. He vomited up two black crows!"

ED JOHNSON

Standing out in my memory is Ed Johnson. He was a cheery, bumptious red-faced man with a snub nose, who always seemed to be making like a sideshow "pitch man", no matter what he was doing at the time. His cheerful chatter would tumble forth like a brook.

One of his favorite ways of selling *two* dozen smoked herring to a housewife, instead of one, was with the following "pitch".

"Good morning, lady—any fresh smoked herring today? They're only a cent apiece, 12 cents a dozen, two dozen for a quarter. Most everybody takes two"—and they did!

Ed Johnson was also the man who would arrive at the ball game with a horse and wagon. Over the wagon seat would be a large and gaudy umbrella, not unlike a beach umbrella of today. And in the back of the wagon was a big freezer of ice cream made by himself. This he would sell by ringing a bell after each play and hollering his wares to the crowd.

At first he served it in a paper box with a disposable tin spoon. Later he went to wooden spoons, and finally he brought to our lives the ice cream cone. The first cones were really conical in shape. After lapping the top and edges of the ice cream, we kids would always bite off the tip of the cone and suck the ice cream down through the hole, winding up finally with the remnants as an ice cream sandwich.

Ed Johnson would always appear each September as a "barker", selling lemonade and hot dogs at the annual Barnstable County Fair and Cattle Show in Barnstable. In later years he owned and operated a summer boarding house in South Chatham called Cockle Cove Inn. It was a moderately priced place, but I feel sure that what it lacked in style, conveniences or variety of its bill-of-fare, it must have been more than balanced by the saucy, impudent showmanship of this unusual "character".

Where Did The Old Words Go?

Since the early 1900's, some words and expressions which were common when I was a boy have faded from use and even disappeared. Here are a few examples.

FEETNINGS

When a man walks on the hard wet sand along the shore at low tide he leaves "footprints". When birds or animals do the same thing they leave "feetnings".

TEMPEST

Today we hear of electrical storms, cloudbursts, heavy rain, etc. Whatever happened to "tempest", meaning a violent downpour with almost constant thunder and lightning? Or the expression, "Tempest in a teapot", meaning a violent outburst over a trivial matter.

This article originally appeared in "The Cape Codder" and has been reprinted here with their permission.

CAL'LATE (*a corruption of "calculate"*)

Among people with a seagoing heritage, when the facts were not clear and some degree of surmise was involved in reaching a conclusion, the speaker often said, "I 'cal'late' such and such," meaning that his opinion was arrived at partly from known facts and partly from deductions.

SHARPIE

There were many "sharpies" along the shore. They were flat-bottomed skiffs, rarely over 16 feet long, decked in forward with a centerboard and cockpit. They were propelled either by oars or a leg o'mutton sail permanently attached to a mast, which was stepped through a hole in the deck, and was un-stepped and stowed with the sail rolled around the mast when not in use. When under sail it was steered by an oar held against the lee gunnel. It was also sometimes propelled by sculling with an oar over the stern. It had no rudder.

DORY

Probably the most common of rowing boats, now very rarely seen. They were of various sizes from about 14 to 20 feet long, flat-bottomed with sides flairing out sharply and the stern pinched in narrow. They were propelled by oars (usually two sets) laid between thole pins. The thole pins were either hard-wood dowels, or more often round pieces of natural hardwood branches, six or eight inches long, inserted in round holes bored in the gunnels. They were often tied loosely together at the bottom with a piece of cod-line, so that when they were removed (as in coming alongside a vessel) they would not be lost or mislaid.

Dories were ideal for fishing vessels which sailed to the Grand Banks of Newfoundland, because in addition to being about the safest rowing boats in heavy seas they could be nested because of their shape, one on the other on the deck of the fishing schooner. No doubt this accounted for the fact that near the upper edge of the stern, there were always bored two holes, a foot or so apart, through which a short piece of rope was passed. Together with a similar loop through a hole bored at the stem, this provided easy fastening for ropes aboard the vessel, used in hoisting the dory onto the deck.

The Grand Banks dories always had removable "kid boards", which could be set vertically athwart the boat against the exposed ribs, thus forming a separate compartment into which the fish were tossed as they were caught by the dorymen. They fished with a hand-line over the side of the dory. Frequently they fished two men to a dory when on the Grand Banks.

HIGHLINE

A man, or a fishing vessel, was "highline" when his catch was the biggest. Some few expert fishing captains had the reputation of usually being "highline". Such men were known as "highliners".

SCULLY-JOE

Small cod or flatfish (flounder), dry salted (corned), then cured by drying in the sun. Often eaten without cooking by cutting strips of it for a snack.

GOGRAM (*goglam, pronounced "goglum"*)

In the summer and early fall the surf is often full of tiny particles of brown weeds. They make the water look like tea. They cling to fishing lines and human flesh. They are unpleasant but not dangerous. Even the fish seem to shun them. This is "gogram" (goglam).

MEADOW BANK

On the "backside" (ocean side) of beaches, such as Monomoy and North Beach in Chatham, where the sand slopes down from the high tide mark to the low, there often appear chunks of peat protruding from the sand. These are the remnants of a marsh which was once on the inside or bay side of the beach. As the ocean side has eroded, new dunes were formed on top of what was the marsh and and now these dunes in turn are being eroded by the sea.

This continuing process of rollover of dunes onto marsh and later erosion result in the exposure to the ocean of the old "meadow bank". Today much of our dunes area on North Beach rests on former marsh land.

NO'TH EAST

It has been only since the arrival on Cape Cod of newswriters "from away" that I ever heard of a "nor'easter" storm. It was always "no'theast" and "nor'west". The reason for this was that when the helmsman was relieved by a new man at the wheel of a vessel, the man at the wheel repeated the compass course to the new man. In the wind it was important that there be no misunderstanding of the directions. So it was always "*nor*'west" and "*no'th*east"; "*sow*'west" and "*south-east*".

LINE STORM

Nowadays, every summer and fall the news media are trumpeting word of "hurricanes." Whatever happened to the old "line storms", which were as certain each year as the sun crossing the equator, north-bound in March and south-bound in September?

FROM AWAY

When I was a boy there were two kinds of people on Cape Cod; Cape Codders and those "from away". I am a Cape Codder; my wife, who has lived here with me for 45 years, is "from away", even though she came from Boston.

DEPOT

Depot meant railway station. It was pronounced "dee-po". Since there have been no passenger trains on Cape Cod for a number of years, the word may have fallen out of use because there were no longer any "dee-po's".

M

One of my pet peeves is with headline writers for our newspapers who always use the Roman symbol for "thousands" when they mean "millions". Why have they stopped using "MM" for millions? You have to read the fine print to find that the headline which reads "thousands" (M) really means "millions" (MM).

BACKSIDE

When I was a boy there was no doubt of a person's meaning when he referred to the "backside" of Cape Cod or of North Beach. He meant the ocean front. The word "shore", as applied to North Beach, always referred to the inner or bay side. Sometimes, however, a vessel "came ashore" on the "backside".

HEALTH EATERS

A derogatory reference by Cape Codders to summer visitors who lie in the sun on our beaches.

WASH ASHORE

This refers to people who arrived on Cape Cod by being victims of shipwrecks, which they survived to become permanent residents of Cape Cod. There are quite a few of such families here.

FLAKE

When a building such as a house was to be moved more than a short distance, it was "flaked". That is, it was cut up into flat panels, carefully marked to identify the locations of each with relation to all the other panels. The panels were then carted to the new site, where they were reassembled exactly as the building was originally.

MEETING HOUSE

A building used as a place of worship. A "church" was an organization of people with certain religious beliefs, dogmas and forms of worship. The "meeting house" was where the members of the church met to worship.

COME-OUTER

A "come-outer" was one who left an established church in protest against new developments in the church. For example, when an organ was installed in the meeting house, some of the more fundamentalists in the congregation withdrew and worshipped together in each other's homes, in protest against the desecration of the meeting house by the installation of an organ, intended to encourage "frolic". I don't know just when this took place, probably in the late 18th or early 19th century here on Cape Cod.

FROLIC

Any gaiety, especially when accompanied by music; or any indecorous behavior by a group of people.

HAIRLEGGER

If you lived in Orleans, Eastham or Wellfleet, it meant anybody from Harwich.

SCRABBLE-TOWN

That part of Chatham along the ocean front near the Chatham twin lights, later called "The Village". It was where men launched their boats to rescue (and to salvage) shipwrecks before the United States Life Saving Service was established in 1872. Each boat competed with others to be first to board a stranded vessel, and thus to have first claim for salvage. Hence, "Scrabble-Town". (A corruption of "scramble")

GOBBLE

Not the voice of a turkey, but you were "gobbling" when you ate fast and greedily. Children were told not to "gobble" their food.

SEA WALL

The long line of debris, especially eelgrass and the like, left along the shore at the high-tide line by the receding water as the tide ebbs.

ROUSING

A sort of shelf, running fore and aft inside a dory, below the gunnels. It had a raised inner edge to keep such things as thole pins and fishing leads from falling out onto the floor or deck of the boat.

YENDER (*a corruption of "yonder"*)

A designation of place when one wished to be evasive.
For example, "Where did you pick all those beach plums?"
Answer: "Over yender."

DUCK

In my youth, "duck" was used only to refer to black ducks.
All other migratory ducks were referred to by other names,
e.g., old squaw, whistler, coot (scots), buffalo head, teal, etc.

GUNNER

A person engaged in shooting waterfowl. Originally applied
to "market gunners", who shipped their kill to the city markets, it came to mean any hunter shooting waterfowl.

WING-BROKES AND CRIPPLES

Any wounded waterfowl. Hence a derogatory term when applied to people who were incapacitated.

QUICK WING FOWL

Any fowl which flew with rapid motion of its wings as con-
trasted to slow-winging birds, such as gulls, crows, hawks,
herons, etc.

GETHERING (*corruption of "gathering"*)

Any group of people coming together more or less informally
for a common purpose, such as a church supper. A "meeting"
was more organized or formal than a "gethering".

SMURRY

When unformed clouds start to obscure the bright sunshine,
the sky was "smurry".

GURRY

The entrails of fish. From dressing fish, men sometimes got "gurry sores" on their hands and wrists.

HOLLOW

Valley. This is still in use in Appalachia; also in the Wellfleet-Truro area, e.g., Lacount's Hollow, Cahoon's Hollow, Newcomb's Hollow, Lombard's Hollow.

CRICK

Up the "crick" is a bad place to be without a paddle (or oars).

QUITE

In the sense of almost. Properly, "quite" means precisely, but in local usage, "quite good", for example, meant substantially but not completely good.

In addition to single words that have disappeared, some once common expressions have been dropped from usage.

ENOUGH FOR A MESS OR A MESS OF FISH

This meant enough for a meal to feed the family or the crew.

CUT OF HIS JIB OR SET OF HIS JIB

This expression was usually used to indicate a lingering doubt or sometimes disapproval of a person.

For example, "He makes a good appearance and talks well; but somehow, I don't quite like the 'cut' (or set) of his jib".

SPEECH OF PEOPLE

I remember that I was puzzled when my mother told me there was something I should not be doing, because of "speech of people". Quite simply, it meant gossip or unfavorable common talk because someone violated a taboo.

DOES NOT DRAW MUCH WATER

A person who was otherwise charming but short of depth of character or intelligence might be referred to as a "fine fellow, but he doesn't draw much water".

This of course derived from the fact that ships which made the long and successful voyages did draw much water —at least in comparison to fishing smacks.

MANY CAN GO AS MATE, BUT FEW AS CAPTAIN

There are many people who faithfully perform duties under the direction of others, many who are good advisors to those who have to make final decisions.

But in an age when the captain alone had the final responsibility, there were few who qualified for that position.

As President Harry Truman said, "The buck stops here."

TOO BIG FOR HIS BREECHES

This meant over-impressed with his own importance; arrogant.

OFF THE EAST END OF STRONG ISLAND

Another local evasion of place-naming.

For example, "Where did you catch all those fish?"

Answer, "Off the east end of Strong Island", when in fact you may have caught them miles from there.

GOING OFF HALF COCKED

Jumping to conclusions or to anger.

NOT BAD

The highest compliment an old-time Cape Codder could give was to say of something that it was "not bad".

PRETTY GOOD

Good, but not good enough to be "not bad".

Fond Memories

From An East Window

MY mother's birthday was May 6th. It has always pleased me to think that not only her family but the migratory terns remember that day. As a boy my bedroom had an east window, and lying in bed in the early morning of a sunny May 6th with a slight early morning breeze from the east, I would hear the sharp and cheerful sounds of the flocks of terns which had arrived from far away during the night to help celebrate her birthday.

Looking out from my window across Black Pond, I could see Little Beach (now called Tern Island), and hovering over it a great flock of terns that had just arrived to nest there. Beyond Little Beach lay the entrance channel to Pleasant Bay, and beyond that the Great Beach (currently called North Beach), and still further the ocean.

I think the terns are the most beautiful of all our local waterfowl. They are swift and graceful in flight, and so sharp-eyed that when they dive headlong into the water they rarely miss catching the small bait fish which is their target. Unlike gulls, for example, terns never eat anything but living fish, which they get by diving into the water. Small sand eels and a variety of minnows seem to be their favorite diet.

By early June, terns lay their lovely speckled eggs in nests which are only little hollows made in the sand. I remember once counting a hundred eggs without moving from the spot where I stood. A visit to their nesting colony during the season of egg laying and hatching, or when the little downy fluffs of chicks had just hatched, was an exciting experience. As you came near their nests, the adult birds would scream "ack-ack-ack" as they got into position for diving on you. Then with a final "ack-ack-ack" and a "yah" they would dive for your head, occasionally actually striking it with their bills.

This was in contrast to the behavior of the herring gulls, which nested then on the islands in Pleasant Bay. Their eggs are similar to but much larger than the terns'. They start laying early in May, weeks before the terns. When disturbed at their nesting area, they show none of the reckless bravery and aggressive defense of their territory that the terns do. Instead they fly about whining and mewing in an unhappy way until you leave.

Unfortunately there has been a great increase in the gull population in recent years. The fact that they lay their eggs so much earlier than the terns, and also eat carrion and eggs as well as young birds, has enabled them to take over what used to be exclusively terns' nesting areas. I understand that the number of gulls nesting there has declined recently, due to access having been achieved by rodents and by man.

(See "The Rites of Spring on Cape Cod", Page 155.)

There was a period of many years in the 1930's, 40's and 50's when the terns nested in large colonies near the end of North Beach. The gulls never took over there, but for the past ten years or more the terns no longer nest there in any numbers. I wonder why. They have apparently moved to Monomoy, which became an island again in the 1960's.

I have been referring mostly to the Common Terns which nest closely together in large colonies. But there were also a few Lesser Terns and Arctic Terns. All through the summer season, from early May to October, the brave and beautiful terns are a part of our environment which never ceases to intrigue and inspire me.

But from my east window there was more to see than the

birds. Every day I could count on seeing a few passing ocean tows, consisting of a powerful tugboat hauling behind it a tow of barges, sometimes three or four in a tow strung out far astern. In the close quarters of Nantucket Sound, I am sure these were headaches for the coasting schooners which depended entirely on sail.

Sometimes we would have a week or more of heavy easterly winds. During that time the sailing ships bound northward around Cape Cod would anchor in Vineyard Sound, awaiting a favorable wind. When the wind would come from the west, they would all weigh anchor together and come roaring down the channels of Nantucket Sound and finally clear through Pollock Rip Slew and past the Pollock Rip Lightship out into the broad Atlantic.

When this happened, it was not at all unusual to count up to a hundred sail of vessels in sight at one time off Chatham. On such a day Cyrus Kent, the marine reporter, must have been busy indeed, identifying the passing ships from his tower atop the building which housed the telegraph office, through which he reported to shipping and insurance interests in Boston.

The day of sailing ships was passing. Even though the seven-masted "Thomas W. Lawson" was built in my boyhood, steam was well on its way to taking over. Many of the once proud sailing ships ended their days as barges carrying coal or other bulk cargo, towed behind an upstart steam tugboat.

But there were also luxurious ocean-going steamships to be seen from my east window. Names like Savannah Line, Merchant and Miners, Eastern, come to mind. These steamers carried passengers and freight between Boston and all the major ports on the Atlantic Coast. There were crack liners, such as the "Harvard" and the "Yale", the "Massachusetts" and the "Bunker Hill", running every night between Boston and New York, leaving after 5:00 P.M. and arriving at the other city about 7:00 A.M. As a boat from Boston went past Chatham in the evening, with its great searchlight probing the darkness far ahead, you could almost set your watch by it, its scheduled time was so dependable.

There were men from Chatham who served as captains or pilots of some of these ships—Captain John Hammond, Captain Burnell Kendrick, for example, and "Uncle Benjie" Atkins, my Grandmother Nickerson's brother, a pilot on the Boston to New York run. He had a sister, Aunt Cyrena, who lived near the head of Pleasant Bay in East Harwich. When he went racing down past Chatham in the evening, he would turn his powerful searchlight atop the pilot house so that its beam fell full on his sister Cyrena's house.

The job of piloting such fast ships on a rigid time schedule through the dangerous waters around Cape Cod, in all kinds of weather, was nervewracking to say the least. Especially when you consider that the pilot was responsible not only for the safety of the ship and the lives of hundreds of passengers and crew, but the owners also relied upon him to maintain an "on time" schedule of arrival upon which the public could depend. I heard rumors that some pilots broke under the strain and had to have long periods of rest and recovery.

But not Uncle Benjie! Once when asked how he stood the strain, he replied, "I have a sweet and gentle sister, Cyrena. Every night she prays for me, and as long as she prays for me I can relax, because I know her prayers will be answered".

I shall never forget the day of Aunt Cyrena's funeral. I must have been ten or twelve years old at the time. Father and mother and the rest of the family were all ready to drive to her services in the surrey. At the last minute I decided not to go. I loved her dearly and wanted to remember her as I knew her, not laid out in a coffin. So I spent what I remember as the most miserable afternoon of my life; alone with my memories of Aunt Cyrena.

Passengers and carriages awaiting the arrival of a train at the old Chatham Depot.

The Chatham Town Hall was located on the site of the present Elementary School building.

The iceman and his wagon were basic necessities once-upon-a-time. Driver is Grover Speight.

The old High School stood on the hill behind the backstop at Veterans Field.

The Shavings Shop on Old Harbor Road, across from Oscar's house, was run by Arthur Edwards.

Top picture: Seaplane hangars at the old U.S. Naval Air Station in Chathamport. Lower picture: Blimp hangar and barracks at the same station.

The NC-4 seaplane, being repaired at the Chatham Naval Air Station, en route to completing the initial flight across the Atlantic Ocean.

The 1912 parade, celebrating Chatham's 200th Anniversary, on Old Harbor Road approaching Main Street.

Nearly 1,000 people attended the banquet commemorating the 200th Anniversary, held in a huge tent near present Chase Park.

The interior of the Weld Manufacturing Company factory, which made precision parts for three-inch shells used in World War I.

The Weld factory was located off Depot Street, on the site of the present Oyster Heights apartments.

View of Main Street at the foot of Seaview Street, looking west.

The Atwood Store and delivery wagons—now the site of the Chatham Public Market.

At one time, guests of the Chatham Bars Inn had to cross a long wooden pier over an inlet to reach the swimming beach.

But they were such happy memories. You approached her little Cape Cod cottage, where she lived alone, by a path along a little-used wagon track which led under the brow of a hill from beside Grandfather Nickerson's barn. Outside her kitchen door she had a small kitchen garden where she raised her herbs and such. This was surrounded by a low white picket fence with a gate. When unlatched the gate swung in, pulled open by a piece of chain attached to a wooden post just inside, and from the chain was suspended a small cannon ball picked up and brought home from a Civil War battlefield.

Once I entered her kitchen on an early fall day to find Aunt Cyrena busily engaged in providing for the winter. On the kitchen range preserves were stewing in kettles, awaiting the process of putting them up in jars. Suspended above the stove, threaded on strings to dry, were slices of apples and peaches from her own trees. To this day I can almost recall the delicious smells of that old kitchen.

There were times when the view from my east window was far from peaceful. In a winter's "no'theast" gale I remember a big steamship passing, literally jumping into the seas. Through the binoculars you could see her propellers come clean out of the water, as she drove her bow down into the trough of a great sea. It was explained to me at the time that under those conditions an engineer had to stand with his hand on the throttle to turn off the power as the propellers came out of the water, lest they tear the machinery apart as they raced in the air.

Every winter there was almost surely one or more vessels wrecked on the backside (ocean side) of the beach. Usually they were schooners laden with lumber and lath or shingles, bound from Nova Scotia, New Brunswick or Maine to New York or Philadelphia. Sometimes if they struck on the outer bar beyond the beach they managed to get off again on a rising tide. But usually, once they struck, they were doomed. If they escaped breaking up completely, they soon wound up on the

151

beach, often after having broken in two. This resulted in their cargoes being salvaged as best they could by local fishermen in their boats. I can remember the great piles on the shore of the harbor, where they were sold at auction by an underwriter's agent, then to be shipped away to the Boston or other markets.

Of course not all the salvaged cargo was recovered by the underwriters. Somehow, some of it got lost on the way from the wreck. I was a small boy when the S. S. "Onondaga" came ashore just north of the Old Harbor Life Saving Station. She had a wide variety of cargo. For years afterwards shoes, chocolates, white rolls of wrapping paper, just to mention a few items, would appear mysteriously in the homes of local people who had "helped" in the salvage operations. Many a house was reshingled with what the tide brought in.

There were four life saving stations in Chatham in my boyhood, and another in Orleans, about four miles north of the Old Harbor Station on the North Beach in Chatham. The other three stations were on Monomoy: one at the point near the Powder Hole boat harbor; another near Inward Point, about halfway back to the mainland; and the third at Chatham, on the beach which then extended at least a half mile off shore from Morris Island. They were named, respectively, Monomoy Point, Monomoy and Chatham Stations.

In the summer only the "keeper" and perhaps his family were there to keep an eye on things. But from the fall through the winter and into spring, the stations were manned with a full crew. These men were almost all local boatmen, who not only knew boats but were also familiar with the local waters. There were no power boats. The lifesavers had only their lifeboats, propelled by oars in the expert hands of the men and guided by the captain (or keeper), with a long steering sweep at the stern.

Sometimes they took turns at cooking, but usually that assignment was subject to arbitration. These were rugged and able men. They not only manned the lifeboats but patrolled the beach at night, and in the foulest weather.

They had a saying, "You had to go out to a rescue, but you did not have to come back."

One of the curious things that I saw from my east window was the constant changing—not only the seasons and the weather, or the light and shadows, but the land and water itself were changing. I doubt if one can see anywhere else in one's lifetime such changes of coastline as here at the elbow of Cape Cod.

We know that in the mid-1800's the entrance to Pleasant Bay had moved southward to somewhere nearly abreast of Scatteree. My father told me that after the great Portland Gale in November of 1898 he sat on the back step of his house, under what was to become my east window, and watched through his binoculars as bodies from the "Portland" were picked up on the end of North Beach, just a bit south of the Old Harbor Coast Guard Station.

I can remember when the Chatham Bars Inn opened in 1914 the entrance from the ocean was directly opposite the Inn. I can remember when there was a South Beach, with water between it and the mainland from Watch Hill to Stage Harbor.

As a boy I spent a few weeks on the shores of the Powder Hole at Monomoy Point, when it was a snug little harbor. In the 1930's and 40's we drove from the mainland all the way to the end of Monomoy at any tide. Monomoy is now an island separated by a quarter mile of water from the mainland. "Shooters Island", where I visited the Monomoy Brant Club in the 1920's, was a quarter mile back from the surf. Its former location is now well off shore. And so on and on, this coastline is constantly changing—but not at a constant rate.

Less obvious are other changes. Tern Island was not an island at all when I was a boy. It was "Little Beach", attached to the mainland about abreast of Chatham Bars Avenue. Between it and the main shore was plenty of water deep enough for a good harbor at the "Cow Yard". This could only be reached by entering between Scatteree and Ram Island Flat, or between Ram Island Flat and the north end of Little Beach. Ram Island Flat is where Cotchpinicut Island, with its high banks topped by pine trees, stood when my grandfather was a boy.

Sometime after opening the Chatham Bars Inn, Charles Hardy and his associates decided they wanted to improve the bathing and boating facilities across the street from the Inn. The water there, at the head of Aunt Lydia's Cove, was relatively stagnant, and the boating would be improved if there could be an entrance to it through Little Beach. So they got a horse-drawn sandscoop and made a little ditch through the beach.

Gradually natural forces widened and deepened this, as the water on the ebb tide flowed out through it instead of around the north point of Little Beach. Gradually sand filled in the harbor or most of it between Little Beach and the mainland. Finally there was a channel dredged through and deep water was created right up to the new dock built then, and now called the Chatham Fish Pier. When I was a boy the water was shallow there, and Howard Eldredge had a fish shanty at the town landing, next to which dad had a small bathhouse, where we changed our clothes to go swimming in the warm water of the cove.

There is currently talk of the United States Army Engineers doing something to improve the entrance over Chatham Bars. Maybe they can, but it won't last long unless it works with, rather than against, the tremendous forces of nature.

(See article "The New Inlet", Page 221.)

The Rites Of Spring On Cape Cod

W E have a saying that Cape Cod has no spring, but moves directly from winter to summer. While this is by no means true, nevertheless the gentle period of spring is all too brief and intermittent. Not so, however, with the *signs* of spring and the exciting feel of recognizing those signs.

It all starts with a day in late February or early March, when you cut a few small branches of forsythia and pussy willows and bring them indoors, where in water and the warmth of the house their blossoms soon develop. Then in March and early April, the crocuses and narcissi push above the ground and start to bloom.

But the most exciting early signs of spring are the mayflowers (trailing arbutus). Their little blossoms hide in the woods under their green leaves, snuggled against the bosom of the earth, amidst a soft, loose mulch of fallen leaves and pine needles. Early in April I start looking for their white or pink blossoms, but usually the beds of mayflower leaves appear to have few, if any. If you get down on your knees and look closely you may find a few tight buds.

As the month progresses, however, they begin to show and by the end of April are usually well past their peak. They seem to do best on a northerly-exposed slope. I usually pick a few, but you must be careful not to pull up the roots with the stems, which are tough and wiry. When I take a small bunch home and bury my nose in them, I get the good smell of the sweet earth and the woods. In late April or early May, I can usually add a few blossoms of hog cranberry (bear berry), whose delicate little pink and white bell-shaped flowers are exquisite.

Meantime I've been watching for the white show of the shadbush, scattered here and there through the woods, the first flowering shrub of the year. At the same period I start visiting the herring brooks, looking for the first run of alewives, as they fight their way upstream to spawn in fresh water. They come in a series of runs, peaking at different times in different streams.

My favorite is Stony Brook in Brewster, where man has helped them by providing fish ladders. Here, at their peak, there is a solid mass of these doughty little fish from bank to bank, much to the special delight of children and old men. No spring would be quite complete either without a sacrificial feast of herring roe, saute'ed with bacon.

Soon too, behind them come the striped bass, following the alewives through the bays to the very mouths of the brooks. In May and early June is the sportsman's time to find this migration of the stripers.

A small vegetable garden (mine is 10 feet by 20 feet) can add to the joy of spring. In April I plant a few peas, to be ready for picking by the Fourth of July—and later a few beans, cucumbers, squash and tomatoes. In May too comes the time to plant a few annuals around the borders of your flower beds. In some years, by Memorial Day, the lilac blooms will still be in bud and in other years they will have gone by.

We used to call it Decoration Day, because that was when everybody went to the cemetery to decorate the graves of the dead. You could always count on that occasion of meeting a distant relative or old acquaintance. For years I used to put at least a sprig of blue wild lupin on the graves of my ancestors, as well as more elaborate tokens at the gravestones of my immediate family.

One of my great pleasures in May is to see the beach plum bushes in blossom. They don't come all at the same time, but spread over a few weeks, depending upon the idiosyncrasies of different soils and exposures. I think they are most beautiful when the flowers are still in tight buds, like pearls, about to burst into full bloom. I had two friends—painters—who each year used to go together to paint pictures of their favorite beach plum bushes. I once told them that if I had to leave Cape Cod forever and could take but one thing with me, it would be one of the beach plums.

In late May and early June, before most of the underbrush in the woods has started its summer growth which hides what lies beneath, it is rewarding to look for lady slippers. Where you find one you may find others nearby. But you may also hunt long without finding any. This lovely pink orchid-like flower grows on a long round stem between two broad green leaves. When I was a child I used to pick a few blossoms and float them in a bowl of water. They looked like lovely pink ducks, swimming.

If you find them, please don't pick them, or at least only a very few, leaving most alone. They grow in places where there is deep soft mulch and plenty of shade in summer. I like to leave them there so someone else can discover them too.

If you happen to be in an area where the poverty grass (Hudsonia) grows, such as some sand beaches or the heathland of Truro, on the few right days in June there is nothing to compare with its bright golden blossoms massed under a sunny canopy of blue sky. It only lasts for a few days, but it is worth the extra effort to find on a bright day.

In April the few Canada geese who have wintered here lay their eggs and hatch their young. Later, if you know where to look, you can watch "Gander" and "Goose" marshalling their young chicks between them as they swim near the shore and begin to learn how to fend for themselves. I don't remember wild geese being here summers in my youth. These are probably the descendants of "wing-brokes and cripples" and of geese who were used as live decoys and were later released, before that was forbidden by law.

Early in May the herring gulls start laying their eggs in colonies on the islands and sandy beaches. The eggs, usually three to a rudely shaped nest on the ground, are from bluish to brownish gray in color and dappled with black specks. There used to be thousands of them on the islands of Pleasant Bay. As a boy I gathered a few eggs and "blew" them by piercing a hole at each end, and then blowing in one end, thus forcing the contents out the other and achieving empty eggshells to add to my collection. Of course this is now forbidden; but you can gather a few major pieces of shells recently vacated by hatching chicks.

It is fascinating, if you have the time and patience, to sit in the warm sun of a May morning and watch a baby chick peck its way out of its shell. If you happen to do this at a place like Little Sipson's Island, you may also witness the mass matings of hundreds of horseshoe crabs as they surge in the warm water at the shore edge. (See "From An East Window, page 147.)

The terns come later. They usually arrive from the south the first week in May and lay their eggs in June. Some of their nesting colonies have been usurped by the gulls, who lay their eggs in May—Tern Island in Chatham, for example. So the terns have had to nest elsewhere. The common terns lay their eggs in simple shallow hollows scooped in the sand, usually in close-packed colonies. The Least Terns do likewise, but their nests are usually more scattered.

I think the terns are the most beautiful of our water birds. Swift, graceful, brave, they eat only live bait-fish, obtained by plunging on it from the air. When a flock is feeding it sounds like a hundred pebbles being tossed into the water. In the fall they fly thousands of miles to the south; but each year they return at precisely the same time to lay their eggs and rear their young here on Cape Cod.

Then there are the *sounds* of spring. In late March on a mild evening are heard the first tentative pipings of a scattered few "peepers" or "pink-winks." These little frogs abound at this season in every wetland puddle. Their shrill chorus reaches its crescendo at night in April and May, to be gone entirely by summer. It stirs an atavistic chord; primal man must have heard it just as I do.

Early in May at night is heard the plaintive call of the whippoorwill, disturbing as it wakens you. Then too at night I hear the "Whooo-whoo" moan of the mouring dove, and wonder if it might be an owl.

But of all the sounds to be heard only in spring, the dawn chorus of the songbirds as they greet each new day is the one I enjoy best. Just at daybreak it starts, and by the time the sun is well up the air is filled with the cheery music of their calls. I often wonder whether these are mating calls, or challenges in defense of their territories, or both. In any case it is easy to drop back to sleep while listening to their songs.

Most people agree that Cape Cod is at its best in the autumn—from mid-September to December. Seasonal visitors, by far the greatest in number, see it only in summer, when the Cape itself seems to be dozing in the sun and fog. Winter can be an exciting time, with its great storms and often successions of bright sunny days, when the contrasts of bright light and shadow make it more beautiful than summer.

But for me the most exciting time is in the spring—brief but different. Each year I thrill to the "Rites of Spring," some of which I have suggested here. If I have given you a few clues so that you may discover some of these rites for yourself, my purpose in writing this chapter will have been achieved.

159

Grandfathers And Grandsons

WHEN I was a boy, there were many useful things my grandfather could teach me; not as many as his grandfather could have taught him, but a lot. During my grandfather's lifetime, the railroad had replaced the stage-coach; the steamship had replaced sail; factories had replaced home industries, where piecework was "farmed out"; the telegraph had replaced the slow delivery of news by courier or by carrier pigeons; and so on and on.

But the telephone had just made its appearance. Internal combustion engines were just beginning to challenge steam. Small electrical motors had not yet replaced belts and shafting in machine shops. Hand tools had not been succeeded by power tools. Hard heavy work was done by hand. There were no chisel (or forklift) trucks for handling materials. There was no machinery for earth-moving (except steam). The pick and shovel and wheelbarrow had not yet been replaced by the bulldozer, the back-hoe or the road scraper.

Snow was removed by hand shovels; there were no snow plows. Air conditioning was an inventor's dream. Even central heating was a novelty. You kept warm and cooked by burning wood and some coal. There was kerosene for lamps, but no electricity in common use. The few paved streets were either cobblestoned in the cities or water-bound macadam in the towns. Black-top had not yet been developed to provide a smooth even surface on which pneumatic tires could roll.

There weren't even any pneumatic rubber tires, except on a few bicycles and an occasional experimental automobile.

So my grandfather could teach me a number of things which he had every reason to believe, from his own experience (he was born in 1833), would be useful for me to know. He taught me that when handling a shovel you should hold it with the hand nearest the blade, which was in the direction towards which you were shoveling. For example, if you were pitching with a shovel, pitchfork, or scoop towards your right, the right hand should be nearest to the blade; if to the left, then the left hand should be nearest the blade. Simple, but something I've seen innumerable, otherwise intelligent people ignore.

If you are "sprigging" the branches from the trunk of a fallen tree, never, never stand on the same side of the trunk as the branches you are chopping off. Always stand on the opposite side, so that a glancing blow of the axe would fly away from you, not towards you. I've seen several chopped legs of people who ignored this simple safety precaution.

The time to plant corn is when the leaves on the white oak trees are the size of a mouse's ear.

When you get your foot stuck in the soft mud of a swamp or muddy creek, don't wiggle it.

If you are going to be seasick, always throw up over the leeward side of the boat.

If you want to back a horse between the shafts of a wagon, you must stand in front of him. If you stand to one side, he will shy away and you'll never get him between those shafts.

There are numerous simple rules of arithmetic that were taught me by my grandfather. If you have an error which is divisible by nine, there probably has been a transposition of digits. A combination of figures should be used wherever convenient, rather than following conventional processes of arithmetic. For example, the easy way to translate Centrigrade into Fahrenheit temperatures is to double the Centrigrade temperature, deduct 10 percent, and add 32. That gives you the Fahrenheit temperature in an easy flash. Opening quohogs (hard-shell clams) can be easy. But you have to sneak up on them when they are resting. If you bang them around, they tighten up and make it difficult to insert the knife blade between their shells. Always use a knife with a thin blade and a rounded, not a sharp, point. Then place the quohog in the palm of your left hand, with the blunt end of the shell away from you. Holding the knife in your right hand, put the edge of the blade between the two shells where the lips meet, and squeeze the back of the blade with the fingers of your left hand, forcing it between the shells. Never push the blade with your right hand until after it is well inserted between the shells. To do so might result in the blade slipping, and a nasty cut on your left hand.

I could go on and on listing the things my grandfather could have taught me, which he had every reason to believe would be useful to me, and often were. But what can I, in 1981, teach my grandson which can be useful to him? The multiplicity of new tools, from computers and electronic devices to CB radios, must seem to him to make irrelevant most of the skills I could teach him.

But in his bewilderingly changing new world, threatened by a nuclear holocaust, perhaps I can guide him to observe some of the ancient verities of all time. The weather, the seasons, reading, awareness of history, the goodness of man as well as the inhumanity of man, the need to reach out to others for mutual aid and support, the importance of the individual. Perhaps I may even persuade him that man's greatest dignity is work—the satisfaction of a job, any job, well done.

Beach Adventures

The Monomoy Brant Club

IN his book, "Shooting Stands of Eastern Massachusetts" (Riverside Press, 1929), John C. Phillips fails to mention the Monomoy Brant Club on Monomoy in Chatham. This may be due to his concentration on goose stands; for he does describe Hopkins' goose stand on Nauset spit in Eastham, and Fred Higgins' stand on Hog Island in Pleasant Bay (Orleans).

The Monomoy Brant Club was unique in several ways. It was organized as a club, and members were assigned to occupy the facilities in groups of their own choosing for a week at a time. Most of the members appear to have been from around Boston, but there were a few Cape Codders.

I was there once for a few days as a guest of Frank Thacher, who was in the insurance business in Hyannis. There were about eight of us in the party, including Frank Paine, a Hyannis architect; E. L. Hurd of Milton and Chatham; D. Edgar Manson of Newton and Chatham; Ted Ricker of the Poland Spring (Maine) family of hotel and bottled water business; and me. We went down by boat from Stage Harbor on a Sunday afternoon late in November in the mid-1920's.

Since this was more than 55 years ago, my recollections may be a bit hazy; but as it was my first experience of this kind, the trip left vivid impressions on my memory. We went in Will Gould's boat on a tide high enough to get across the flats to an anchorage in the "Flat-Fish Hole", which lay between the camp on Shooters' Island and the main outer beach of Monomoy Point. The location was some two or three miles below Chatham Twin Lights, perhaps a mile short of Inward Point.

The camp consisted of at least three buildings located on a low hillock of hard ground (not sand), on which there was considerable vegetation including a stand of fair-sized trees. I think they may have been silver leaf or some similar deciduous trees. The main building included kitchen and dining facilities; the other two were primarily bunkhouses. I was in one of them with Thacher, Paine and Ricker.

Before dinner on the evening of our arrival, Frank Paine produced what to my inexperienced palate were epicurean hors d'oeuvres to go with our before-dinner drinks. Although Prohibition was then in full force (if not effect), it would have been unthinkable to be at the Brant Club, I learned, and not have a "Monomoy".

This drink was made as follows: to a lump of sugar in a short glass add a drop or two of Angostura bitters: then a generous slug of good Medford rum, a slice of fresh lemon slightly squeezed, two or three whole cloves, and fill the glass with boiling water, stir and quaff. A variation of this is to add ice instead of boiling water.

Years later, after a wedding, a group of us were in the bar-lounge at the Ritz-Carlton Hotel in Boston. I asked the bartender for a "Monomoy" and started to tell him how to make it. He interrupted, assuring me that he was familiar with "Monomoys", which he proceeded to demonstrate to perfection.

But to get back to Shooters' Island. In addition to Bill Gould, who was in charge of the operation, there were a cook and an assistant gunner. They had formerly worked both spring and fall; but when the spring shooting was outlawed, they worked full time only in the fall and winter. And they had plenty to do. Supplies as well as sportsmen had to be brought down by boat.

Although they had no "fliers" or other live decoys, they had plenty of wooden and cork decoys for geese, brant and ducks. The shooting was done from "sink boxes" off on the outer edges of the marsh, and hence were usually under water at the top of the tide.

They were big enough to hold two men comfortably and could be occupied until the water at high tide lapped over their tops and filled them. This led to the need for considerable wading at times. In preparation for this each man had a small section of metal stovepipe, about four inches long, custom-made to fit snuggly inside his rubber boots just below the knee.

By hauling the legs of his oilskin foul-weather pants down outside his boots, and then taking several turns of tarred line outside of that and tying it tightly over the stovepipe, he was able to wade without getting wet in water almost to the top of his oil pants, which were pulled up under his armpits. This was especially useful in crossing tidal creeks on the way between the camp and the boxes.

Each morning the gunner or his assistant was supposed to go out and bail the water out of the boxes and make sure that the decoys were out in good order. Then after breakfast the sportsmen would tramp out at dawn across the marsh to shoot from the boxes. I think that this stretch of marsh, as well as the upland and beach, was owned by the Brant Club.

Just beyond, towards Inward Point, was a similar spread known as the Bristol Club. And of course at Inward Point itself were several gunning camps mostly owned by local men who shot in the public domain—and perhaps now and then did a bit of poaching on the Brant Club marsh.

I remember lying in a box one day with Ted Ricker. Some geese came to our decoys and I shot my first goose. But for the most part the birds were brant, "trading" back and forth along the outer edges of the marsh in flocks of from a dozen or so to 20 or 30. I was told that the fall and winter gunning was nothing like it had been in the spring. This is borne out by my recent observation of brant in Pleasant Bay. For several years now I have noticed that they seem to be more plentiful in April and May than in the fall.

For some reason I had to leave before the end of the week. So I was rowed across "Flat-Fish Hole" in a skiff to the beach, then walked across to the ocean side before starting up the beach for Chatham, where Monomoy joined the mainland at that time at about Holway Street or a little north of that. Between the mainland and the beach abreast Chatham Twin Lights was a considerable body of salt water a hundred yards or more in width reached by a shallow tidal flow from Stage Harbor. As I started to walk up Monomoy Beach towards Chatham, the dunes cut off my view of Chatham and it was not until I got abreast of Island Pond, which lay between the beach and Morris Island, that I could see the mainland of Chatham itself.

Shooters' Island and the Monomoy Brant Club have long since washed away. In the mid-1940's remnants were still there. But now the spot where they once stood is hundreds of yards offshore in the breakers of Chatham Bars. I feel sure that the Brant Club must have kept records, if no more than a log book and an account book. I know they had annual dinners of the members in Boston, so I suspect they had meetings of which some sort of records were kept.

Perhaps someday such records, running from the late 1800's to the 1930's, may be found. Perhaps some descendant of a former member may have them. If so I hope they will not be just tossed away; for they could provide a glimpse of a way of life which will never return.

Note: Records from 1862 to World War II are now in the possession of The Chatham Historical Society.

Twelfth Of October
Weekends

I T was a chilly, wet early afternoon of a Friday, with rain in intermittent squalls driven shorewards by a southeasterly wind. But this didn't deter me from driving my Model A Ford station wagon, equipped with nine-inch tires for over-sand use, down the length of Monomoy from Chatham to the old lighthouse at Monomoy Point. It was our "twelfth of October weekend" when eight or ten of us gathered at the old lighthouse for a few days of sociability and surfcasting for striped bass.

On the way down I came across George Bearse gathering driftwood for the fires at the camp which he owned. He had bought the light and the light-keeper's house, built about 1830, from the Federal Government after its use had been discontinued. He had installed an electric generator in an outbuilding, so the lighting was by electricity. The keeper's house was commodious and comfortable, with several bedrooms on the second floor, and a large comfortable kitchen, dining room and living room on the first. It even had a bathroom with a flush toilet. Such luxurious quarters were most unusual on the beach. The keeper and his family had lived there alone, about eight miles from the nearest mainland.

When I arrived at the lighthouse, Ed Kidder, Earl Allen and Bill Courtnell were there, comfortably dry and warm, sipping beer. The rest of the men, including Maynard Whittaker, Win Dow, Carroll Harvey, Bill Elwell, Bob Morris and Jay Bryant had not yet arrived, as they were driving down from Boston that afternoon.

I tried to persuade them to go with me down to Point Rip, about a mile away at the very tip of Monomoy. But they were much too comfortable to leave, even when I pointed out that we might shoot a few "coot" (scota). The wind was just right to catch them swinging over the point in the late afternoon, as they flew from their offshore feeding grounds to spend the night resting on the more sheltered waters behind Monomoy. So I drove off alone.

I had gone less than half the distance when I came upon Ruth Collins, standing on the slope of the beach and casting her tin-clad drail straight into the wind and out just beyond the break of the surf. Behind her, spread over the sand were about a dozen beautiful striped bass. Such a catch was unusual and she was pretty excited and happy.

Even without her invitation, I would have joined her. As I stepped down beside her and started casting my own "tin-clad", she had another one on. For the next hour or so, it was rare indeed that one or the other of us was not reeling in a bass. Finally, after repeated glances at her watch, she reluctantly left. She said she had weekend house guests arriving and that they must already be there. So she drove off in order to greet them before dark.

I stayed on until after sundown and then drove back to the lighthouse with twelve beautiful bass, averaging about eight or ten pounds each, in the back of my wagon. They were the only fish caught by us over the whole holiday weekend. Such are the vagaries of surfcasting. But there was a fish for each of the "city fellers" to take home.

One of them who hadn't done any surfcasting before remarked, "Surfcasting is a strange sport. It's like going into the woods, blindfolded and at night, to shoot grouse with a rifle."

But in spite of no more fish being caught, we had a lot of fun. This included some wonderful meals prepared by that master camp cook, Earl Allen, and some slightly alcoholic poker playing, as well as hours of futile surfcasting along the ocean front. We fished assiduously over the high tide at morning and evening. On the low tide in the afternoon we went clamming at the Powder Hole.

One of our friends from the city, who had not had enough to drink at lunch, brought along a bottle which he sat up on the flat ahead of where he was digging for clams. He dug up a clam which was obviously not still alive, and upon a dare started to swallow the meat. The result was definitely therapeutic for him, as he promptly vomited it and most of the whisky, much to the amusement of the rest of us.

At dusk a couple of us went over to Lighthouse Pond to lie in the tall marsh grass in hopes of shooting a black duck or two as they came in for the night. But no luck; perhaps because it was illegal.

But dinnertime was fun. It included singing, led by Allie Griffin, who also kept us all laughing at his jokes and stories, and drinking. There were two or three guests who were not staying with us, but who had been invited for dinner when we met them while surfcasting.

Towards the end of dinner, George Bearse went outdoors to relieve himself over the low-board fence which enclosed a small brick patio outside the door. He came back chuckling.

"At last I've got even! When I was a boy of ten, I got skunked on, and my mother made me stay outdoors and take off all my clothes, but tonight now, I got even—there was a skunk just outside the fence."

These "October 12th weekends" at the lighthouse came to an end with the advent of World War II, when most of the men were scattered afar by their duties. But before the war was over a few of us revived the practice, though on a more modest scale. We started, as I remember, with a new group

171

who went down to Sturgis Rice's camp on the North Beach in Orleans, and while we had a lot of fun, the group was smaller and perhaps more restrained.

The last year that we went there, we spent the final morning cleaning the camp so as to leave everything shipshape and departed right after lunch, so the "city fellers" could drive home and arrive well before dinnertime. We left camp on time in our two beach wagons, but we had gone only a short distance along the backside of the beach when we spotted signs of fish just beyond the surf.

Of course we stopped and started casting, following the fish along the beach as they moved back and forth just beyond the surf. We loaded the backs of our wagons with forty or fifty bass, forgetting all about time. One result was that we were so late in leaving that one of the men didn't get home for dinner on time. I learned afterwards that it was his wedding anniversary too. Whether that triggered his divorce not long afterwards, I never knew.

In the fall of 1946, I started a series of "October 12th weekends" at my own camp on the North Beach, about opposite the Chatham Bars Inn. This was a one-room building, formerly a one-car garage, which I had moved there in 1926 to use for duck hunting. It had four bunks across one end and a sink and hand pump at the other. Because of the small space, we were limited to four in number, but all of us were big men. In addition to myself, they were Harry Damon, Carleton Francis and Frank Thompson, who even then dwarfed us two-hundred pounders with his more than two hundred and seventy-five pound bulk.

One afternoon, while we were staying there, we all drove to Orleans on errands; Francis and I in my Model A station wagon, and Damon and Thompson in Thompson's V-8 station wagon, which was much faster on the beach than my Model A.

After finishing our errands, we all stopped at the bar in

the Southward Inn for a drink. Francis and I left soon to fish Nauset Inlet before returning to camp, leaving the other two to follow. At dusk Carlie and I returned to camp, expecting to find the others there.

We started to prepare dinner while waiting for them, thinking, of course, that they must have "got into fish" somewhere on the beach. But time passed, quite a lot of it, and we ourselves were "feeling no pain" before we heard a halloo from the dark outside, followed by the appearance of a very tired Damon and Thompson on foot.

This is what had happened. With Thompson at the wheel they had come skittering down on the "low beach", the tide being low. The speed of the V-8 on the hard-packed wet sand had fooled them, and without knowing it, in the darkness, they drove right past the turnoff to the camp all the way to the point of the beach, and then right off the point into the water, which was fairly deep there.

As they scurried out of the car, sitting half submerged in the water, Frank suggested they should go back and turn off the lights to save the battery. They climbed up on the beach to look around and see where they were. Then, as now, Chatham Light was flashing well to the north.

Seeing this, Frank exclaimed, "My God! We're on Monomoy, but how did we get there?"

They trudged their way the three miles or more in their wet clothes and rubber boots to camp, where they found Carlie and me waiting for them, not at first quite believing their story. But when we did, they took Harry's boat which was moored abreast the camp to go across to the mainland and telephone the Coast Guard for help in retrieving their car.

Upon their return we all went in my car to the scene of the accident. There was the V-8 in the water up to the bottom of its windows. We had with us only some light rope, one end of which we fastened to each car to keep the V-8 from drifting away on the incoming tide, which runs strong at the Point.

Presently we saw coming towards us on the beach the lights of the Coast Guard Dukw. Just as it reached us our line between the two cars parted. The steel cable on the stern of the Dukw was jammed in its guides, and try as we might we couldn't clear it enough to fasten the ends to the car in the water. So we just had to watch it disappear slowly beneath the surface.

A couple of days later, the weather being fine, Frank got a small plane to spot the car on the bottom and managed to rig lines to it and haul it out. They towed it up the beach to the mainland where it was bathed over and over again with fresh water. The engine was disassembled and put together again. In a few days the V-8 was operating, little if any the worse for the experience.

In 1947 I built my new camp beside the old one on North Beach. This was bigger, with a small back entry, a 14-foot by 16-foot kitchen-living room, and a 12-foot by 16-foot bedroom with two beds and two bunks. Beginning that fall and for many years thereafter, our "October 12th weekend" head-quartered there, occasionally using the old camp or a friend's camp to house the overflow in numbers.

There was usually one and sometimes two good cooks in the crew. I remember particularly such gourmet chefs as Ed Dybing and Norman MacDonald, whose bouillabaisse was the most delicious I've ever tasted. Frank Thompson, who was a hotelman (Snow Inn and Wychmere Harbor Club), ran the commissary, so we always had top quality supplies. The last two or three years we were there he even brought along his chef from the Club.

We always had at least two beach wagons on hand, a motor boat and skiff moored in front, and at least one beach wagon stationed on Monomoy. Some years we even had Frank's war surplus DWCK, which ran both on water and land. I remember, it got stuck once on a sandbar too shallow to use the propeller and too mushy for the wheels to take hold. There was a lot of serious surfcasting, especially at daybreak and at dusk. We dug clams, went scalloping, and of course played a lot of poker.

Some of the meals were innovative. Chester Slack, for example, usually brought along the dough so we could have fried bread at least once. It was he too who introduced strawberry short-cake with whipped cream for breakfast; it made a perfect breakfast. We usually had freshly caught fried mussels at least once, and of course steaks and lobster. We never knew how many to expect for a meal, as friends kept dropping by, but that never seemed to present any problem.

Once Norm MacDonald had spent most of the afternoon preparing a roast of lamb and all the goodies that went with it. Some of the men had been fishing Monomoy, so we were holding everything for their return. When they came in with two buckets of clams they had dug at the Powder Hole at the end of Monomoy, all plans were changed. It was one of those years when clams were extremely scarce, almost none to be found on the North Beach, so Norman's gourmet dinner was put aside while we devoured steamed clams, though a few did nibble at the lamb.

The old-fashioned castiron, wood and coal-burning kitchen range was our sole source of heat. All the cooking was done on it or in its oven, except of course the broiling, which we did outside on a charcoal grill. The stove took a little getting used to.

I remember one occasion when Morton Furber was in charge of baking a ham. He didn't realize that the shelf under the oven door tipped forward a bit, so when he pulled the ham forward and rested it on the shelf, the whole thing catapulted upside down onto the floor. But no harm was done. It was delicious, even though one might encounter a grain of sand, picked up in the process, when chewing on a bite of ham.

We were usually there at least three or four days, but

always included October 12, a legal holiday, in our stay. When the 12th fell on a Wednesday, we obviously had to include both the Sunday before it and the Sunday after. But this simply meant that we had more of a turnover among the guests, some arriving as others were leaving, staying only a part of the time.

The last day was always clean-up day with many chores, such as getting the beach wagon back from Monomoy to the mainland, taking the motor boat and skiff up to its Ryder's Cove mooring, and really cleaning the camp. This included scrubbing the floor of the main room with sand, soap and hot water, after which if the weather permitted we aired out the whole place in warm sunshine and breeze. We knew that I'd be back in a few days with my wife Barbie, and we were trying, with only moderate success I admit, to win her approval of our efforts.

Barbie and I spent many happy days and nights at the camp, which we named "Bar-B". For a few years, beginning in 1948, we lived there more than half each week in the summer, while I commuted by beach wagon to work at Orleans. Our son Jan, (thirteen years old in 1948), tended our two or three lobster pots out front in the channel, keeping us well supplied with lobsters, and we entertained frequently for dinner. Sometimes the guests came under their own power, but usually I picked them up at the Town Beach in Orleans and drove them back late in the evening.

We stayed overnight at the camp every month of the year, but usually we gave up soon after the duck hunting season was over. It could be really cold on the floor of a bitter winter morning when the fire was low. However we had little trouble keeping the temperature near 70°.

Fishing Tales

Striped Bass Fishing

MY earliest recollections of striped bass fishing are of a day when, as a boy, I happened to be on the North Beach in Chatham with my father. There was a power dory with a rowing dory in tow just offshore of the surf. In the rowing dory was a seine, and there were three or four men in the two boats, among them, as I recall, Rufus Nickerson and his brother Joe.

Dad said they were about to seine a school of bass which they had spotted near us in the surf. First they rowed ashore and landed a man with one end of the seine on the slope of the beach. He attached the bottom corner of the net to his foot and held the upper corner in his hands, while the other men rowed off paying out the seine as they went around the school of fish. When it was all out, they rowed in and brought their end of the net to shore. Then carefully the men began to purse up the seine from both ends. As soon as the fish became aware of the net they tried frantically to escape, and some of them did, but not by going *over* or *around* the net.

As it was drawn to shore, there were moments when the *bottom* of the seine was not securely down on the sand, in spite of the leads. Those bass would put their noses down and try to burrow through sand and water, in the undertow, *under* the bottom edge of the net. Some escaped this way. But most of the school were brought flipping and flopping up onto the dry sand.

For more than 50 years this method of catching bass has

been outlawed. But until then it was a common method used by local fishermen, when the autumn run of bass was on.

I remember another time when I was swimming in the surf and suddenly found myself surrounded by a school of striped bass. I was not sure at first what they were and scrambled back to the beach accompanied to the edge of the undertow by dozens of big fish.

As I grew up I heard men talk of "heaving and hauling" for bass; so I decided to try it. The equipment consisted of a good length of heavy cod line wrapped around a straight stick, something over a foot long. At the end of the hard-tarred cod line we bent two or three yards of softer and slightly heavier line and at the end of this a lead drail, fairly heavy, in which a stout hook had been imbedded when the lead had been molten. The softer line at the heaving end was to save some of the wear and tear on your fingers.

The fishing method was to uncoil as much line from the stick as you thought you could heave, then take the end nearest the drail, whirl it around your head a few times and heave the drail out over the surf. As you retrieved the line, hand over hand, you hoped for a strike, and sometimes you got one.

The lead tended to turn black from the chemical action of the salt water. So it had to be scraped bright from time to time with a knife. Some of the old-timers became very proficient with this method of fishing and could heave a lead drail as far as 50 yards over the breakers. Needless to say, the bass had to be close in to be caught this way but they often are when chasing bait in the fall.

It was not until some time in the 1920's that I first saw anyone fishing with a rod in the surf. At the time I remember thinking it was a pretty effete way to fish, influenced in part, no doubt, because it was a summer resident from New Jersey who was doing it. Before long, however, surf fishing with rod and reel became very popular locally. The rig consisted of a split-bamboo rod about five or six feet in length, plus a detachable wooden butt about two and a half feet long, to which was fastened a heavy spool type reel filled with 12 or 16-pound test linen line. Also strapped around your waist by a leather belt was a "butt socket", into which the butt of the rod was inserted when retrieving. These were usually of leather. But some used a beer can for a butt socket. The most popular reels were Pfleuger Capitol, Penn Surfmaster, and Penn Squidder, but there were many other makes.

The lure was almost invariably a tin drail with a hook imbedded in it, shaped with a slight bend to resemble a squid and to give it more action. Sometimes we pointed the hook with a strip of pork rind to give it even more action. The tin remained bright in the water (as lead would not) and required only an occasional rubbing in the sand to keep it shining. The linen line had very little give to it, and as a result, a backlash when casting almost invariably resulted in a sound like a pistol shot and a drail sailing out to sea. To lose half a dozen drails in this manner in a few hours of fishing was not unusual. But in those days they cost only 35 cents (cheaper by the dozen) at the local hardware store. Each day after fishing, the line had to be strung out in the air and dried, because if it was left wet on the reel it tended to rot and lose its strength.

During the 30's we organized the Lower Cape Surfcasters Association, which awarded arm patches for proficiency in casting the "tin-clad" jig. The neophyte first achieved his 25 yard patch, then 50, then 75, and finally he might make the 100 yard patch. Both men and women were members, and some of the women were better casters than most of the men. In the summer we had a big clambake, and after the bass fishing season was over an annual meeting and dinner. This club was very successful and lots of fun. It brought together people from all walks of life with a common interest in surf casting.

And it also served as a mutual aid group, for it was during the 1930's too, that "beach buggies" (which were mostly Model

A or Model T Fords) first appeared on the beaches in numbers. They were all two-wheel drive and under-powered for use in sand. So, getting stuck and having to be shoveled out and jacked up, and having driftwood boards or planks put under the wheels to get out, was common operating procedure. Learning to drive on the beach with this equipment required quite a bit of doing, and occasionally help from others. The Surfcasters Association finally just died out and disappeared with the advent of World War II and gasoline rationing.

All during the 1930's and until the late 1940's, Monomoy was directly accessible by land from the mainland. And it was preferred by many to other surf-casting areas. Before dawn when the tide was right in late September and October, a dozen or so beach buggies would arrive at Light House Bar or Point Rip, and by sunrise we would be landing bass. Men who had jobs could often be in time for work at 8 a.m. and have several bass in their wagons before that hour.

It was in the 1930's too that George Bearse let a crowd of us use his Monomoy Lighthouse as a fishing camp for an annual October 12 weekend of fishing and camaraderie. In later years some of us continued this practice on North Beach, either at Sturgis Rice's camp in Orleans or at mine in Chatham until after 1960.

During the war years, gasoline rationing prevented using motor vehicles on the beach for fishing. But I had a flat-bottomed, center-board sharpie with a leg-of-mutton sail. There were no motor boats racing around to disturb us because of gasoline rationing (and even if there had been, the biggest outboards in common use were only five or ten horsepower), and I caught a lot of striped bass in Pleasant Bay. It was rare indeed to troll a line behind my sailing skiff between the islands and the beach and come home empty-handed. We also did some casting from the shore with good catches at places like the mouth of Crow's Pond and at Pleasant Bay narrows.

In the late 40's and early 50's things began to change. Until then almost all surf casting had been with jigs, usually tin or tin with feathers or bucktails. Now it was discovered that striped bass would take surface plugs such as were used on western lakes for pike. Gradually plugs of every description began to take over as lures, replacing jigs. It was about this time too that glass rods in one piece, some as long as nine or ten feet began to replace the rods with a split-bamboo tip and wooden butt. Even back in the 30's, some surf casters had used single pieces of "Burma cane", which were longer and whippier than the split bamboo. But they were inclined to take a "set" to one side or the other. The glass surf rods were far better, though much more expensive than the Burma cane.

During July and August when most of us never expected to catch bass in the surf, people started fishing (of all things) with sea worms. Then night fishing started! When drails (with accompanying backlashes) were most commonly used, our fishing stopped after sundown, except on the full of the moon. But with the advent of nylon-braided line, and later monofilament, and especially the backlash-free spinning reel, which came into use in the '50's, night fishing became popular.

I have never been able to see much sport in sitting in the dark on a stool waiting for a fish, usually a skate, sometimes a bass, to take my hook, when you can't see what is happening. But it is popular with many people today who put high value on the catch, higher than they do on the catching.

Since the late 1940's Monomoy has been an island again. Nauset (North) Beach is attached to the mainland in Orleans and this has resulted in a concentration of so-called beach buggies there. But the beach buggies have changed too. Instead of being light or stripped-down vehicles, they have become heavy campers, converted milk delivery trucks, and the like, designed for overnight camping. They contain complete living facilities and lumber along at low speeds until they reach their chosen location. The fishermen set up camp for as long as the regulations permit them to stay. This is a far cry from chasing signs of fish up and down the beach and casting tinclads. These are mostly bait fishermen, whose lines just set there in the surf gathering weeds, while the fishermen doze over their cans of beer.

The fishing in Pleasant Bay has changed too. No longer is day fishing reliable. By day, powerful outboard motors up to 100 horsepower or more race about, towing water skiers behind them and breaking up any schools of fish which might be on the surface chasing bait. Most of the fishing is at night now, or early in the morning when the motorboat jockeys are still abed. And there is little fishing with jigs and plugs.

Instead the fishermen use live eels as bait or tow behind their boats contraptions which look like an umbrella frame— a "Christmas Tree"—loaded with multi-colored lures, sometimes catching two or three fish at once, but hardly "sport", I'd say. But these "meat-fishermen" are not worse, I guess, than the seiners. Nor are they worse than some of us who set trawls at night on the flats, when the low tide came at dusk and at dawn, hauling them out soon after sunrise before the gulls could get to work on the catch. The difference is that these men call themselves sportsmen!

Speaking of bass fishing in Pleasant Bay I should mention a commercial method no longer used there. This consisted of building a weir, which was a long fence of netting running from shallow water out to deeper water. It ended inside a circular trap which was supported by poles set in the sandy bottom.

The fish would encounter the fence and follow it offshore in an attempt to get around it. When they came to the end of the fence they found themselves inside the circular trap. As they followed around the walls of the trap they were deflected away from the small opening through which they had entered, and rarely if ever found their way out. Later a "trap fisherman" would come and purse up the circular part of the net and bail the fish out into his boat.

I recall three such weirs which were put out regularly each season. Bartlett Bassett had one at the west end of Strong Island. Rufus Nickerson had one just north of the Old Harbor Coast Guard Station, and there was a third one on the beach side of the bay north of Strong Island. This method of fishing is still used on the Chatham bay side of Monomoy, between Inward Point and the Powder Hole. But its use has been declining for years.

I have written this memorandum about bass fishing so that my grandson Peter, who is an enthusiastic fisherman himself, can know a little of how it used to be before the waters of Pleasant Bay were filled with high-powered outboard motorboats and the sands of Nauset Beach were occupied by heavy motor vehicles designed for camping.

A War-Time Fish Story

IN the fall of 1942 we closed our home which was about five miles out from both Orleans and Chatham, and moved into an old house on Old Harbor Road in Chatham which I had inherited from my Uncle Joshua. It was a good house, but not as comfortable as our own. However it had many advantages in wartime, when the German submarines were in control of our coastal shipping lanes. It was heated by a furnace in the basement, which burned coal but could run on wood, and the hot water supply was heated by a coal-burning stove. We could walk to the shops and our seven-year-old son walked to school. Gasoline use was kept at a minimum. We lived there for two winters.

One October evening a friend of ours, Ann Plum, was at our house for dinner. The next day was opening of the quail season, and we decided that she and I would hunt them over the many acres of open land which surrounded her house. So at dawn the next morning, I was at her house for breakfast, and we hunted through the early morning hours without seeing a sign of a quail. By 8:30 or so, it was apparent that this was going to be one of those perfect "bluebird days" of October: warm, brightly sunny and only a light breeze. Such a day was too beautiful to waste.

I suggested that I had enough gasoline in my Model A beach wagon to run us down to the end of Monomoy and back, and since our purpose would be surf casting for bass, a food supply without ration stamps, we could justify such a trip with clear conscience. At the point rip on the tip of Monomoy, we picked up two or three bass with our tin-clad jigs. By this time it was getting toward noon, and since we had food for the larder, we started back up the beach for home.

As we got up by "Nigger Bar", about abreast Shooters' Island, we saw two young Coast Guardsmen running toward us, waving us down. In those days every foot of our shoreline was patrolled, day and night, by Coast Guardsmen in pairs with a dog, as a protection against any landings from German submarines, and of course to keep a close check on whatever might come drifting in to shore.

They were excited, and at first we guessed they had encountered something of military importance. But no! They said that the surf, abreast where we were on an inner road, was full of fish.

So we drove over to the water's edge and started casting. I have never seen such fast and furious surf fishing. For the next hour or two there was scarcely a time when either Ann or I didn't have a fish on. We loaded the back of our wagon with bass, at least fifty or sixty of them. Towards the end, I remember, she was so exhausted that she sat down on the beach to reel in her fish. I was "pooped" too. At length we quit. By this time it was nearly three o'clock and we were hungry, since we hadn't eaten since our breakfast at dawn.

The Chatham Coast Guard Station at that time was on top of Morris Island, on the bluff overlooking the inlet to the east. As a gesture of thanks to the young men who had "found" our fish while on patrol, we stopped at the station and gave the cook as many bass as he would accept. While we were there he was just taking some hot apple turnovers out of his oven. They were beautiful and smelled so good! Nothing would do, but we must sit down and have some of them with generous glasses of milk. I've never tasted better, before or since.

By the time we got home and had given away as many bass as we could to friends and neighbors, there were still some left in the wagon, which I disposed of to a fish buyer at the Chatham Fish Pier. As the sun set we both felt that it had been a day to remember.

Fishing With Uncle Ernest

A MONG the happy memories of my childhood are the annual fishing trips to the ponds in the Brewster woods with my father and his brother Ernest. These took place regularly in the first week of May.

Uncle Ernest would arrive by train in Chatham from his home in Pawtucket, Rhode Island, and spend the night at our house. The next day we three would hitch up the "democrat wagon" and drive over the sandy, rutted road to Grandfather Nickerson's home in East Harwich, arriving in time for supper, and of course an evening of reminiscences and yarns before bedtime.

After an early breakfast, the next morning we would start off with the horse and wagon for the ponds. It would take at least an hour's driving through old woods roads to get to our first stop at the east end of Rafe's Pond. On the way we would enter the real woods at Freeman's Way, going by the "Old Mansion", where a house had once stood, but there were only the lilacs and apple trees beneath which the green grass was lush, even in early May. We always stopped and looked around for the deer which could sometimes be found feeding under the old apple trees in the early morning.

Then there was the long slow climb up the road past "Hangman's Hill", where it was said a man had hung himself. Soon we turned off to the right on a lesser woods road, in which there was a fork where a small blind had been built from which to shoot deer and foxes as they came along the way. There was usually a discussion about which fork we should take, but eventually we arrived at a little beach on the east end of Rafe's Pond.

By that time father was willing to forgo Uncle Ernest's steady talking for a bit. So they usually split up, Ernest fishing the south side of the pond, and Oscar (father) fishing the north side.

Then we went to fishing, always counting on catching enough pickerel for our midday meal. Our tackle was quite rudimentary. We each had a bamboo pole about 14 to 16 feet long, to the tip of which we tied a piece of tarred "mackerel line", not quite as long as the pole, and to the end of that we tied on a medium-sized triple-hooked spinner-type "spoon hook". If we were lucky enough to catch gudgeons (minnows) or small frogs, we sometimes "pointed" the hook with them. We would cast our lure out into the pond and then "drail" it through the water by wading quietly along the shore, repeating this process every few yards.

If the day was sunny the pickerel would be in the shallow water among the newly forming lily pads. We would catch them by throwing out the spoon hook and then slowly retrieving it as we waded cautiously along in the water.

I usually went along with father, not so much because I was tired of listening to Uncle Ernest, but because at the edge of the pond under the steep bank of the north side duck hunters had built elaborate blinds, and these were fascinating for a boy to inspect even though this was not the season for ducks. I usually took time out to explore them and to investigate the little shelter behind the long rampart of the blinds, which stretched along the shore.

Then there was the sound of rustling in the dead leaves under the brush, which led to the discovery of happy-looking red-breasted towhees seeking their breakfast under the old leaves. I could be distracted too by seizing the opportunity to pick a handful of mayflowers (trailing arbutus) if they had not all gone by.

When we met again, back at the wagon, we usually had enough pickerel for our next meal. Then we would discuss where to go next. Sometimes it would be to Lower Cliff Pond, or it might be to Upper Cliff. If it was to Upper Cliff, we would decide whether to go first to one of the three "nooks" on the southerly side—"Riddleton's, "Hopkins" or "Grassy"—or perhaps to "Shoot Flying Beach", which separated Upper Cliff from the Black Pond which lay between it and Lower Cliff.

"Shoot Flying Beach" was so called because it was there that hunters could shoot geese and ducks as they flew across between the ponds. In any case we would fish at several of these chosen spots, sometimes varying our catch with a black bass, especially if we had been able to catch a small frog with which to point the hook.

By noon we were hungry and the men would gather a few stones which they would arrange in a small open-sided circle, within which they would build a fire. When we had a good bed of coals, they would take a piece of cellar window wire mesh, fold it once, and place the fish between the folds and over the fire to broil, very slowly.

It was there that I learned that fish should be cooked as fresh as possible and *very* slowly, until just at the end of the cooking. We would eat our fill of broiled fish, with pilot biscuits and peach halves right out of the can, all washed down with fresh water dipped out of the lake. These lunches really must have been good for me to remember them so well more than a half century later!

Then after a short nap we could continue our fishing. Once I remember we caught a huge turtle at "Grassy Nook", as it was migrating between Cliff Pond and the little mud pond just across the beach from Cliff.

By the time we made our way back to grandfather's house,

we were happily weary. But not too much to keep us from enjoying a hearty supper, followed again by yarns and story-telling before bedtime.

Early the next morning we would be off again for other ponds: Grassy Pond, Bushy Beach Pond, Jot's Pound, Green Land Pond and Long Pond. There we would repeat our program of the day before. But this time we would drop Uncle Ernest off in the afternoon, either back at Grandpa Nick's or at some other relatives of his or his wife's (she was a Cahoon) in East Harwich.

Then came the long drive back to Chatham, while a boy became sleepy as he watched the sand from the ruts fall back from the spokes of the wheels as they turned.

A Day With Harry Damon

O
N a beautiful spring morning in May of 1941, Harry Damon and I set out in my little sharpie to find some of those small to medium-size striped bass which were plentiful in Pleasant Bay that year. Our boat was a flat-bottomed, center-board sharpie, designed to sail with a "leg o'mutton" sail with a mast that was stepped through a hole in the forward deck, and steered with an oar stuck over the lee gunnel. Or you could unstep the mast, roll the sail around it, and stow one end under the deck so that you could row with a pair of oars.

Captain Joe Kelley, a retired Coast Guard station keeper, had built it for me. Designed to take two people it was among the last I remember seeing of what had been a very common type used for duck hunting and general chores on the water. But on this particular morning I had "gone modern" and was using my new five-horsepower outboard motor. Outboards had progressed by then to the point that they would start more often than not, which was a big step forward.

We headed up the channel between Doane Flat and Wrinkle Flat towards Strong Island meadow. As we approached the east end of the island, Harry called my attention to the rocks on the point of the island which were sticking up out of the water. To be sure there are rocks there, but not normally exposed. What he had seen proved to be some seals sitting on the barely submerged rocks.

This fact had no sooner been established, he spotted some more "seals" on rocks to the east towards the North Beach. But there are no rocks there. What we had seen were three deer wading up to their bellies in the water covering the flat. As we approached them they galloped off in clouds of spray towards the beach. All this didn't prevent us from casting our lures for bass, and as usual we caught two or three on the downstream side of the rips, where the tide running over the edge of a flat drops off into deeper water.

We had a date to meet our wives and the children, Harry's two little daughters and my six-year-old son, for a picnic at noon on the beach at "The Narrows", where the water runs through Pleasant Bay into Little Pleasant Bay, between Sipson's Island and Potonimicut. They had driven there by auto and were waiting when we arrived. After our picnic lunch, my son Jan, casting off the shore with a "tin clad" jig, caught his first striped bass, a six pounder.

In the early afternoon Harry and I started back for home in the boat. As we were between the west end of Strong Island and the mainland of Nickerson's Neck, we saw swimming toward the island on the surface of the water a big black snake, its head well out of the water and its neck arched. We made a few casts towards it with our fishing lures but without success, except that Harry did lay a lure right on the snake, which after writhing up the leader for a foot or two dropped off and disappeared into the water.

That was, indeed, a day to be remembered.

Storms And Rescues

Chatham Old Harbor Life Saving Station—1912

Hurricane Edna

On Friday afternoon, September 10, 1954, my wife Barbie and I drove the eight miles down the North Beach to our camp. Our radio reported that tropical storm "Edna" was moving up the coast in our direction. But the near calm and heavy fog all night gave no immediate hint of the weather to come.

Next morning while we breakfasted about eight o'clock, we learned from our radio that "Edna" was heading straight for Nantucket. Even allowing for the scare tactics of news reporters on radio, we proceeded to secure loose or movable objects outside the camp.

All morning the wind was from the east, gradually increasing, with heavy rain at times. By noon our barometer had dropped from 30° to exactly 29°, and the radio was reporting extreme precautions all along the coast, especially in the area of Wareham to New London. Evacuees from along the shorefront were being brought into the Wareham Town Hall. I brought our Jeep station wagon around from its usual parking place on the easterly side of the camp and snuggled it up in the lea of the west wall.

At 12:30 the barometer had dropped a little to 28.95°, and the wind was blowing much harder from the east. In fact as we looked out our west window across the bay towards Chatham, we could see the wind pick up surface water in solid scuds of spray, and we were looking from the windward side of the water! The ocean high tide was at 11:00 A.M., but looking from where we were we saw no seas running through the cuts in the dunes on the ocean side, nor were there any other signs of extreme high level of water at the top of the tide. The marsh to the southeast of our camp was not even flooded. Meanwhile our radio was reporting that the "eye" of hurricane "Edna" was due to hit between Nantucket and Falmouth about 1:30 or 2:00 P.M.

At one o'clock our barometer stood at 28.84°. In all this wind we were surprised to see a few terns flying along over the edge of the water near our shore. By 1:30 our barometer read 28.70°, and the wind velocity was increasing, still from the east. The weather bureau report said that the eye of "Edna" would pass within an hour over the center of Nantucket, with gusts up to 140 miles per hour. Our barometer still continued to fall rapidly: 2:00 P.M. at 28.55°; 2:30 P.M. at 28.37°; 3:00 P.M. at 28.22°; 3:10 P.M. at 28.18°; 3:30 P.M. at 28.15°.

Suddenly the wind dropped and shifted to a light southwest breeze. The sun shone brightly through the murky overcast. Anticipating renewed gale winds from the southwest and west, I moved our Jeep from the west to the north side of the camp, even though blue sky was showing occasionally through rifts in the clouds. Then we saw a big four-engine B-29 weather-reporting bomber overhead, evidently following the eye of the storm.

In my log I noted, "Am still amazed at the score or more of terns seen in the air at the height of the storm."

At 3:50 P.M. the barometer had risen to 28.30°, the sun was shining brightly and the wind was strong southwest. But there was a heavy black murk in the sky to the southwest. I moved the beach wagon around close up to the east side of the camp for fear the gale will come now from the west and northwest. At 4:30 the barometer read 28.40°, and a gale was blowing from the west with violent gusts and heavy overcast. By 5:00 P.M. the barometer had risen to 28.50°, and I quote from my log written at the time.

"Wind from N.W. *with heaviest gusts of the day*. The camp is really quivering, especially the north end wall. Am sure glad I put the beach wagon around on the east side, backed up in front of the window over the sink. It *should* be low tide here (inside of beach) about 7:00 P.M. but no bare flat is showing. Have been listening all day to radio Station WEEI, which has been doing an excellent reporting job on the storm 'Edna'. But WEEI just went out—must have lost their transmitter. They had recordings and direct transmission from 'correspondents' in Wareham, Martha's Vineyard, Nantucket, Provincetown, Providence, and telephone reports from Dennisport and Wellfleet.

"We must be on the leeward cycle of the hurricane. The camp is really creaking and the north wall seems to be flexing itself. We are now playing 'gin' and having a drink. I don't think Barbie is very happy; but this is something I've always wanted to do. Barbie knocks off every few minutes to wipe up water and sand leaking in around windows, while I write in the log. If my writing is a bit shaky, it's the vibration, not the liquor.

"Now (5:15), barometer reads 28.65° and I think winds are much heavier, especially heavier gusts, since we passed through the eye of the hurricane; 5:35 P.M., barometer 28.80°, wind less violent; 6:10 P.M., barometer 29.00°, light shows on western horizon. Winds while still strong (gale force) are subsiding. Camp no longer quivers violently. Wind N.W. 7:20 P.M., barometer reads 29.22°; wind now strong W. to N.W. Took a ride in beach wagon to see the surf. Rainbow. Full moon showing. I guess the storm is over!"

By 8:30 the barometer read 29.36°. We had started a fire in the cookstove, which we hadn't dared to do all day for fear that the camp would burn if a gust blew in a window or moved the camp off its foundation. We cooked and ate our dinner and went to bed.

Next morning, Sunday, September 12, we drove about

to check on conditions. Saw a few fishermen and a boat which had dragged ashore on its moorings. Down near the point of the beach on the last grassy dune above the tide's reach, we saw a large number of terns sitting amongst the stubble. Many of them were young, just learning to fly, and a few were still downy. Perhaps those terns we had seen flying yesterday at the peak of the storm were looking for lost young or for food for them.

The Rescue

A GROUP of Chatham men, mostly local boatmen and fishermen, stood huddled together on top of "Mill Hill," in the scant lee of the old windmill. It was midmorning and bitter cold, with the wind blowing hard from the northwest, driving before it occasional spits of snow.

Their eyes were all turned towards the west, across Stage Harbor, Hardings Beach, and the great pack of drift ice solidly offshore from the beach for a mile or so. Their attention was riveted on a schooner with distress signals flying, anchored out beyond the ice pack, but just perceptively dragging her anchor inexorably toward the grinding edge of the ice. They knew that without help the vessel was doomed, and with her all her crew.

So where were the men from the life saving service? There were four life saving service stations in Chatham: one at Old Harbor; one on the beach ocean-ward from Morris Island; one halfway down Monomoy Point, known as the Monomoy Station; and one at the "Powder Hole", near the tip off Monomoy, known as the Monomoy Point Station.

Obviously no help could be given by sending out crews from the two ocean-side stations. But what about the two stations on Monomoy Point itself? Could they launch a boat in the teeth of the onshore gale on the inner side of the point and fight their way against the wind and waves to the vessel in distress?

Just before noon, word reached the group of men on

"Mill Hill" that the life saving service had decided that under the conditions no rescue could be attempted. They could only pray that the ship would stay clear of the ice pack, and perhaps by the next morning the wind would have dropped or changed direction so they could reach her with a lifeboat, the only means of propelling such a boat being with oars.

In spite of the fact that all four life saving crews were mostly local men and expert boatmen, their fellow citizens gathered on the hill were indignant when they learned that no attempt at rescue would be made that day by the life saving service. From where they stood on the hill, the angle of their vision was such that they could see what the men at the stations could not—that the vessel was slowly but steadily dragging her anchors. Tomorrow would be too late; for it seemed certain that she would founder in the ice pack before then.

Somebody in the group came up with an idea. If they could launch a boat from the South Chatham shore to windward of her, they could row downwind, pick off her crew, and land them abreast the Monomoy Station. Besides they had just such a boat at their disposal, left over from before the establishment of the United States Life Saving Service, and well maintained for use in the commercial "wrecking" business. There were plenty of men in the group on the hill who were tough and well-experienced in handling such a craft under difficult conditions, and they could drag their boat on wheels to the windward shore for launching.

It *could* be done, though at considerable risk. If not the crew on the vessel would surely perish, while the men on shore stood by. Under those circumstances the answer to the problem seemed obvious. The only difficulty was to choose the five men to man the boat and to drag it to South Chatham in time, before dark.

Somehow the five were selected, four to row and one to serve as helmsman and coxswain. Somehow the boat was dragged to a place beyond the ice pack for launching. Somehow they managed to pick the crew off the wreck and row them down-wind to the safe shore and the warmth of the Monomoy Station before daylight had faded.

They made sure the survivors were safely settled in the life saving station. They even accepted a few cups of hot coffee. But they all stubbornly refused to stay the night, they were so thoroughly disgusted and angry at the failure of the United States Life Saving Service to attempt a rescue that they chose to walk the three miles or so back to Chatham mainland.

The names of those five men are unknown to me. But they were a breed apart—the kind of men whom I saw as a boy working their cat boats to and from the offshore fishing grounds, salting their catch and sometimes salvaging cargo from wrecked ships. The story I've told is the way it was told to me, and it rings true to my ears.

Scrabbletown

BEFORE the United States Life Saving Service was established in the early 1870's, "wrecking" was a voluntary, private occupation. Since all shipping depended upon sail, and there were thousands of vessels passing around Cape Cod every year, inevitably some were stranded on the sandy shoals near Chatham. There were always a few which were totally lost, but many more were saved after running aground.

In what was known as "the village", near Chatham's twin lights, there were several crews of "wreckers". These were made up of local young men who worked in teams, each team maintaining its own lifeboat for going to rescue wrecks.

There are stories that these men were not far removed from being pirates, or "mooncussers". It has been said that "Wicked Hill" (now Seaview Street) got its name because on dark and stormy nights men tied a lantern to a lame horse, and then walked the beast back and forth to give the impression that the lantern was a riding light on a vessel safely at anchor, thus enticing unwary mariners to their doom on Chatham Bars. I feel sure such stories were the fabrications of mean minds, of people who overemphasized the high competition between salvage crews.

I've heard that when two boats of wreckers were racing to be the first to board a stranded vessel, the one who came aboard over the stern had a better chance of getting the job than the one who came over the bow, because the former would reach the captain first, since he would usually be near the helm. I've heard too that it sometimes happened that the "wreckers" would put out kedge anchor lines to hold a stranded vessel from freeing herself on a rising tide long enough to make a salvage deal with the captain, and then reverse the process after the bargain had been made.

To be sure, salvaging was a lucrative and highly competitive business. But there was another side, a grimmer one. If the ship was in real danger of breaking up, or if loss of lives seemed imminent the first obligation of the "wreckers" was to save lives. There were many heroic rescues. There was no pay and no salvage involved. It was often a case of the Chatham men risking their own lives in attempts to save others. They had a rule amongst themselves that no two brothers could go in the same rescue boat; for if one boat should be lost and the men drowned there was always a chance that the other brother would survive. Better to risk losing only one brother, rather than two in the same boat.

It was against this background of high competition between crews of "wreckers" and high risks in saving lives with no reward except in heaven, that the part of Chatham near the twin lights and facing the bars came to be known as "Scrabbletown".

Captain Joe Kelley

I N the early 1900's a disaster befell the crew of the Monomoy Point Life Saving Station, one of four life saving stations in Chatham. The entire lifeboat crew (except for one) was lost in an attempted rescue. Captain Joseph Kelley was assigned to lead the crew which replaced those lost. He had a reputation for daring leadership and good discipline. There were many stories about him; but one of the best was about a rescue during a northeast storm.

It was a bitter cold winter day, wind howling, with snow squalls. From the lookout tower at the Monomoy Point Station there could be seen a vessel in distress, signaling for help off to the southwest towards Nantucket. In those days the lifeboats were propelled by oars pulled by men. They had no other power.

What to do? The old slogan, "You have to go, but you don't have to come back", seemed to apply in this case. If the life saving crew could reach the vessel in distress, there would be no way they could get back to Monomoy against the gale. And to make matters worse, action had to be decided upon now or never; for in a few hours the winter night would fall.

Kelley made the decision to go. His oarsmen, guided by him at the long helmsman's sweep in the stern, made their target and pulled up under the lee of the vessel. On boarding her, Captain Kelley found that she was taking water fast. His original plan of spending the night aboard while his crew manned the pumps would not work. It was evident that she couldn't stay afloat till morning even with that extra help. What to do?

He ordered the vessel's crew into the frail-looking lifeboat, where he made them lie down beneath the thwarts, thus acting as ballast under the oarsmen's feet. He himself manned the steering sweep in the stern, facing his men. In his belt around his coat was a service revolver.

He told the rescued crewmen, "If one of you tries to stand up, he'll foul up the men at the oars. So I'll shoot him down."

Then they headed for Nantucket far away to the leeward. As night fell the weary men managed to pull safely through the snow squalls into Nantucket harbor.

In later years Captain Joe was in charge of the Old Harbor Station on the North Beach in Chatham. His home, where he visited with his wife and family on his one-day leaves, was on Old Harbor Road. On the front of it he had erected a tower similar to the watchtower on the life saving station. There was an unobstructed view between it and the tower at Old Harbor Station. On every clear evening he and his wife held long chats by blinker-light signals, this being before the days of radio.

After his retirement I used to see him often, and I remember some of his advice about boatmanship. He once built for me a flat-bottomed centerboard skiff, decked forward with a small cockpit, steered by an oar held over the leeward side while under sail. The sail was a "leg o'mutton" sail permanently attached to a small mast which was stuck thru a hole in the deck when in use.

In advising me about sailing it Captain Kelley said, "When you have a sea that sort of mounds up but doesn't break, don't worry about it. But when you have a sea that starts to curl, stay clear, if you can, or you're in trouble."

Bucking The Tides

ABOUT 2:30 of a Saturday afternoon on January 3, 1948, Barbie and I and our 12-year old son Jan left our home in East Harwich and headed for our Camp B (Bar-B), about eight miles down the beach from the Orleans mainland. I had figured we had plenty of time before high tide (due after 5 P.M.) to get through the low places, in spite of yesterday's northeast storm, for the tide-tables showed diminishing heights of tide. But as so often happens, it was later proved that my amateur forecasts of tides are no more reliable as applied to North Beach than are the forecasts of the United States Weather Bureau as applied to the Outer Cape.

Even as we left the upland in Orleans, seas were occasionally lapping across the beach between the dunes near the end of Smith Neck Road, near Mayo's duck farm. We drove down the inside route behind the dunes; but south from the Orleans Coast Guard Station, which was on Little Pochet Island, there were several places where the seas were lapping through between the dunes. I figured we could make it to camp long before high tide.

But long before we reached the cut-through north of the Old Harbor Coast Guard Station, it was evident we could not make it. So we turned disappointedly back for home, still, I thought, well ahead of the high tide due around 5:30. But we got only as far as a half a mile north of Sturg Rice's camp, still a couple of miles short of the Orleans mainland, when our way was stopped by sea water running across the beach between the dunes. Wading out into it with hip boots showed that it was clearly too deep to ford. With dusk coming on and the high tide still to come, it would be hours before we could cross.

Fortunately the key to the lock on our camp was the same as that for Sturg's. We had purposely arranged that so we could check on each other's camps from time to time. This time it was more than just checking!

We went back to Sturg's camp and spent the night there as snug as bugs in rugs. We used our own food and linen, since we had come loaded with supplies for our own camp. But we were surely grateful for the warmth of his fire and lamps and his comfortable beds. For dinner we had cheese canapes with Canadian Club Whisky, fried chicken, asparagus, celery, candy and tea. For breakfast we had orange juice, bacon and eggs, toast and coffee, with Jimmy Taylor's North Beach beach plum jelly.

Before 10 o'clock Sunday morning we had cleaned up and were on our way south for our camp—this time on a *falling* tide. As we drove south we saw hundreds and hundreds of Canadian geese and black ducks, great flocks of both, some in the air and some resting on the marsh or on the water of the bay just beyond it.

Just south of the Old Harbor Coast Guard Station we encountered a huge shallow pool of sea water which had formed in the middle of the beach, as the recent storm had brought waves which had torn away much of the higher dune area near the ocean and had spilled over onto the middle of the beach behind them.

At that time the telephone lines connecting the Coast Guard stations ran the whole length of the "backside" of Cape Cod. A mile or so south of the Old Harbor Station, the pole line turned sharply to the west and ran across the beach to the bay, which was crossed by a heavy underwater telephone cable to the mainland. Our camp was very near where the pole line ended in the cable connection.

Near the place where the pole line made its turn to the west was the "half-way house", which was a very small building used as a checkpoint by Coast Guardsmen on foot patrol. Here they punched in their keys to the time clock as proof that they had actually patrolled to that point. Even though this was the southern terminus of the required patrol, it was still called a "half-way house", because most of such buildings were halfway between the many Coast Guard stations on the backside of the Cape, and the three on Monomoy, and were the common termini for both the station to the north and the one to the south.

This particular one had been set behind the dunes well back from the ocean. But on this day in January we saw that it had been washed by the seas which had eroded the dunes in the recent storm. As I write this account, thirty years later, the location where it stood is out in the ocean, well beyond where the surf breaks on the beach today.

We finally arrived at our camp about 10:30 that Sunday morning, some 20 hours after we had started from home. After a hearty Sunday dinner we were planning to leave about one-thirty, to be ahead of the rising tide's driving water across the beach between the dunes. But we were having such a good time that we decided to stay that night and not even attempt to beat the tide.

So even though the temperature outside was in the low thirties, with a very strong wind blowing from the northeast, we had the temperature inside up to the high 70's with the fire from the out-wood and coal-burning kitchen range. Next morning, of course, our fire had gotten low during the night, but by the time we had finished breakfast the camp was again warm and snug. Reluctantly, well before noon, we left for home, figuring that the low tide on the backside would be about 12:30. We arrived home in the early afternoon with the happy feeling that this had been another day to remember.

The North Beach
At Chatham

Its History

Y Grandfather Nickerson was born in 1833. I was born in 1901. When I was a boy, he told me that when *he* was a boy, he went with his father one day to go clamming on the flat by Cotchpinicut Island in the Old Harbor at Chatham. It was a tall island, he said, with a high bank and with pine trees growing at the top of the bank. He remembered it well, because while his father dug clams, boy-like he took time out to scramble up the bank and climb one of the tall pine trees, in the top of which he had spied a crow's nest—and yes, he stole the eggs from it. For in those days crows were mortal enemies of man. In fact there was a time hereabouts when a man had to kill so many crows before he could marry.

That was the first time I ever heard of Cotchpinicut Island; for by the time I was a boy there was no Cotchpinicut Island protecting the Old Harbor at Chatham. All I ever saw with my own eyes to indicate that it might have existed was a big sand flat which we called "Ram Island Flat". It was a good place (and still is) to build a stand in the ice at low water and shoot ducks and geese when the weather was bad and very cold.

Later, of course, I learned more of Cotchpinicut Island from others, including William C. Smith's "A History of Chatham", in which among other "early land problems", he describes the early ownership claims to "Monomoit Great Beach", which were finally settled in 1729.

In 1711 the Indian heirs gave a deed to nine colonists to all of the Great Beach, "from Sandy Point home to Sipson's Bounds, together with that one island called Cotchpinicut Island, lying between said Monomoy and the Great Beach". Sipson's Bounds' southern boundary ran "from the north side of Cotchpinicut Island easterly to a great rock in or near the channel called Untumsket Rock, thence easterly to and across the beach to the ocean". (*Ref. P. 205, Part II "A History of Chatham", William C. Smith.*)

When the Island was there it protected the Old Harbor lying between it and what is now North Chatham. My Great Great Grandfather Atkins had a dock and fitting-out place at the Cow Yard on the Old Harbor back of Cotchpinicut Island and just south of Scatteree Point. I have a picture of his little topsail schooner, "Morning Star of Chatham", Captain Joshua Atkins, Departing from the Port of Naples", with Mount Vesuvius in the background to show it was *the* Naples.

The "Monomoit Great Beach" referred to here came to be known as the "South Beach", and was so known in my youth until it finally was washed away by the sea. This name distinguished it from "North Beach" which extended southward from Orleans to about opposite Strong Island in olden days. The North Beach was also known as Nauset Beach, to distinguish it from Monomoit Beach (the South Beach). Between the two beaches was the entrance to Monomoit (Pleasant) Bay.

When Governor Bradford came from Plymouth in 1622 in the "Swan" to trade for corn and beans, accompanied by his Indian friend and guide Squanto (Tisquantum), it was through this inlet that he sailed into Pleasant Bay. And it was here on the shores of Pleasant Bay on that voyage that Squanto died. This forced the Pilgrims' trading party to return northward around the Cape to Plymouth, since they had no other pilot for the waters to the south.

It was on the point of the North Beach, a little to the

north of Strong Island that in 1626 the first recorded shipwreck on these shores occurred—that of the "Sparrowhawk". Later in my grandfather's time, her hull reappeared on the backside (ocean side) of the beach, was identified, and turned over to a museum in Plymouth. In the intervening 200-odd years her remains had not moved, but the beach had. So that the "Sparrowhawk", abandoned on the inside of the beach, washed out on the outside—the beach having "rolled over on itself" in the meantime.

When grandfather was a young man he devoted part of his time to codfishing, as did most of his neighbors. Their small sailboats were moored in Pleasant Bay or some of its coves. There were days when it was too rough on the bars in the inlet for them to go out into the ocean. Grandfather told me that he used to go up on the hill back of his barn and look through his spyglass down the bay between Strong Island and Fox Hill at the bars to see if it were too rough.

Sometimes the little fleet of small-boat fishermen would sail down to just inside the point of the South Beach, where the deep water ran right close to the shore, and nose their bows into the edge of the beach. Then they would jump ashore and climb a dune for a look at the bars to decide whether they thought it would be safe to go out.

Gradually, "by fits and starts", the entrance worked its way southward. As it did so the North Beach grew longer and the South Beach grew shorter, 'til within my memory the South Beach disappeared entirely, and today (1963) the point of the North Beach is a half mile or so southeast of Morris Island. As the inlet moved south, the mainland, the other beaches on the shore, and Cotchpinicut Island were subjected to erosion, as the opening to the ocean came opposite them. This accounts for the sandy cliffs all along the easterly shore of Chatham and on the east of Strong Island. It also explains why Cotchpinicut Island disappeared. By 1912, when the Chatham Bars Inn was built, the inlet was directly opposite the front entrance, about where I built my camp on North Beach in 1926.

By that time, however, the point of the North Beach was more than a half mile south of my camp. I remember that under certain conditions of sea tide we had to be careful in sailing my "sharpie" across from the camp. Occasionally a sea would break on the shallow bar lying between the camp and the Chatham Bars Inn and divide the two channels, one lying just inside the beach and the other running along the mainland shore.

When the Chatham Beach Club was built in 1928, the inlet was almost opposite it, the point of North Beach still being to the north. Since then the point has moved rapidly southward. As late as 1945 it was north of Morris Island, but today (1963) it is well to the south of it, even south of the new cut-through, which is south of Morris Island. In fact from the point of the North Beach today you can look through the cut-through, past the outer shore of Hardings Beach, to Harwichport.

Even though the ownership of the South Beach was finally settled in 1729, there remained conflicting claims to parts of it, due to the salt meadows on its westerly side which were valuable for fodder. One might have supposed, when the South Beach had washed away completely, that claims of ownership would have disappeared with it. But such was not the case.

In 1924 a claimant to meadowlands on the North Beach in Chatham gave deeds to Oscar C. Nickerson and to George S. Bearse, both of Chatham. Most of this beach, lying within the town of Chatham, had been *created* within the previous 75 years. In the meantime several camps and a Coast Guard station had been built on it.

In 1958 the question of title was finally resolved by the Superior Court of Barnstable County. Each of the owners of camps then existing wound up with a clear title. Bearse and Nickerson agreed on a division, giving each a clear title to portions of the beach. Among the claimants was Mrs. Eleanor H. Edson who had no camp, but was claiming under a title to the *South Beach*, which *used* to be where the North Beach was in 1958. She got clear title to a portion of the beach too.

But most important, the Town of Chatham got clear title to nearly four miles extending northward from the point of the North Beach to just south of my camp, opposite the Chatham Bars Inn. Back in 1926, my father, Oscar C. Nickerson, had given deeds to me and to B. Ralph Bevins to all the beach southward from a point 500 feet south of the Old Harbor Coast Guard Station. After Bevins' death in 1950, I acquired his interest from his estate. Shortly afterwards I deeded to the Town of Chatham what is now nearly four miles at the southerly end of the beach. When the law suits were settled in 1958, Bearse also gave a similar deed to the Town, thus giving the Town unquestionable title.

Since 1958 I have given all but about six acres of my remaining beachland to the Town, and my brother, E. Carleton Nickerson, and George S. Bearse have given additional tracts. The result is that except for an area less than about a mile each way, north and south of the Old Harbor Coast Guard Station, all of the North Beach lying in the Town of Chatham is owned by the Town. Likewise all of the beach from the Chatham boundary line north to Eastham and lying in the Town of Orleans (except for one 500-foot strip) is owned by the Town of Orleans.

This entire beach lies within the boundaries of the Cape Cod National Seashore, authorized by Congress in 1961 and established by the Secretary of the Interior in 1963.

The Act of Congress authorizing the establishment of the Cape Cod National Seashore provides, however, that the Federal Government may not acquire title to town-owned lands without the concurrence of the town. Thus the towns of Chatham and Orleans may have to decide whether they will continue to own their own beaches, or whether they will turn them over to the Department of the Interior as part of the National Seashore.

Meanwhile the beach is constantly changing, as it has since before the days of the Indians. But it is always there, no matter how much it changes and no matter that ownership was "finally settled" in 1729.

The New Inlet In 1987

I N 1963 I wrote a piece about the North Beach at Chatham. What follows is intended as a sequel to that piece.

In January 1987 the sea broke through the North Beach about opposite Chatham Light. By now (May 1987) this new inlet has become well established, and there is every indication that it will remain as the entrance to the Pleasant Bay estuary for many years to come. It is now over a half-mile wide and the ebb tides run out through it at speeds estimated to be five or six knots, thus assuring its continuance.

The question arises, "Why did it break through *here* and not much farther to the north, as had been the case in previous cycles, the last of which was about 150 years ago?"

There seems to be one substantial principle involved. There must be sufficient relatively deep water on the inside of the beach, where the tide is hours later than on the outside, so that once opened the breach is subject to strong and sustained outward-running currents on the ebb tide. When the previous breaches occurred, there was just such a situation inside the barrier beach opposite to and even well north of Strong Island.

But during the last 150 years, the frequent overwashes from the sea, between the dunes and into the easterly end of Pleasant Bay, merely deposited vast quantities of sand onto the inner marsh lands and into the easterly end of the Bay itself, until gradually there was no deep water along the inside of the beach to the north. There were only marshland and sand flats which were often exposed at low tide.

To be sure there were within my memory overwashes from the sea which could be crossed only at low tide, notably one in the early 1940's which stayed open for several weeks. But the lack of deep water on the inside of the beach prevented a strong outward current on the ebb tide. Thus it would always be only a short time before the cut would be filled in with sand and so disappear.

I remember seeing in one such cut the imprint of a hoof in the black muck of what was once salt meadow. William C. Smith, in his "A History of Chatham," tells of cattle being left to forage on the beach. Or was the hoof-mark that of an ox used to haul salt hay from where it was harvested to boats waiting to take it to the mainland?

But to get back to our *new* inlet. There has been another factor at work these many years. As the North Beach continued to extend southward, it was fed not only by sand eroded from the cliffs at Eastham and Wellfleet, but also by the movement of sand from its own ocean front towards the south. This resulted in the northerly portions of the beach becoming narrower as the point extended southward.

For example, the site of the Old Harbor Life Saving Station, which fifty years ago was about a quarter-mile in from the ocean is now in the surf. And the same is true of the site of the "half-way house" south of the station, where the Coast Guard patrols punched in with their keys, which was well towards the middle of the beach. The broadest part of the beach was at or near the point, and the narrowest continued to be some miles north of the point. Coupled with this movement was a sporadic erosion of the dune line on the inside of the beach, thus contributing to its narrowing. Finally in the storm on January 1987, the last thin line was washed out at the northernmost place where there was "deep" water on the inside. Thus we have the new inlet.

What of its future? First of all there will always be an inlet to Pleasant Bay somewhere. The Bay itself, and its many springs and streams leading into it, generates sufficient quantities of "new" fresh water so that it must flow out somewhere. It is quite possible that in the next two or three centuries the easterly end of Pleasant Bay will become a salt marsh. This has happened at Nauset in Eastham, where marshes now fill the harbor in which the French explorers anchored in 1605. But there is still a Nauset Inlet.

I believe that the newly created island, currently being called South Beach, will attach itself to Monomoy, and there will again be quiet water between it and the mainland. But the northerly end of this South Beach will gradually erode, and the point of the North Beach will continue its way southward again. During this process there will again be erosion of the mainland and of Morris Island as the inlet moves south. But this process will take years, even decades, to accomplish natures's design. There is nothing new about this, if we look at the past, and remember the changes even in one man's lifetime.

When I was a boy, the beach extended for more than a thousand yards offshore from Morris Island. There was a life saving station there which was moved back in my childhood, and there was the Chatham Beach Hotel. When the Chatham Beach Club was built in 1928, we built a footbridge about 360 feet long across the water (which flowed in from Stage Harbor) to the beach. The inlet was still north of there. Just north of the new inlet lie the remains of a schooner, which was wrecked on the point when I was a boy, and I remember playing on her hulk afterwards.

I have mentioned the widening of the beach at or near the point, as it makes its way south. There is a curious cadence to this process. First a bar makes up in a southeasterly direction from the point. The surf breaking on this bar creates a special roar. In the days before power boats, local fishermen, coming in from offshore in their sailboats, listened for it when visibility was poor. They called it "the roaring bull".

Gradually the bar becomes a beach, and as it does so hooks around in a southwesterly direction until eventually its end joins onto the main part of the beach. This leaves a hole on the middle of the beach which usually has an outlet into the waters on the inside. I can think of about a half dozen such holes I have seen, and in which I have found quohogs or shot ducks and geese. There still exist some of these, or their remnants, notably "Hartwell's Hole" and "The Hospital", now four miles or more from where the point of North Beach was last summer. This process will continue as long as there is a South Beach. Thus there is a succession of "roaring bulls", which ultimately become additions to the point of North Beach.

Then there arises the question of ownership. Before the new inlet opened, creating an island of that portion of the former North Beach which lies south of the inlet, the ownership to what has now become an island was clearly in the Town of Chatham, even though it lay within the authorized boundaries of the Cape Cod National Seashore. If and when the new South Beach joins onto Monomoy at some point beyond Morris Island, where will the title of the town end, as it joins land owned by another agency of the Federal Government and operated as a "wilderness area"?

As far as the newly established point of North Beach is concerned, that part of the beach has already been owned by the Town of Chatham, since it was given to the Town in the 1950's. As it again extends its way southward, the accretion to it will likewise belong to the town. Under the terms of the Act of Congress in 1961, authorizing the establishment of the Cape Cod National Seashore, any land belonging to the Town may be acquired by the national government for the park service, only with the concurrence of the Town.

Thus Chatham now owns *two* ocean-front beaches, part of the North and all of the South. What will be Chatham's policy for the long term, with respect to these valuable but constantly changing assets?

FOOTNOTE: Regarding town's ownership of beach land.

The Chatham-Orleans boundary line runs across the beach about opposite to Strong Island. The Town of Orleans has owned the beach from there northward since sometime in the 1850's. If the breakthrough in 1987 had occured where it did about 150 years ago, the point of the North Beach would have been in Orleans. As it worked its way southward over the intervening century and a half, the ownership of the beach which thus acreted would be in the owner of the land to which the acretion was made. Thus the Town of Orleans, if it owned the beach then as it does now, would have become the owner of the newly created North Beach in Chatham. This is just the situation now existing at the northerly end of the beach owned by the Town of Orleans. There the progression of Nauset Inlet to the *north* has, over many recent years, resulted in the Town of Orleans being the owner of the northerly end of its Nauset Beach, which lies within the boundaries of the Town of Eastham.

One Cape Codder's Reflections

SOME reflections on the first three quarters of the 20th century from the point of view of one Cape Codder. . . . .

I was born in 1901. I am writing this in 1978. During this span of 77 years, the world has seen greater changes in man's ways of life than in any like period since the invention of the wheel, or the shift from a nomadic hunting economy to one based upon agriculture.

In the third quarter of the century these changes have had increasing impact upon the underdeveloped areas of the world, as the effects of development and invention in the industrialized nations have spread worldwide. And these changes have not only affected the material aspects of man's life, but the social and religious as well.

It occurs to me, therefore, that a bird's eye view, as seen from a tiny "back-wash" on the edges of the mainstream, namely from a Cape Codder on Cape Cod, might be worth writing down. This is not intended to be an autobiography, although it will be bound to include some personal experiences of my life. Nor is it intended to be any more than some reflections, as the title implies.

My family has lived on Cape Cod since the middle of the 17th century, a span of more than 300 years. My comments, then, may include some relating to my forebears as well as to myself.

TRANSPORTATION

When I was a boy growing up in Chatham, the roads were dirt roads and the vehicles were horse-drawn, for the most part. I can remember the building of a water-bound macadam road to replace the dirt road past our home on Old Harbor Road. I was fascinated at the maneuvering of the engines and cars in the terminal yard of the Chatham Railroad, which had been built only 14 years before I was born.

The first blacktop roads were made by spreading hot liquid tar or asphalt, from a sprinkler at the rear of a horse-drawn wagon, over the hardening surface of the dirt roads. This was then covered with sand spread evenly by men with shovels. Such little traffic as there was, together with the sun, created a thin but hard surface which was a big improvement, but under today's traffic would hardly have lasted more than a few months.

In winter when a heavy snowstorm sometimes piled deep drifts on the roads, the men living along them turned out in force and shoveled through the deepest drifts, always being careful to leave a good layer of snow in the cuts to accomodate the runners of sleighs. The more experienced shovelers always carried a little piece of salt pork rind in their pockets, which they used to grease the metal surface of their shovels so that the snow could not stick to them.

When the automobile first appeared during my childhood, it was not used in winter; it was put on jacks under the axles in the barn to save the tires. So no thought was given to snow removal for clearing the roads for automobile traffic. In fact the first trucks I remember had hard rubber tires and came into use on the main roads only after they had been "hardened" with oil.

The first passenger car I remember was a Cadillac two-seater, which cranked from the side and was steered by a tiller operated from the back seat. (Really designed for back seat drivers!) By the time I was 12 years old my father was the proud owner of a Studebaker touring car. Among my chores was crawling under the car with a can of hard grease and keeping the grease cups full and their caps screwed down.

Until then, if you were going only four or five miles, it was on foot; up to 10 or 15 miles, it was by horse and carriage. For greater distances it was by train.

For example, when I was nine my father took me to Provincetown for the dedication of the Pilgrim Memorial Monument. We took an early morning train from Chatham to Harwich, where we transferred to an excursion train from Boston crowded with other passengers going to the big event.

In Provincetown the long train ran out onto the wharf, where dad and I climbed onto the roof of a shed from which we were better able to see the parade and the arrival at the dock of President and Mrs. Howard Taft. After the impressive dedication exercises on High Pole Hill, we went aboard one of the numerous Navy ships at anchor in the harbor, the battleship "Connecticut." I was much impressed with the bright dress uniforms of the Marines.

Similarly when we went, as almost everyone did, to the annual Barnstable County Fair and Cattle Show in Barnstable, we went by train, usually a special excursion train run just for that event.

Even later when I was in Chatham High School, the boys and girls from South Chatham and the northwest section of town came to school by train, riding between South Chatham and Chatham depots. The timetable was arranged so that the incoming train arrived a few minutes before school and the afternoon train left shortly after school. My cousins, who lived in Sagamore, also went to and from the high school in Bourne-dale by train.

Sometimes on Sundays or holidays we went by carriage to visit friends or relatives in East Harwich and Harwich.

By the time I was graduated from Chatham High School in 1917, all this had begun to change. The automobile had begun to take over as the means of personal transportation. Henry Ford had shocked the business community by announcing the $5.00 a day minimum wage in his factory, thus attracting the best workmen from all over the country, at a time when the going rate for common labor was less than $2.00 a day. He was turning out Model T's, which sold for around four hundred dollars or a little more.

Woodrow Wilson had just been re-elected President on the slogan, "He has kept us out of the war", which had already been raging for two and half years. Of course he declared war in April 1917 within a few weeks after his inauguration in March. But he had been elected in November 1916 because he'd kept us out of the war!

There were many other manufacturers of automobiles, many more than there are now. But the Model T dominated the burgeoning market. Even the multitudinous jokes and songs about it helped sell it. Anyone who could spin the crank under the radiator, while pulling out the wire choke which stuck out under the radiator on the right-hand side, could operate one. Of course cranking had to be done with the spark lever under the left-hand side of the steering wheel retarded, and you had to rush to advance it before the engine stalled, at the same time advancing the hand throttle under the right-hand side of the steering wheel just a little.

There was no foot-operated accelerator. The clutch pedal for the left foot remained in neutral until the hand brake was released, and then you pushed it to the floor for "low" and released it to spring back for "high". The brake pedal was on the right, and when it got worn you could always stop the car by pressing down on the reverse pedal between the other two.

The gasoline tank was under the front seat on the right. To check on your supply you removed the seat cushion, unscrewed the cap on the top of the tank and inserted a measuring stick with marks on it like a ruler. By seeing how far from the end was wet, you knew how much gasoline you had. To fill the tank there were no gasoline pumps such as we now have. Instead the gasoline vendor (often a grocery store, repair garage or the like, since there were no service stations) would fill a five-gallon can and pour the contents usually through a soft chamois filter into the tank.

For ordinary repairs you needed a pair of pliers, a wrench, a screw driver and a wad of chewing gum—and of course a flat iron bar and a hammer to replace the clincher tires, which blew or punctured at an average rate of about once per 100 miles.

But Americans were on wheels in privately owned and operated vehicles. All we needed, we thought, were better roads. And that wasn't too big a problem when normal driving speed was 25 to 35 miles per hour, and you expected to have to shift into low speed to go up almost any hill.

All this brought great changes to Cape Cod. To be sure most summer visitors arrived by train and stayed for at least half the summer. But gradually the auto traffic took over, at first only chauffeur-driven cars of the wealthy, but soon owners driving family cars.

Along the main roads and especially in the villages people began taking summer boarders in their homes. Presently summer boarding houses run by "mom and pop" developed. Then in the thirties and forties there sprang up roadside cabin colonies—small separate buildings offering overnight accommodations. Along with these came small roadside restaurants. It wasn't until after World War II that there were any motels as we know them today on Cape Cod.

Meanwhile, as more of the well-to-do came by train and in their autos, they discovered the joy of having their own summer homes on the Cape. They did this in Chatham, I noticed, after having stayed for a vacation at such hotels and inns as the Chatham Bars Inn, Hotel Mattaquason, Old Harbor Inn, Hawes House, and Dill Cottages. They included both the wealthy and the merely comfortably well-off families. They included tycoons, school teachers, lawyers, white collar junior jobholders, salesmen, and increasingly skilled working men with grease under their finger nails.

As a result we Cape Codders were exposed to a greater variety of people than most people who lived in small cities. This was very stimulating intellectually and socially, as well as economically. We looked forward in the spring to their coming. I must admit though that we heaved a communal sign of relief when they left in the fall.

In the winter we had plenty of time to reflect on and digest our contacts with our summer visitors. And we were thrown back upon our own resources for the winter months. Remember that there were no movies until World War I (1914–18), no radio, television or electricity, and even when that first came it was for lights only, and was turned off around midnight.

TOWN SERVICES

In those days the operation of our town was much simpler. The selectmen also served as "Overseers of the Poor", (welfare had no such meaning as it has come to have now). Each year the town raised and appropriated sufficient money, usually not more than $1,000, to care for its poor, most of whom lived in a big two-story almshouse on Old Harbor Road, opposite the end of Depot Street. While I was still a boy this was abandoned, and the poor were boarded around in families by arrangements made with the Overseers of the Poor.

The poor were usually elderly people, destitute, with no families of their own to take them in. If they had any family it was there that they lived, proudly avoiding "going on the town". Almost every family in our neighborhood, when I was a child, included some indigent relatives who usually earned their keep by baby-sitting or doing household chores or odd jobs around the place. Both they and their families took pride in not being dependent.

We had no fire department. When a fire broke out in the woods, often set by sparks from the smokestack of the engine of a train, the able-bodied men were expected to drop what they were doing, grab a shovel and go the fire. We did have fire wardens, but it was their principle job to organize and direct the men who came to fight the fire. This was usually done by shoveling dirt along the leading edges of the fire, thus narrowing its breadth and eventually choking it off.

But if it really got raging and into the tops of the trees, it often became necessary to build a backfire. To do this the fire warden would line his men up along an open place, usually a sandy road downwind of the fire, and start a new fire which they forced to burn to the windward. Then when the main fire reached the backfire there was nothing for it to feed on.

House fires presented a different problem. They were rare indeed, but I remember two that happened in 1916 or 1917. One broke out during the performance of a play written by Carol Wight based on the local scene. As the play was drawing to its end, it was interrupted by an announcement that a house was on fire on Main Street.

Actually two buildings burned that night. First, the one housing Ryder's Barber Shop and Freeman's Haberdashery; then the house next door of Oscar Howard, which caught from the first building. Dr. Frank Worthing's house, next to Howard's, was threatened and it caught fire, but was saved by a large and energetic "bucket brigade". This was a human chain which passed buckets of water from a nearby cistern along the line to those at the end who threw the water onto the threatened areas of Dr. Worthing's house.

Meanwhile others were busily engaged in removing the contents of the house, which they piled across the street. All three buildings were located on the east side of Main Street, opposite what is now the entrance to the Kate Gould Park, southerly towards Chatham Bars Avenue.

The other big house fire occurred soon after and destroyed a large summer home on Sea View Street (Wicked Hill), near where the first tee of the Chatham Bars Inn golf course is now located. With these demonstrations of need, it was not long (the next town meeting, I think) before the town voted to buy a modern fire engine.

Since there was no "town water", the engine had two big chemical tanks, hose, ladders and other equipment, including a bell mounted in front of the driver which was operated from the front seat by pulling on a rope. There was no windshield. This didn't matter much because its maximum speed was around 25 miles per hour. It was manned entirely by volunteers, who organized themselves and drilled regularly. It was like a social club, and the members got paid a small fee only when they responded to a fire.

In my boyhood Chatham had no police department. It didn't really need one. Each year the town meeting elected several constables, usually men of mature years and some political standing in the town. They appeared in their blue uniforms on special occasions, such as town meetings, parades, or a large gathering such as a big dance. I think they were paid by the day for each appearance and were subject to call by the selectmen when needed.

It wasn't until sometime in the twenties that we had a police department, and even then at first it consisted of one man, full time. He was Everett Eldredge, a local man who had won distinction in the Navy as a pugilist under the name of "Gunboat Eldredge". He was tough physically. One of his hobbies was deer hunting with bow and arrow. He also liked to vacation out in the woods, subsisting on what he could catch to eat.

But he was best remembered by the numerous young people whom he took under his wing when they "ran afoul of the law". Taking them into custody was a last resort. He preferred to counsel them, usually ending with a stern warning against future transgressions. In most cases this was enough, and later most of them felt a deep and warm appreciation of his fatherly guidance.

200TH ANNIVERSARY AND OTHER ENTERTAINMENT

In the summer of 1912, when I was 11, Chatham celebrated the 200th Anniversary of its incorporation as a town. Preparations began the winter before this big event. I remember sitting with Alfred Harding, the town clerk, in his little office in the back of his store on Main Street. He was in charge of the badges and souvenirs, and I arranged with him to hawk these items from a large basket on my arm on the days of the celebration.

The big parade (with two bands) was scheduled for the morning of the first day, but because of heavy rain it was postponed to the second day, which turned out to be brightly sunny. Most of the organizations in the town were represented by elaborate floats (horse-drawn, of course). The G.A.R. of Civil War Veterans was well represented.

There was a grand ball at night in the Town Hall, which stood about where the Intermediate School now stands, between the High School and Main Street. There was a meeting room with kitchen facilities on the first floor, with the selectmen's office behind it in one corner, reached by a separate outside door. On the second floor was the ballroom, where town meetings were held. It had a stage, and theatrical productions were also presented there.

It was here I saw my first movie. It was shown as a part of a week-long "medicine show" of the Kickapoo Indians, held each summer. Their pitchman used the intermissions to sell "Sagwa", a secret formula good for man or beast, and alleged to cure anything from heaves and spavin in a horse to liver complaints, indigestion, headache and neuralgia. Today we get much the same pitch on television commercials, only more sophisticated and somewhat restrained by laws to protect the consumer.

When I was old enough to start going to dances in the Town Hall, I remember being amused by signs on the walls reading, "No Turkey Trot, Bunny Hug, Spitting or Throwing Peanut Shells on the Floor."

Before the movie theatre was built on Main Street (about 1914), Charlie Lake used to show movies regularly in the Town Hall, using a small booth built in the balcony for his projector. Between reels he showed a slide on the screen reading, "3 minutes, please, while we change the film". Pearl White in the "Perils of Pauline" was a favorite serial.

There was also a third floor, which was used as quarters for the Independent Order of Red Men, a fraternal society.

On Sundays we all went to church, walking the mile or so from our house on Old Harbor Road to the Methodist Episcopal Church. In those days the minister always wore a Prince Albert frock coat (no robes). The sermons were usually based on the Old Testament, with frequent references to the God of Isaac and the God of Jacob. As a small boy I got into trouble when my parents caught me mimicking in our pew the exaggerated gestures of the preacher.

I remember too being fascinated by the crosshatch of seamy lines on the back of the thoroughly scrubbed and carefully barbered neck of the old gentleman who always sat directly in front of us. I found it hard to understand, and to this day I still do, why Jacob, who was a scoundrel, should have been regarded as a hero, and his brother Esau condemned for having "sold his birthright for a mess of potage".

Also on Sundays I went to Sunday School, which was conducted in the half-basement vestry of the church. I well remember one of my Sunday School teachers, named Bradford Bloomer. Weekdays in season he was a lobster fisherman. In the summer he lived alone all week in a camp on the edge of the "Powder Hole", a harbor for small craft near the end of Monomoy Point. He would go down there with his powerboat Sunday evening or Monday morning and return with his week's catch on Saturday.

But most important, once each summer he would take the boys of his small Sunday School class with him to spend an unforgettable week at the end of Monomoy. Each day he would go to haul his lobster pots, but we boys had a wonderful time roaming about the area.

But to get back to the 200th Anniversary. There was a series of baseball games. Such games were usually played at the "Cattlefield" (on Bar Cliff Avenue). But on this occasion the games were at "Rockwell Field" on "Rink Hill" overlooking the Mill Pond, and in the same general area as the other daytime events of the celebration. Field events included three-legged races, in which each pair of contestants had the right leg of one strapped securely to the left leg of his partner. There was the greased pig chase, in which a small pig was heavily coated with lard. If you could catch the pig and hold him, he was yours. Then there was the "greased pole", a mast set in the ground with a five dollar bill in an envelope fastened at its top. If you could climb the greased pole and reach the five dollars, it was yours.

There were also many more serious events. At Rink Hill, near where the old windmill is now located off Cross Street, a huge tent had been erected on the bluff overlooking the Mill

Pond. Here in the middle of the big day, a banquet was served and the diners listened for a couple of hours to speeches appropriate to the occasion. I remember that it was there that I first tasted frozen pudding (with rum in it).

Afterwards there were dory races and demonstrations of the work of the Life Saving Service (now the Coast Guard) in the Mill Pond, observed by the crowd on the banks of the bluff. At that time there were four life saving stations in Chatham, manned for the most part by local men. So the contests of capsizing and righting the lifeboats, the breeches buoy drills, and the rowing race between two of the stations were of great interest.

When the celebration was all over and the accounts of the various committees (some 20 of them) finally rendered, there was a surplus left over of $143.37. This was spent towards the printing of a 120-page booklet entitled," The Chatham Celebration 1712–1912". Included in it was a record of receipts and expenditures, which I summarize as follows:

RECEIPTS

(a)	From friends, including $100 from Norfolk Hunt Club (21)	$ 217.00
(b)	From summer residents, not natives (27)	309.00
(c)	From summer residents, natives (12)	216.00
(d)	From natives, not residents (22)	125.00
(e)	From residents, not natives (26)	98.50
(f)	From native residents (87)	214.50
		$1,199.00

From Town of Chatham appropriation	750.00
Income from sale of dinner tickets	803.75
Ball tickets, badges, pennants, etc.	252.00
Total income	$3,166.75

EXPENDITURES

For tents, grounds, etc.	$ 287.36
Parade committee	99.87
Dinner committee	1,022.21
Committee on speakers (7 dinner tickets)	7.00
Basketball committee	17.25
Baseball committee	106.99
Old home social and reception committee	73.54
Water carnival committee	178.15
Reception and ball committee	136.98
Music committee (including $268.45 for Salem Cadet Band and $84.00 for its transportation)	449.12
Decorations committee	201.25
Police committee (for deputy sheriffs and constables)	63.90
Historic sites committee	42.45
Printing and advertising	112.02
Committee on souvenirs and badges	164.50
Committee on reception of invited guests	32.00
For Veterans of Civil War expense	7.14
For postcards and printing of secretary	21.75
Total expenditures	$3,023.38
Balance of receipts over expenditures	$ 143.37

Certain facts should be borne in mind in thinking of the 1912 celebration. For example, censuses of the Town of Chatham show that its population in 1910 (1,564) was less than it had been in 1820 (1,630). Censuses from 1765 (678) show a gradual increase until it peaked in 1860 at 2,710. Every census taken at five-year intervals after 1860 showed a steady, but gradual decline till it was 1,564 in 1910.

The dinner tickets sold for $1.00 each, even though it was a sumptuous menu, including turkey, ham, tongue, mashed potatoes, vegetable salad, olives and pickles, rolls and butter, assorted creams and sherbets, frozen pudding, assorted cakes and coffee. Approximately 800 dinner tickets were sold, but with the tickets given away to invited guests, the cost was about $200 more than the revenue.

There was no police force, that function being covered by deputy sheriffs and constables. There were no automobiles in the parade, only horse-drawn vehicles and people on foot or horseback. And five years later, when I was graduated from Chatham High School in 1917, I was one of a class of seven.

IMPACT OF WORLD WAR I

In the five years from 1913 to 1918, several major events took place in Chatham which influenced deeply its future development.

In 1913–14 the Marconi Radio Station was built in Chathamport. There were five or six 400-foot steel masts erected. They were lined up precisely to aim at installations in Potsdam, Germany. The engineers had a difficult time preserving this alignment and the spacing between the towers. They had to avoid having any of them set in one of the numerous fresh water ponds in that area. The materials for the construction came in on freight cars to the railroad terminal in Chatham. From there they were hauled in wagons to the construction sites.

In addition to the power plant and work building, the Marconi Company built several houses for the families of their employees and even a small brick hotel. These buildings were clustered together near the head of Ryders Cove and are still in use today.

The radio station was ready to go into operation about the first of August, 1914. But World War I broke out on

August 4th. Immediately the United States Government took over the station and posted Marine guards to protect it.

So it was never used as it was originally intended, for communications with Potsdam. In fact by the time the war was over in November 1918, the technical advances in the use of radio had become so great that the 400-foot masts were obsolete; later they were torn down. The radio station has been in continuous operation ever since, primarily for ship-to-shore communication.

I remember being in the operating room one evening in the 1920's, as a guest of the superintendent, Fred Heiser, who pointed out to me men at various desks who were "working" ships in the North Atlantic, the South Atlantic, the Mediterranean, the Red Sea and the Pacific, all at the same time.

The men usually stayed on for long periods, long enough at least to meet and marry some of the local girls. For example, my cousin Gladys Nickerson married Tom Cave, and her sister Madge married Leslie Strong, both of whom came originally as operators at the radio station.

About 1912 an eccentric and talented young mechanical engineer from a wealthy Boston family, who owned a lovely old summer home converted from a year-round home in North Chatham, decided to stay in Chatham and make his life work here. Gould Weld built a large steel and hollow-tile factory, with a private sidetrack, on what had been the local baseball field. He called his project the Weld Manufacturing Company.

For a number of years this land had served as the baseball field, with home plate about where the westerly end of the factory building stood. The baseball field was moved to private land known as the "Cattle Field", on the southerly side of Bar Cliff Avenue just west of Old Harbor Road.

Weld Manufacturing conducted experimental engineering projects for the rapidly growing automotive industry. Gould Weld was a "nut" on internal combustion engines as related to automobiles. The machinery, such as lathes, was run by leather belts served by overhead shafts just under the roof and running lengthwise in the building.

Then came the war! Long before the United States became a participant, Weld's shop was turning out "gains" for three-inch artillery shells for the Imperial Russian Government.

The factory was very busy; machinists and other skilled workmen came to Chatham. The area was enclosed with a high steel fence topped by barbed wire and patrolled by armed guards. The plant worked around the clock, seven days a week. A steam plant on the premises provided the power and light. Industry and high wages had come to Chatham.

A problem was that the "gains", which were only a few inches long, had to be made to extremely close tolerance, and there were too many rejections by the inspectors.

When the war ended the company went bankrupt. Gould Weld was killed in an automobile accident while driving his chain-driven sportscar. His business partner ran away under dubious circumstances. The succeeding management was inept. Then of course the Imperial Russian Government collapsed.

For several years Edwin Eldredge used the building as a repair shop. Finally about 1925 it was bought by my father, and was used for the storage of building materials by the Nickerson Lumber Company until 1975. At the time of this purchase, the lumber yard, store and office were across the railroad track on land belonging to the Chatham Railroad Company, about where the Elementary School now stands. In 1926 the lumber company's operation was moved across the tracks, a new store and office were built on Depot Street, using the land behind it and the factory building for storage of lumber and building materials.

For a brief period in World War II, it again became a factory, turning out heavy packing cases and pre-built doghouses and yards for the military. In October 1975, Nickerson

241

Lumber Company closed its Chatham plant, and the approximately four acres of land and the buildings on it were sold.

In 1916 the United States Navy purchased the land at the end of Nickerson's Neck and by 1917 the Naval Air Stations was in operation. Construction continued all through World War I. In fact the second and largest airplane hangar was not completed until 1919, long after the war had ended. But they did have in 1917–18 a hangar for seaplanes, a huge one for blimps, and scores of barracks and other buildings.

One of their problems was the inadequacy of an immediate supply of fresh water. This was solved by installing wells and pumps about where the northeastern side of Riverbay Estates now is and piping the water from there.

The planes which were flown from the station were wood-framed biplanes with two pontoons (Curtis Wrights, I think), and later Liberty flying boats, in addition to the blimps. The first west to east trans-Atlantic flight took off from there in 1919. But by the early 1920's the station was abandoned and most of the buildings were torn down by wreckers. For years we called that point "Concrete Acres", because of the thousands of tons of concrete rubble left from the foundations and paved areas.

In my boyhood there had been a clubhouse in East Harwich on Pleasant Bay, just north of where Wequasset Inn now stands. This was the base for sailboat racing for many years. But by 1918 it had fallen by the wayside. In that year a new Chatham Yacht Club was organized, with a class of "Bay Birds". There must have been about 50 of them, and the summer races, twice a week, were a source of great enjoyment to both participants and onlookers.

Later a splinter group established the Stage Harbor Yacht Club for racing in Stage Harbor and Nantucket Sound. But the races and regattas on Pleasant Bay in the summer are colorful indeed, with nearly a 100 boats competing at times.

SCHOOLING

In the spring of 1917, I went with the senior class of Orleans High School on their annual trip to Washington, D.C. In those days, it was customary for senior high school classes to spend the previous two years raising the money to pay for such a trip, which was looked forward to as a really exciting and educational experience. For some reason the Chatham senior class did not go that year, so my father arranged for me to join the Orleans class.

We left by train from Orleans, changed at Tremont (near Middleboro) to a train for Fall River, where we took the overnight boat to New York. We spent a day and a night in New York, visiting the Museum of Natural History and seeing the sights, including a dazzling performance at the Hippodrome. I remember the show included animals and big choruses, almost like a circus. Then we went by train to see the sights and wonders of the nation's Capitol, before coming home by train at the end of our week. For most of us it was our first trip beyond eastern Massachusetts, and we were much impressed by all we saw and heard.

In September 1917 I entered Phillips Exeter Academy as an "upper middler". My good teachers at Chatham had prepared me well for the strict discipline of the teaching at Exeter. While I did have to study hard, I had little difficulty in graduating as a senior in June 1918, and being accepted for entrance to Harvard College in September.

At Exeter I came in contact with boys and faculty whose world was different from any I had known. I had never seen a football game, a professional baseball game, a rowing shell or a ballet, nor heard a concert of professional quality.

The boys were from all over the United States, in fact some from foreign countries. I remember one Physit Arthachinta from Siam, who was bright and charming. As an example of how very unsophisticated I was, I still remember the incident when a boy asked to "borrow" a nickel from me for a telephone call, and then never paid it back, much to my surprise.

In September 1918 I spent the weekend before college opened with my sister and her husband in South Weymouth. He was working in the Navy at Fore River Shipyards in Quincy. Sunday morning he took me to see the launching of a new submarine. At midday dinner I did not feel well, left the table and went to lie down. That was the last thing I really knew until several days later, I had influenza, and I was lucky to be alive. Several of my friends and acquaintances died of it in that awful epidemic.

My entrance to Harvard was delayed for a week or two until I recovered. Then all the freshmen 18 or older having been inducted into the Students Army Training Corps (S.A.T.C.), I found myself segregated with the others under 18 (I was 17), in what was called the Junior Company, not actually in the service, though we were in uniform. We were housed in the dormitories in the yard. I was in Holworthy Hall. We had the same classes and drills as all the other freshmen.

In October I had the idea of getting parental permission to join the Marines, having found that I could meet their physical requirements. I shall never forget meeting my father between trains at the South Station in Boston, where we sat on stools at the horse-shoe-shaped counter in the lunchroom and discussed the situation.

He remarked (this being late October 1918), "Either this war will be over by Christmas or it will last a long, long time. So why don't you wait till Christmas. If the war isn't over by then, I'll give my consent for you to join the Marines".

Since Christmas was less than two months away, this seemed reasonable and I agreed. The war ended with the Armistice, November 11, 1918.

We and our allies had won the "War to End Wars", the "War to Make the World Safe for Democracy". Forever after the world was to be blessed with unending peace.

Nevertheless the boys who joined the Marines in October 1918 didn't get back till years later, after fighting with the White Russians against the Bolsheviks in Siberia. My father was wise and I was lucky.

My freshman roommate was Bill Brewster, whose father was a teacher at Andover Academy. He was an enthusiastic fencer, and among many other things, introduced me to using toilet paper for a handkerchief when one had a cold. (There was no Kleenex then).

At the end of my freshman year, I got a job for the summer as a tutor for 10-year-old Billy Miller, who was living with his grandparents at their summer home in Chester, Nova Scotia. I was there for three months, from mid-June to mid-September. It was the first freedom from war in the lives of the young people who had lived it for four years. Billy's father and uncle were back from war. It was a gay and busy summer. And again I learned about another kind of world.

In my sophomore year I acquired two more roommates, Dennet Withington, from Honolulu, and Dick Linton, from Wailuku, Maui. There was quite a group of us living in the same building. Many of us wound up as seniors together in the west entry of Holworthy Hall. In my sophomore year I joined the Pi Eta Club. In those days there was no "commons" for dining. We "ate around". Pi Eta was where I ate my meals except for weekends.

The contacts at mealtime were most stimulating. I remember Bernard Fay, a Frenchman whose English was almost as bad as my French. We made a practice of conversing bilingually; he in English, I in French. Sometimes the results were amazing!

There were several people who later became known nationally in their fields; among them Roy Larson, who joined

Henry Luce in starting and developing "Time" magazine, and later "Life," "Fortune," etc.

In my senior year I was general manager of the Pi Eta Show and club treasurer. Of course the show lost a little money, but it was a great experience for me. It wasn't until two or three years later, when Dick Aldrich (later to be a Broadway producer) ran it that the show showed a small profit.

At Harvard I became intrigued with rowing, to which I had been introduced at Exeter. I rowed on the class crew in my sophomore year, as a substitute at New London my junior year, and on the varsity in my senior year. The class crew was more fun.

TRAVELING AROUND

In the summer of 1921 my father got me a job as a deck hand on the American Hawaiian Line freighter "Ohioan". We sailed in June from Boston, and from Brooklyn on the day of the Dempsey—Carpentier prizefight.

In San Francisco I left the "Ohioan", and after spending a week or so with the family of another lad who had come on as crew in Brooklyn, but who lived in Sausalito, I shipped out on the "Admiral Dewey" for Seattle. For the first time I was seasick, all the way from the Golden Gate to the Straits of Juan De Fuca at the entrance of Puget Sound.

As we were leaving San Francisco Harbor, battening down hatch covers on the forward hold, I heard my name called from the passenger deck above. There was Homer Howes, who with another man was making a traveling audit for Bemis Bag Company. He was on crutches as a result of polio. The last time I had seen him was when I used to pick him up as he crawled down from Carleton Crosby's house in East Harwich to swim in Pleasant Bay, and took him for rides to Orleans or Chatham.

I left the ship again in Seattle and stayed there for over a week, including a weekend on the glacier at Paradise Valley on Mt. Rainier. There were other side trips, such as to Snoqualmie Falls.

I remember going out to see the University of Washington. Some of its buildings were made of huge logs. I wandered down to the boathouse where I just happened to run across Ed Leader, the Washington crew coach. We had a long talk about rowing, especially about the crew at Harvard, which was having coaching problems at that time. Little did I know that he was just signing up to go as head crew coach at Yale! I learned then that distance from home is no excuse for talking freely about things you wouldn't discuss with a neighbor, or competitor.

I went on with Homer Howes and his partner for a few days at Vancouver. Then on to their next assignment in Winnipeg, stopping off on the way for a day at Lake Louise and at Banff. I finally left them at Winnipeg, continued by train to Port Arthur-Fort William at the head of Lake Superior. After a few days of futilely seeking a job to work my passage down the Lakes, I booked by boat to Owen Sound and thence by rail to Toronto.

On arriving in Toronto (about noon on a Saturday), I immediately went to the railroad office to get the rebate due me on my transcontinental railroad fare, because I had ridden in a car designed for immigrants, with three berths in a tier instead of the conventional two, and consisting merely of tightly woven mats instead of spring and mattress. The men at the office were just leaving, but when I explained my plight they went back and got me the money that was due me.

With this new wealth, I took the ferry to Niagara Falls and managed to get a cot on a porch of the hotel overlooking the Falls for three dollars. Then back to Toronto, and again by boat to Montreal. There I bought my ticket home and stayed a few days in Montreal on what money I had left.

Finally I arrived home in Chatham with two suitcases full of dirty clothes and $1.37 in cash. I could not understand why my parents had been worrying about me!

After getting my A.B. degree, and rowing at New London in June 1922, I immediately returned to Chatham and started to work for my father in his Nickerson Lumber Company. While in New London in 1921 and 1922, I went for Sunday cruises as one of the Harvard crew squad on both J.P. Morgan's "Corsair" and Vanderbilt's "Vagrant". I mention these things, as well as having described briefly some of the events in my life from 1917 to 1922, because thenceforth my whole experience has been on Cape Cod.

There weren't many people of my age hereabouts in the winter in those years. Most of the ambitious young people were drawn away by the lure of opportunities in the cities. I threw myself enthusiastically into my work and into civic affairs, even serving one three-year term on the Chatham School Committee.

One of my ex-roommate's brothers, Lothrop Withington, had married "Karkie" Whipple, whose father Sherman Whipple, a successful Boston lawyer, had a big country estate, "The Forges" at Plymouth. I was often invited there for weekends, along with many other young people. This was a lot of fun and provided an exciting contrast to the quiet life in winter on the Cape.

REAL ESTATE SPECULATION

In the early 1920's there was a tremendous speculative boom in real estate in Florida. This was followed in a small way by similar land speculation on Cape Cod. Hyannis was headquarters for a lot of land speculators and brokers who were seeking to buy acreage cheap and sell it quick at a big profit.

On one of those Plymouth weekends I chatted with Ralph Hornblower of the Boston banking firm of Hornblower and Weeks. He told me that they owned some real estate in East Orleans, consisting of three houses and a substantial acreage, which they would like to sell as a part of settling the estate of Dr. Vernon Briggs. I asked him the price, which was $25,000. In spite of the fact that this seemed an enormous sum to me, I reported it to my father and to Elnathan Eldredge, who was in the real estate and insurance business in South Orleans. Together with other Eldredge brothers, they occasionally entered into joint real estate ventures. This looked to them like a good opportunity for profit, so they proceeded to buy it, and even cut me in for an equal share with the others as a "finder's fee".

Elnathan and I were the joint managers for the group and this was an education in itself. We sold off the three houses and then sold options to buy the remaining land at a handsome profit to us on several occasions. Each time the prospective sale fell through, because the buyer couldn't sell his option or conclude his deal with his prospective customer, we kept the option money. Finally we sold the remaining land at a very good profit to Tom Nickerson of Harwichport, and he ultimately made a good profit on it too.

I mention these incidents because they were typical of what was happening on Cape Cod in the mid-1920's. But it was not really healthy. Not only was it speculative, but most of it was dealt in relatively undeveloped tracts, with little intent to do much else except sell the land to another speculator.

One exception (and there were several) was the development by the Orleans Associates of what had been Asa Mayo's farm at Pochet in East Orleans. They laid out their lots beautifully under the direction of Harold Hill Blossom, a well-known landscape architect. Their model houses were well designed by a famous architect, William Chandler. But by 1928 they too were in bad trouble and wound up in bank-ruptcy.

In an attempt to salvage the debt they owed Nickerson Lumber Company, we bought the property that remained unsold in their development at the foreclosure sale, hoping to make a quick resale. But from then until the late 1940's we never succeeded in selling enough lots to pay the taxes and mortgage interest, even though at one point in the 1930's we offered most of the lots at $675 each and you take your pick.

It wasn't until the 1950's and 1960's that we could get anywhere near the prices at which the Orleans Associates had sold lots in the 1920's. Today (1978), I doubt if even the poorest of the 119 lots there could be bought for as little as $12,000. Such have been the vagaries of Cape Cod real estate values!

There was one land venture, not for profit, in the 1920's in which Heman A. Harding, a lawyer in Chatham and I were involved, upon which I look back with pleasure. Between Depot Street, where the Chatham Police and Fire Station now are, and the site of the former Chatham High School was a considerable tract of unused land, including a swampy area on the easterly end of it. The land was good enough and big enough, we thought, for a municipal baseball field. It belonged to Joseph W. Nickerson, whose home at the corner of Depot Street and Old Harbor Road adjoined it. He gave us a very fair price for it. (I think it was around two or three thousand dollars).

So we set about to raise the money by public subscription to buy it as a gift to the town. We decided to call it Veterans Field in honor of all the Chatham men who had served in the armed services. But we agreed upon (and stuck to) one unique condition. We would accept contributions only from residents of Chatham. We actually refused several gifts offered by sum-mer residents, feeling that this should be a memorial to Chatham men by Chatham people only. I am happy that it worked out so well, and that Veterans Field was brought in to being as a strictly indigenous project.

BUSINESS AFFILIATIONS

Some of the endeavors with which I became involved in the 1920's were significant forerunners of the development and growth of Cape Cod which has occurred since World War II. I shall mention a few of them, primarily because they were typical examples of what was happening here in general.

For example, early in the 1920's the Hyannis Cooperative Bank was organized, and I went on its Board of Directors shortly after. Monthly meetings were held in the directors' room of the Hyannis Trust Company. A single teller's window in the Trust Company's office was assigned to the Cooperative Bank, and a teller was employed to represent the Cooperative Bank there.

In 1941 the assets of the Cooperative Bank were approximately one million dollars, and the decision was made to build our own bank building. This was done on a piece of land at the extreme west end of Hyannis, donated (or sold at a nominal price) by the Makepeace family, which was a part of their homestead land there. Tom Otis, the President of the Cooperative Bank, was the husband of Will Makepeace's daughter. I am sure that the Makepeace's were influenced by him in their altruistic decision to make the land available.

In those days every loan was passed on by the full board, based on the recommendations of the Security Committee, who inspected every prospective loan property before the meetings of the board. The decision on each loan was made only after thorough discussion by the board.

I remember John Bursley, a successful farmer and a real gentleman from West Barnstable. One of his favorite tests for eligibility was to find out which branch of the family the applicant came from.

He would say, "I don't know the applicant personally; but if he is of the "X" branch of the family he should be a good risk. But if he is from the "Y" branch of that family we should be pretty cautious."

Then there was Louis Arenovski, who first came to Cape Cod as a pack-peddler, and who had become very successful with his clothing store on Main Street in Hyannis and in numerous real estate ventures. He was on the committee which inspected the applicant's property. If their home was well kept and neat, especially if there were several small children, he would usually favor taking the risk even though their financial figures were marginal.

The Hyannis Cooperative Bank has grown since those days to the point where such homespun simplicity has been supplanted by modern methods. It now has seven banking offices and a computer center. I like to think, however, that even though its assets are approaching 200 million dollars, it still retains its original flavor of grass roots simplicity.

It was early in the 1920's too that I went on the board of the Cape Cod Hospital, which had opened in 1920 in an old wooden residence, with only one surgeon in charge of its medical activities. I had been on the board about a year when, in order to keep the hospital open, we had to borrow money for running expenses. We were about to start our first public fund raising campaign, but we needed money before that. The Hyannis Trust Company made the loan on a note to be paid, we hoped, out of the proceeds of the public campaign. But they required that each of the directors endorse the note personally. I was one to do so, though at that time my signature was worth very little. Today (1978) the hospital has over 100 qualified physicians on its active staff, employs nearly a thousand people, and provides services of which we did not even dream in the 1920's.

Somewhat later, in 1932, together with a group of other Cape Cod lumber dealers, I was involved in the acquisition of a retail building materials and mason supply business in West Barnstable from Waldo Brothers and Bond, whose main business was wholesaling masons' supplies from their Boston plant. We continued the retail operations at West Barnstable for a short time, but as soon as possible converted it into a wholesale business serving primarily retail lumber dealers on Cape Cod and the Islands.

We opened in April 1932 and by the end of that year had lost 10 percent of our original investment of $30,000. By the end of January 1933, it became evident that we were well on the road to financial disaster. We established a credit policy whereby any customer whose bill was not paid by the middle of the next month was required to pay cash. This policy has been continued to this day and accounts in substantial measure for the outstanding success of this enterprise. Without it we would have been so deeply mired in debt that we could not have survived, let alone grow as we have to where sales last year (1977) were nearly nine million dollars.

One decision, made in February 1933, probably accounts more than any other for the survival of the Barnstable County Supply Company in that crucial first full year of operations. Remember 1933 was the very bottom of the depths of the "Great Depression." It was the year of the "Bank Holiday", when every bank in the United States was closed for a period. Everybody's pay rate was cut, typically by about 25 percent; so even the employed were "on short rations."

We officers and directors of the company were drawing no pay at all. Even our traveling expenses were not allowed. Early in February we proposed to our employees (some six or eight in number) that they could choose between a pay cut of 20 percent or drawing no pay at all for the third week of each month. If they chose the latter, we promised that if there were any earnings for the year 1933 they would go first to make up the pay they had foregone for eleven weeks, and only then would the remainder, if any, be kept for the company. When the results for the year were in each employee got his full pay and there was $136 left over for the company. Such an agreement would be forbidden by law today. But it saved their jobs at full pay; otherwise I am sure there would have been no company and no jobs in the ensuing year.

In the 1930's I became involved in our trade associations and served as a director of the Northeastern Retail Lumbermen's Association, headquartered in Rochester, New York and as President of the Massachusetts Association. Paul Collier, who was Executive Secretary of Northeastern, was an able pilot in steering us through the mazes of the New Deal regulations, including the N.R.A. and the later wartime price controls and rationing requirements. This was quite an education for me.

I remember that Joe Miskell of the Wood Lumber Company of Falmouth loved to tease me by saying, "You went to Harvard, I know, but we're the ones who have given you your education." In a sense he was quite right.

In 1941 I was invited to become a director of the Lumber Mutual Fire Insurance Company of Boston. Its home office at that time was an impressive building just off Kenmore Square. Its primary business was insuring lumber and woodworking businesses. That company too went through a series of crises, both minor and major, during the 33 years that I served on its board.

There have been substantial changes in its ways, and today it is one of the strongest little mutual companies in the business. Even though I must admit I have never thoroughly understood the accounting methods required for it by the Commonwealth of Massachusetts, it was a great educational experience. It also brought me into contact with groups of outstandingly able men on its board.

In January 1954 my father, who had founded our Nickerson Lumber Company, died in his 88th year. I had feared that the taxes due to his death might wreck the finances of the company. But due in large part to the able counsel of my sister's husband, Morton R. Creesy, his executors were able to liquidate most of his property so that very little tax money had to be provided, either directly or indirectly from the business. This left us free to embark on a program of expansion (on borrowed money, of course) which led to a rapid growth of the business during the late 1950's and 1960's.

In 1954 we were invited to become a stockholder in the Lumbermen's Merchandising Corporation (Elmco), located in Philadelphia. At that time it had about 80 stockholders, each owning the same number of shares, and did an annual volume of less than 20 million dollars. This company acted as buyer of forest products and building materials for its stockholders, who were scattered over the northeastern United States from New England to Maryland. Its credit terms were even more stringent than those we had established for the Barnstable County Supply Company. The roster of its stockholders was made up of some of the most successful retail building material dealers in the Northeast.

It was an honor and a privilege to be invited to be a stockholder, and the contacts made there were extremely educational. I later served on its Board of Directors, as Chairman of the Board for two years, and then on its Executive Committee. Today it has stockholders of like caliber from Maine to Florida and as far west as the Mississippi River. Last year its sales volume exceeded 200 million dollars. My experience with Elmco was also an important part of my education.

Perhaps I have been writing too much about myself. My purpose is solely to give a "thumb nail" sketch of some of the experiences of one Cape Codder, whose career has spanned the time from when Cape Cod was a stagnant backwash with a declining population, to now when its population has increased fourfold and its land values have increased astronomically. Perhaps somewhere in what I am writing is a nugget which will provide an idea or a better understanding of the times for some future reader.

CAPE PLAYHOUSE IN DENNIS

There was one cultural activity in which I became involved in 1927, and with which I had considerable to do in the 1940's and later. It was the Cape Playhouse in Dennis.

In 1926 I met Raymond Moore, who was about to build the Cape Playhouse theatre in Dennis, and became so intrigued with the idea that I persuaded my father to extend credit for the building materials for it. By the time the building was finished, the costs had very substantially exceeded the estimates, and Moore found himself with a lot of bills he could not pay. He had financed the project by selling preferred stock in Cape Playhouse, Inc. (a Massachusetts corporation) to a number of civic-minded residents and summer residents whom he had interested in bringing this cultural program to Cape Cod.

Moore and his lawyer (I think his name was Weinberg) retained the common (voting) stock. He wanted my company to accept preferred stock in payment for the very substantial balance owed us for building materials. I refused to do this, but did agree to take a series of notes in full payment, with the agreement that if all the notes were paid on time we would accept stock in payment of the final note. This was done over a period of two or three years, and that is how we came to be stockholders.

I think Ray Moore was definitely annoyed by this, and for the next several years our relationship was rather cool. In the early 1930's too, it became evident that he wasn't going to be able to meet the dividend payments on the preferred stock. This stock carried a proviso that if several dividends were passed it then had full voting power. If this happened, Moore's common stock would for a time become a minority interest.

So Ray Moore persuaded most of the holders of preferred stock in the Massachusetts corporation to exchange their shares for preferred stock in the Cape Playhouse Inc. (a Delaware corporation). These new preferred shares had no voting power, no matter how long the preferred dividends might be in default. All the common stock in the new Delaware corporation was held by the old Massachusetts Corporation. Thus Moore could not lose control, since the remaining preferred stock in the Massachusetts corporation was only a small minority, most of it having been exchanged for the non-voting preferred stock of the Delaware corporation.

During the 1930's Moore married a wealthy woman, built the Cape Cinema, and developed his lovely gardens nearby along Chase Creek. In the fall of 1939 he came to me and asked if I would be agreeable to his naming me in his will as one of three trustees of his estate. The other two were to be Charles Wharton, a New York theatrical lawyer, and Francis Hart, a long-time friend in the theatrical world. He wanted to use me as a representative of local civic interest, replacing a man in whom he had lost confidence, (for reasons that I knew to be well justified).

A few weeks later I mentioned to my wife Barbie that I had agreed to this, whereupon she got me to promise that immediately upon Moore's return to Cape Cod in the spring (he had left for the winter), I would go to him and tell him I had changed my mind.

But Moore never came back in the spring. He died in New York in February 1940. Plans had to be made at once to get the theatre open and running for the summer season. Charles Wharton declined to serve under Moore's will. This left Francis Hart and me with the responsibilities in which we were ably aided by Kenneth E. Wilson, a Hyannis lawyer, who had been Moore's recent attorney and who continued as ours. Richard Aldrich, a New York producer, had been acting as Moore's general manager of the theatre, and we were fortunate to have him continue in that capacity.

We quickly discovered that Moore had died with almost no liquid assets, and that the Playhouse treasury was bare. So we arranged in March for an increase in the mortgage held by the First National Bank of Yarmouth to provide for funds to get the theatre opened for the season. We were therefore amazed in April when we were invited to attend a special meeting of the directors of the bank at eight o'clock in the morning, to be told that the bank was selling our mortgage to David Stoneman, the lessee of Moore's Cape Cinema. The mortgage was one of the old type, written for short term, but with the tacit understanding that so long as interest payments were maintained it would not be foreclosed, even though technically the payment of the principal was past due. Hart and I, accompanied by Wilson, of course protested vigorously but to no avail.

Later that very morning a hearing was scheduled before the Judge of Probate at Barnstable, at which Hart and I were seeking to be appointed as temporary administrators of Moore's estate. Our case was called at 11 o'clock, and immediately Attorney Gershom Hall asked the judge to deny our appointment, since we were inexperienced, and it would not be in the best interest of his client, the holder of the mortgage on the theatre. Fortunately we had gone to the judge before court opened and told him of our morning's experience at the bank. So he asked Mr. Hall how long his client had held the mortgage.

When Hall replied, "Since sometime before 10 o'clock this morning," the judge denied his request and appointed us.

But this did not solve our problem, since there was still time, if he chose to do so, for Stoneman to foreclose and take over the theatre before that season's opening. Wilson had left the court before we did, but had asked me to report to him on what took place. This I did by going to his office in Hyannis.

When I told him the story, he asked me to go with him down the hall to the office of his father-in-law, Charles W. Megathlin, who at that time was President of the Cape Cod Trust Company, with its main office in Harwich, and repeat to him what I had just described. Mr. Megathlin was obviously disturbed by the turn of events.

When I asked if his bank would take on a mortgage to pay off the old one, all he said was, "I'll take it up with my board and see what we can do."

Within a few days it was all arranged and we had a new mortgage with the Cape Cod Trust Company and the old one was paid off. For many years, through good times and bad, that bank (now the Cape Cod Bank & Trust Company) has continued its friendly support.

Fortunately Richard Aldrich continued as manager. He was a friend of Hart, and I had known him casually since the mid-1920's, when he was business manager for Cheney's "Jitney Players", a "strolling" company who presented their shows from a platform at the rear of a truck parked on the lawn of country estates. I had also known him when he was business manager of the Pi Eta Show at Harvard in which I had taken part in 1921.

Arthur Sircom was the very capable director of the Playhouse productions. Ray Moore's original scheme of introducing a new star or stars each week, supported by a resident company, was still being followed, and Sircom's job was to rehearse the resident company for next week's show while they were performing in this week's.

Then by Sundays, at the latest, the star would arrive and would rehearse with the company for the coming weeks's production. It was a bit tough, but it worked, due in no small measure to the talent and devotion of both cast and director. It wasn't until World War II that the "package show" took over, whereby cast and star moved together from summer theatre to summer theatre.

An interesting sidelight occurred in July of 1941. Gertrude Lawrence, who had appeared several times as a star at the Cape Playhouse, was to marry Richard Aldrich on the fourth of July in Dennis. The ceremony was to be at midnight on July 3rd.

About 5:30 that evening I got a frantic call from Hart, who with his wife Muriel Williams, a regular in the stock company, were to be the witnesses. Gertrude had just learned that the minister who was to marry them was named Carl Schultz. Since her country was at war with Germany, she just wouldn't be married by a man with such a German name. Especially she objected because of the implications which might be inferred when the notice of her marriage appeared in the London papers, as it certainly would.

"Can you find us a minister with a good English name?" asked Hart.

I said I'd try. So I called the Reverend Paul Wilkinson in Orleans. At first he was reluctant, but upon my repeating with emphasis the name of the bride and why I was asking him, he was eager to perform the ceremony. I called Hart back and he took it from there. That is how Gertrude and Dick came to be married by Paul Wilkinson at Dick's house in Dennis.

In December 1941 America was in the war. Aldrich was about to go off in the Navy. What should we do about the season of 1942? In March we had a soul-searching session in New York. Wilson, Hart, Aldrich, our accountant and I discussed the subject for most of a day, and we finally decided to proceed and open for the 1942 season.

The decision had to be made then in order to get the productions lined up in time for a late June opening. We were all in agreement that we should do this; but I feel sure we never would have had we dreamed that by June no autos would be allowed to move after dark on Cape Cod with any lights stronger than their parking lights—not even low-beam head-lights.

This restriction was necessary, because by June of 1942 German submarines had control of the seaways along our Atlantic coast, and Cape Cod had to be blacked out at night so they could not lie offshore and sink every ship as it was silhouetted against a background glow from the land area. The black-out was very effective. From offshore no lights showed from Cape Cod.

For the Cape Playhouse it was financial disaster, even though we rearranged the time for our shows so that people could get home before dark. After all, the gasoline rationing left little fuel to be used for going to the theatre. The upshot was that the season resulted in a loss of more than $15,000, which was a lot of money in 1942.

We thought we had substantially solved the problem with a loan from a wealthy summer resident of Barnstable named Kent. And we also got some real help from Gertrude Law-rence. Dick Aldrich was overseas in the Navy. Gertrude was at the peak of her career, with the lead in the Broadway production of "Lady in the Dark." With wartime taxes at their peak the final increments of her fabulous pay was in a tax bracket which must have been over 80 percent.

I went to New York and at a meeting with her and her lawyer, David Holtzman, got them to lease the theatre for 1943, to hold it for Richard when he should return from the war. It may have been a weak agreement, but Gertrude, the bride, did just that for her Richard. The lease was just about enough to cover the taxes, interest and insurance. So we were saved again!

As 1944 drew towards its close it became evident that the war might be over in 1945. At this point Kent became sensitive about his loan and pressed for payment, which was technically due. We had slipped into default as to the payment dates, but it was obvious that the Cape Playhouse would be a good investment to own when the war was over.

The situation became really critical in December 1944. At that point I went to see an old acquaintance of mine, Philip Mather, who was a summer resident of Chatham. One of his daughters had worked as an apprentice at the Cape Playhouse. He was then living in Boston. I laid the whole miserable problem before him. The result was that between Christmas of 1944 and New Year's Day 1945 he came to Hyannis for a conference in the office of Thomas Otis, the lawyer who had taken over our case for Ken Wilson, who was away in the Navy. Mather magnanimously loaned the money to pay off Kent (at a very low rate of interest, some of which he later forgave), so early in January we were saved again!

When the war was over, Mather and I had learned a lot about the theatre, enough to know that we wanted Aldrich back again for the 1946 season.

The postwar period saw the introduction of the completely "packaged" shows. Although Aldrich advertised it as "Richard Aldrich's Cape Playhouse", his actual ownership never was any more than a few shares of the outstanding capital stock. Mather and I got a friend of his, Victor Phillips, who had retired to live in Chatham, to serve as treasurer, and largely through his untiring efforts we got in practically all of the outstanding shares.

Thus finally, in the 1950's, we were able to abolish the corporations and establish the Raymond Moore Foundation as the owner of the theater properties.

Some Thoughts On Aging

As I approach my 79th birthday next March (1980—or rather as it approaches me), I feel constrained to write down some of my thoughts about aging. Apparently much, if not most, of what has been written and done about this has perforce been by those who are not yet more than the proverbial "three score and ten".

Of course in any discussion such as this we should first define what we mean by "aged". After all, "old" is a relative term. To the boy of 15, a man of 25 is old enough to be a fount of wisdom and knowledge, while the same man is regarded as untried and inexperienced by a man of 50. But for my purposes here, let us define as "old" anyone 70 or older.

I am reminded of the story told about Justice Oliver Wendell Holmes and Justice Louis Brandeis, who were walking along a street in Washington after a session of the United States Supreme Court on Justice Brandeis' 70th birthday. Approaching them came a really gorgeously proportioned, beautiful woman. As she passed by, both men followed her briefly with their eyes; whereupon Justice Holmes turned to Justice Brandeis and with a heartfelt sigh said, "My! What wouldn't I give to be 70 again!"

Once when I was about 50 and was President of Cape Cod Hospital, I happened upon the head nurse, Miss Barton, whose face wore a deeply troubled expression. I asked her what was wrong.

"I have three very sick patients," she said, "each of whom desperately needs a full-time special duty nurse. But I have only one such nurse available, and I must decide to which of the three I shall assign her."

I thought for a moment and considering that a person at the age of 21 has more of life to lose than at age 80, I said, "Is anyone of the three young?"

Promptly she replied, "That, Mr. Nickerson, depends upon how old you are!"

So being "young" or being "old" is indeed relative, and it is difficult to avoid an objective point of view on the subject. But being now nearly nine years beyond the "three score and ten", I shall try.

Probably the pervading feeling one has after 70 is that of gradually (or sometimes abruptly) slipping out of the main stream of activity. No longer are your decisions or even your opinions considered "relevant" by those who are still in the main stream of things. To be sure they are usually courteous about it, but gradually you realize that they are paying less and less attention. Your ideas are based upon past experience; theirs, on future expectations. Often, to them at least, there seems to be little connection between the two.

I recall that in my youth and middle age, even though I fully recognized the inevitability of death, I reacted as if I expected to live for ever. Plans and dreams were in terms of decades or longer. But now I have a sense of the shortness of time—at least for me.

I remember, and now understand better, the impatience of Ernest Bradford, the 80-year old Chairman of the Board of the Hyannis Cooperative Bank, when there were delays in getting the work started on the bank's first branch office (in Orleans).

"Let's get going!" he said. For him the time was short for such activity.

Of course all this is understandable and natural. I know that my mental agility, as well as my physical, has lessened materially. I forget things—often such little things as where I put something only a few minutes ago. My mind moves more slowly, and it is often *after* the event that I think of what I should have said. If I walk too far today, I feel like taking a nap afterwards. If I want to pick up something from the floor, I don't just bend over and do it—I kneel first.

Sometimes there are bursts of the old energy. This tends to be true in meetings of boards or committees where decisions are being reached; and probably from *my* point of view it is important to stay on in such capacities as a stimulant, an antidote to fading away.

It also is probably why I should continue going out in my boat, walking in the woods, scratching for quohogs, all of which I can do at my own pace. But the fact remains that my eagerness to do things has waned, and now I have to push myself a bit to do things instead of just "dozing by the fireside."

I suppose the biggest hazard of aging is boredom. Not just boredom by itself, but by what it leads to. Boredom leads to lethargy, and lethargy leads to stagnation, and then to a loss of interest in life.

But for some boredom leads to overuse of alcohol or other stimulants to offset it. Or boredom leads to contentiousness. If life is so dull, then argument or quarrelsomeness may give it some spice.

As my father used to say when he was in his eighties and no longer able to walk about freely, "The hardest thing in this world to do is nothing."

So I find myself making big projects out of little problems. Cashing a check at the bank is no longer accomplished on the run, but it involves a short walk with the chance of at least exchanging "hello" with a few people. Pruning a shrub is no longer a hurried procedure, but a slowly executed "project". Reading the daily paper is no longer only hastily skimming the headlines, but includes reading a few articles in full. (Strangely, this often demonstrates how misleading headlines can be.)

And I sleep more, too much probably. Bed feels so comfortable and relaxing, particularly in the morning, when there is nothing special to do when I get up.

But as I look about at my contemporaries, I conclude that aging is a time when you must keep moving, physically, mentally, and perhaps emotionally. Otherwise it is a time when you just fade away.

But each of these categories should be approached with moderation. Don't climb ladders or skip rope; but do the easy thing, like walking, scratching for quohogs, pruning the bushes, picking berries. Mentally I no longer strive to get a quick and conclusive answer to questions, but I find that solutions now come best if the problem is allowed to mull for a while—an hour, a day, or even longer. Emotionally, it is important that you still care—about people, about causes, about issues.

I suppose that a devout person, which I am not, gets special comfort in old age from his religion. I don't know about that at first hand. But I do know that I am increasingly aware of the natural world about me—of the sun, the rain and the fog; of insects, birds and animals; of trees, shrubs and the grass; of the ocean and the bay; and of all the sensations of color and sound, of smell and taste, and the feel of the world around me.

With age comes an increasing compassion for others and a tolerance for their frailties. I am more aware of my own shortcomings and try to develop a method of suggestion to others, rather than a flat statement about what should be done.

I worry about the state of the world, the nation, the local community, my family, my friends—more than I used to, especially in the wee hours of the morning when I lie awake for no good reason. But I don't do much about it.

I find that I glance through the obituaries in the daily newspaper, which I rarely used to do. All too often there are familiar names—people whose lives have touched mine. And I enjoy recalling the happy times I've had with many friends who are no longer here—people with whom I have fished or hunted, worked or contended, played or fought.

I go to the cemetery now and then; and as I look at the gravestones of many of the "old folks" I knew, I realize that they died younger than I now am, and that in the eyes of most people, I too am now one of the "old folks".

Cape Cod Needs Vigilant Devotion

Excerpts from talks given in November 1983 to the Lower Cape Lifetime Learning Program in Orleans and the Truro Neighborhood Association.

SEVENTY-FIVE years ago, in 1908, I was attending the Atwood School in Chatham. This was one of six primary schools in the town, which then had a population of about 1,600, a little more than half of what it had been 50 years before. Daily, five days a week, 36 weeks of the year, I trudged along the sandy road in the dust or mud to and from school with my black tin dinner box in my hand. School buses hadn't been heard of. The nearest thing to them were the horse-drawn "barges" which met the trains at the depot two or three times a day.

While I was still going to the Atwood School the road past our house was paved, not as it is done today, but with water-bound macadam. It wasn't long after that hardened surface roads were connecting the towns and villages on what is now Route 28, from Chatham west and from Chatham to Orleans, as well as from Sandwich along the north shore of Cape Cod and thence on to Provincetown. The main streets of some villages were paved with gravel or oyster shells. Between East Harwich and Harwich Center was a hard-surfaced road known as the shell road (now a part of Route 39), where the men used to try out their trotting horses.

The problem of snow removal in winter was handled differently. After a heavy snowfall the men who lived nearby turned out with shovels to dig a way through the big drifts, leaving enough surface on which sleighs could run. Today, even as the snow begins to accumulate, the plows are out pushing it aside and later sanding the road surface to provide traction for the wheels of our automobiles. We see no sleighs.

The main dependence for travel beyond one's immediate environs on Cape Cod were the trains. Passenger service was good, with several trains daily in each direction, most of them stopping at every little station located only a few miles apart along the way.

In the summer of 1910, when I was nine years old, I went with my father to the dedication of the Pilgrim Memorial Monument in Provincetown. We took the train from Chatham to Harwich, where we transferred to an excursion train to Provincetown.

My next visit to Provincetown came a couple of years later. One of my playmates was Bill Barclay, whose family had long been seasonal visitors to Chatham. His father had an automobile called a "Cattle Ax"—a Cadillac touring car with a top that could be folded back. You had to crank it by hand. One wonderful day I was invited to go with Bill and his parents on an all-day trip to Provincetown. The roads had been hardened all the way through to the Cape's tip. Although the trip was slightly hazarduous, it was entirely practical for an experienced chauffer (and mechanic) like Mr. Barclay.

By the time I was 12 my father too had an automobile, a Studebaker touring car which he kept in a shed at his lumber yard, a half mile from home. By 1917, when I was graduated from Chatham High School (in a senior class of seven), automobiles were commonplace, especially the Model T Fords ($397 F.O.B. Detroit).

During those years of my adolescence, many other things were changing on Cape Cod. People acquired telephones. You cranked a handle on a box and the operator answered, "Number, please." She would also give you the correct time on request, and was usually a warm personal friend. If the party didn't answer, the operator would sometimes suggest you try to get them at a neighbor's house. The telephone girls knew about everything that went on in the village.

During this same period electricity came into our lives. In Chatham, for example, there was a local generating plant which supplied current for home and street lights, but only until 11 P.M. After that you relied on the usual kerosene lamps.

Just before the outbreak of World War I in 1914, other exciting things were happening on Cape Cod. Marconi built a radio station for sending in Chatham and for receiving in Marion, Massachusetts. These replaced his earlier station in Wellfleet. But a few days before it was ready to operate, the war started and the United States Government seized the property and assigned Marines to guard it. It still functions as R.C.A.'s major ship-to-shore message carrier.

While a few local fishermen still clung to sail only for their boats, most of them were switching to motorboats for their work. Many of them were one-cylinder marine engines with a heavy flywheel—"one lungers" they were called. There were still no fast motorboats, with either inboard or outboard motors.

The local milkman delivered early in the morning milk from his own cows in quart glass bottles. It was neither pasteurized of homogenized. You could count on the cream rising to the top in the neck of the bottle.

The grocer came with his order-cart to take orders which he would deliver the next day. The butcher came with his butcher-cart selling meat. The scissors grinder came once or twice a year with his work tools strapped to his back. Pack-peddlers stopped by selling needles and thread and other things light enough to be carried in a back pack. In summer the organ-grinder with his monkey visited us, and the hurdy-gurdy man, pulling his hurdy-gurdy by its shafts. The Grand Union teawagons made their rounds.

There were no cash-and-carry food stores until the A&P started opening them. These were small grocery stores, in which a clerk waited on you from behind the counter; there were no check-out stations, because there was no self-service. This would come later, with the packaging of products which had formerly been measured out from bulk containers, as the customer waited.

But things were changing. The Zaimes brothers ("the Greeks", they were called) came to Chatham with their store full of fresh fruit and produce, some of it out-of-season. Their horse-drawn wagons covered the Mid-Cape area, bringing fresh produce to customers who heretofore had known only what they or their neighbors had raised.

During this period new hotels and summer boarding houses were opening. Several golf courses were built. The automobile and the roads they could use made possible the great changes on Cape Cod.

The way tourists are accommodated has changed completely over the years. In the 1920's and 30's, many private homes had paying guests who stayed sometimes for only one night or often for periods of a week to a month. Then roadside cabins began to take over much of this business. But the first motel did not appear on Cape Cod until around 1950. Today there are motels everywhere.

In the 1920's tearooms were popular. Elderly ladies, often in chauffeur-driven cars, were prone to take an afternoon drive with friends, topping it off with tea (and other delicious goodies) at a tearoom, such as Alice Wight's Champlain Tearoom in Chatham or Margaret Richardson's Sign of the Motor Car in Dennis. But where is the tearoom now?

Another change has been the lengthening of Cape Cod's season. Before World War II it was from late June until right after Labor Day. While that is still the peak of the tourist season, many places serving visitors stay open much longer. The Chatham Bars Inn, for example, is open from the end of April until the middle of October, and is planning to remain open year-round. And Columbus Day weekend, Veterans Day, Washington's Birthday and Patriot's Day often see our streets crowded with cars "from away".

Further economic and social developments have come as Cape Cod's year-round population has grown from less than 30,000 in the 1930's to more than 150,000 today. The driving time to Boston has shrunk from three and a half to four hours to only one and a half to two hours. The passenger trains have disappeared (since these talks were given, some have returned). Airplane service, not even dreamed of when I went to Atwood School, carries scores of thousands each year. I even know of one man who commutes weekends from California, saying it is really no further (in time) than when he used to commute here from central New Jersey.

By the 1920's the Cape was booming. Tracts of land were being sold by and to speculators. There were a few real estate developments, often only on paper. If you wanted to buy a home lot, you probably got it by finding someone with more land than he needed, who would sell you a piece of it. Building permits, zoning bylaws, historic districts, environmental conservation programs had not yet appeared on the scene.

In the late 1920's Cape Cod seemed to be poised for extraordinary growth and development, even though agriculture was still a significant part of its economy, with such cash crops as turnips, asparagus, strawberries, and of course cranberries.

Harvesting the latter by hand had been replaced by the

use of scoops or "tip-ups", which could be handled only by a strong man. Gone were the days when men, women and children picked cranberries by hand into six quart measures, working between strings lining the bogs into rows and supervised by the owner or his foreman. Gone too was the time when few boys showed up for the opening of the new school term until after the cranberry harvest. And no longer did women sit beside the trays in the screen-house picking out the bad berries as they were pushed toward the waiting barrels. Machines were taking over.

But then came the stock market crash in the fall of 1929, followed by a general economic collapse, resulting in 1933 in the closing for a time of all the banks in the country. Unemployment was high, prices were low, survival was the goal for all through the 1930's. Land which had been selling at what was considered good prices couldn't be sold at any price. But year after year the taxes had to be paid.

In 1939 came World War II, in which the United States became an active belligerent on December 7, 1941. The next year (1942), German U-boats had control of our entire Atlantic coastal waters. Here on Cape Cod, every foot of our ocean front was patrolled night and day by Coast Guardsmen with dogs.

At night we had a complete blackout—not a glimmer of light could be seen looking landward from the sea. The use of headlights on automobiles, even on low-beam, was forbidden. You could use only your parking lights. And you were allowed only six gallons of gasoline per week for the typical family car. Basic supplies such as meat, sugar, fuel and shoes were strictly rationed. Motorboats could not be used for pleasure, only for business purposes.

Building materials could be purchased only if you first obtained a certificate showing what you were to buy and why, and they were hard to come by. There were few industries on Cape Cod that were a part of the war production effort.

Those who were not in the military left for jobs in the factories and shipyards.

Even doctors and nurses were hard to find. Most of those who had been on the staff of Cape Cod Hospital, for example, were in the armed services. Their places were filled, as best they could, by people who were old or in any case less qualified.

It was not until 1947 that all these restrictions were finally lifted. Then Cape Cod started to recover from the barren years of the 30's and the war years of the 40's, at first slowly and stumbling a little. But by the 1950's the pent-up demand for the things Cape Cod had to offer began to take hold, and in the 60's and 70's the Cape was burgeoning. Its year-round population increased and still is growing at one of the very highest percentage rates in the country.

Zoning bylaws, building restrictions, wet-lands protection, conservation areas, bike paths, a limited access highway (Route 6), public water systems, regional schools, fire departments, paramedical rescue squads, police departments, all these and other changes have come pell-mell in the last 30 years. We are still striving to adjust to the needs of more people in the same space. With the help of people who care, people who love Cape Cod, we will.

A major change during the past few years is the creation of condominiums and similar high-class multi-unit housing. This has been aided by the rapid increase in the prices of land during the past decade.

The percentage of the total population of Cape Cod over 65 years of age has been increasing. Over half the patients admitted to Cape Cod Hospital, for example, are over 65. These elderly people are often accustomed to apartment-house living in their past. Even if they have been used to living in a single family house, they often welcome getting rid of the responsibilities of caring for such a house and its grounds. Under current zoning bylaws, such condominums are strictly regulated, especially as to where in each town they can be located.

But will these restrictions be loosened in the future? Perhaps they won't, because with density of population come problems of water supply and sewage disposal. In any event it seems likely that Cape Cod will see many changes in the future, just as it has seen in the past.

Probably the greatest change that has come to Cape Cod, since it was first settled by Europeans, is exemplified by my friend who commutes from California. This is in contrast to the major factor in determining the original boundaries of our Cape towns—the walking distances to churches.

In the early colonial period of the Plymouth Colony, church and state were one. Only church members could vote, and the town meetings were held in the church. So it was desirable that the boundaries of the political unit (the town) should be such that church members could walk to church and to town meetings.

There have been many cycles of change on Cape Cod. Originally devoted to farming, the inhabitants became fishermen and sailors. In the first half of the 19th century its population grew with its maritime activities.

Its men became deep-sea sailors familiar with ports of Europe as well as those of the Mid-East, the Far East and the Pacific Northwest. Its people were not simple peasant-type rustics, but world travelers.

Then came steam replacing sail, and the population of Cape Cod dropped sharply from the mid-1800's to the early 1900's.

But by the 1920's, Cape Cod, mimicking on a small scale the Florida land boom, had its own speculative land boom. This collapsed about 1929, and from then until 1946 you could hardly give land away. This of course was followed by the increased activity in real estate, sharply rising prices for land, and a tripling or even quadrupling of population.

275

But the greatest single impact for the Lower Cape, especially for the towns of Eastham, Wellfleet and Truro, was the Act of Congress in 1961 which authorized the establishment of the Cape Cod National Seashore. In spite of the fact that more than one half of all the ocean front of Cape Cod, from Provincetown to Chatham, was already in public ownership, the case was presented as if there was only one alternative to private development and destruction of natural values.

So today we have the Cape Cod National Seashore, occupying a major portion of these three towns, including about nine miles on the Cape Cod Bay shore of Truro and Wellfleet, where the park runs from Bay shore to the Atlantic Ocean. This leaves little land under the control of the towns in Truro and Wellfleet.

While the value of protecting the land within the Seashore is obvious, its impact on the town itself can be full of problems. One effect of the withdrawal of so much land and its preservation as natural areas is to enhance the value of the remaining land and to encourage its more intensive use. As land values go up there is the temptation, for example, to build high-rise structures on it.

There is also the inevitable conflict between national and local interests. The people of Truro want only what is best for Truro. The Cape Cod National Seashore, however, is concerned with what the Federal government conceives to be in the best interests of *all* the inhabitants of *all* 50 of these United States—of which Truro is but a miniscule drop. The Park Service, in turn only a part of the Department of the Interior, has its planners in Denver, Colorado, where its technicians devise plans to carry out national policies which have been determined in Washington. These policies which affect Truro in its relation to the Seashore are determined on a national level; and since most national parks are quite different from this one, national policy has to be determined to accomodate the greatest good for the greatest numbers—or at least what the then current office-holders conceive that to be.

For example, fallen deadwood may not be picked up in national parks, in spite of the fact that national forests permit it and state forests encourage it. As applied to Cape Cod National Seashore, this means that driftwood, classified as deadwood, may not be picked up. When national policy ran up against the age-old local custom of picking up driftwood on Cape Cod, a compromise was finally adopted by the Federal Agency: driftwood can be picked up when found below the high-water mark. But driftwood above the high-tide mark must not be touched. Question: by what miracle does driftwood get above high-water mark?

Another example, one currently being worked on: it is national policy of the Park Service that mosquitoes should not be controlled by pesticides in so-called "natural areas". For more than 50 years the Cape Cod Mosquito Control Project, acting for the state and for all the Cape Cod towns, has devoted itself to controlling the mosquito population of Cape Cod. When national policy to protect mosquitoes collides with local policy to destroy them, there is a problem.

I guess what I'm saying is that whether the problems arise from national policy, from population trends, from economic changes, or from whatever cause, the future of Chatham and Truro, of Eastham and Wellfleet, in fact of all of Cape Cod, depends on the continued vigilance and devotion to civic duties which have sustained our Cape Cod towns in the past. The future will depend on all of us, our vigilance, our ability to solve problems.